Eye

Eye of the Tiger

My Life

FRANK BRUNO

WARNER BOOKS

A *Warner* Book

First published in Great Britain in 1992 by
Weidenfeld and Nicolson

Copyright © Frank Bruno and Norman Giller

This edition published by Warner in 1993

A CIP catalogue for this book
is available from the British Library

ISBN 0 7515 0148 4

Phototypeset by Intype, London

Printed in England by Clays Ltd, St Ives plc

Warner Books
A division of
Little, Brown and Company (UK) Limited
165 Great Dover Street
London SE1 4YA

Contents

Illustrations

Sugar Ray Leonard visits before the Tyson fight (*Daily Mirror*)

Shaking hands with Mike Tyson before the fight in Las Vegas

The whole family at Buckingham Palace: showing off the MBE (*Sun*)

Collecting the MBE (*Sun*)

In Robin Hood and the Babes in the Wood panto at the Bristol Hippodrome (Martin Chainey)

With Harry Carpenter (Press Association)

Author's Note

My grateful thanks to writer Norman Giller, a good friend, for helping me get my thoughts and feelings down on paper. He normally writes in partnership with Jimmy Greaves, but I thought he would like to listen to a cultured voice for a change (only joking, Jim). I did the talking, the living and the fighting, and I left the writing to Norman, who has known me since I was a starry-eyed youngster first starting out in the world of professional boxing. I would not wish to pretend that I have written the book. But, more important, I have *lived* it. All the sentiments expressed in the book are mine, and when you have finished reading it perhaps you will conclude that I am not – as was once suggested – 'as thick as two short planks'. I dedicate the book to the four most important women in my life: my Mum, my daughters Nicola and Rachel and, most of all, to a lady called Laura. Thank you for paying me the compliment of reading the book. It is much appreciated, know what I mean!

June 17, 1991

Simon Block, Esq
Secretary,
Southern Area Council
of the British Boxing Board
of Control,
70 Vauxhall Bridge Road,
London SW1V 2RP

Dear Simon,

I would like to formally re-apply for my licence to box.

As you are aware, I have not boxed since my world title challenge against Mike Tyson in Las Vegas in 1989.

The rest has done me the world of good, and I am now looking forward to actively returning to the sport that I love. I have undergone all the necessary medical checks, and I will provide you and your colleagues with the relevant paperwork when you have decided on a date to consider my application.

I look forward to hearing from you.

All best wishes.

Yours sincerely,

Frank BRuno

-x-

Eye of the Tiger

Chapter One

The Violent Playground

The British Airways jet climbed a couple of thousand feet above the paradise island of Jamaica where my wife Laura and I had just spent a week recovering from the pressure and controversy of my first comeback contest. I was drifting off into a doze when the captain suddenly announced: 'Please keep your safety belts fastened. We have a technical problem and are having to return to Kingston.'

Just those few words were more terrifying than anything I had ever experienced in the ring. Give me a Mike Tyson punch to the jaw any day rather than that feeling of fear and helplessness when you know your pilot is having problems. There were ambulances and fire engines roaring alongside us as we landed, but – thank God – they were not needed. It was an unnerving incident that further strengthened my belief that I was right to be continuing my boxing career. Just a couple of weeks earlier I had told journalists that I could get killed in a motorway pile-up or in a plane crash. You are at risk in just about everything you do these days, even making love. At least with boxing you can minimise the danger and you are in control of your own destiny.

I hope by the time you finish reading this book you will understand why I have found it necessary to box on after the sort of experiences that would convince most people that the time had come to put their feet up. On the way to explaining my decision to return to the ring I want to share with you the ups and occasional downs of a career that could have come right out of a *Rocky* film script. The difference is that this is for real. I've got the scars and the scrapbooks to prove it.

The book will serve as a sort of therapy for me as I weigh up all the pros and cons of boxing, and I shall lie on an imaginary couch as I look back down the mountain I have climbed to get where I am today. If you are surprised by some of the phrases and opinions coming your way please don't blame the ghostwriter who is helping me get my memories down on paper. The facts and feelings in this book are all mine. I promise you that I am not the thick-headed, no-brains boxer portrayed by my dummy on *Spitting Image*. There are times when I mangle the English language when I talk, know what I mean! But I pride myself on having a pretty sharp brain, and while I've got no educational qualifications to show off I reckon I have qualified for an honours degree in the University of Life.

The best thing that ever happened to me before my boxing career was to be sent to a boarding school where they knocked the bully out of me. Oxford could not have done a better job for me than Oak Hall, a school for scoundrels tucked away in the rolling hills of Sussex. When I arrived there as a reluctant pupil at the age of eleven I was a young tearaway with an uncontrolled violent streak. In five years they managed to teach me not only the three Rs but also the importance of discipline, and they managed to get me equipped for survival in the jungle of the outside world. Well, almost. It took boxing and a lady called Laura to put the finishing touches to my education, and if it were not for them I would possibly be telling this story in a prison cell. But let me start at the beginning . . .

I was born in Hammersmith General Hospital on 16 November 1961. My lovely Mum, Lynette, was a district nurse in South London for many years and a big fuss was made of her at her local hospital when I arrived, all nine pounds of me. Little did she know she was cradling ten tons of trouble in her arms. I have told of my early days in a previous book (*Know What I Mean?*) but I shall now dig deeper into my memory as I retrace my steps so that you understand the environment that helped shape me.

We lived in a neat terraced house in Barmouth Road, Wandsworth, that was kept like a palace by my Mum who loved living there surrounded by all her friends and leading a full and rewarding life dedicated to spreading the word of God. Mum preaches from the pulpit at the Pentecostal church in Fulham, and she can really get the congregation worked up with words that pour from deep in her soul. She has mixed emotions about what I have achieved. Mum is proud yet at the same time concerned that I have made a name for myself in a sport that can be violent to the point of viciousness. Every time I climb into the ring she is at home praying that neither I nor my opponent gets hurt. She will be the first to breathe a sigh of relief when I finally decide to hang up my gloves.

I was a real handful for Mum as a kid. She often tells of how I used to smash my way out of my wooden cot before I was a year old. So I can trace the violent side of my nature right back to the cot. On my very first day at school I waited until Mum had deposited me at the playground and then the second her back was turned I took off on my five-year-old legs and raced back home. Mum tried sweet-talking me back to school but finally had to lead me ear first! I needed the strong hand of a father, but by the time I was picking up the reputation of being a bully boy on the streets of Wandsworth my dear Dad, Robert, was losing a battle with diabetes and had been paralysed down one side by a stroke. Yet even though he was weak and bedridden I still lived in fear of him whenever complaints were being made about my having misbehaved (usually by neighbours whose sons I had whacked). I used to be summoned into the bedroom to face my father, who would direct me round to the side of the bed so that I was close to the half of the body he could still move. Suddenly from beneath the bedclothes he would produce a curtain rod and would hit me like a headmaster using a cane. 'This is for your own good, Franklyn,' he used to say. 'And there will be more to come if you don't do exactly what your mother tells you. Behave yourself or else . . .'

The thought of that curtain rod frightened me much more than, in later years, the prospect of facing the fists of such as Bonecrusher Smith and 'Iron' Mike Tyson. There's an old saying, 'Spare the rod and spoil the child.' I would much rather have been spoiled!

My fear of my father never turned into hatred, and I loved and respected him. It was the most devastating experience of my life to see him wasting away in his final months. He was in constant pain, and when I used to come home on school holidays Mum had to show me how to give him his injections so that she could go out on her nursing calls. When Dad cried out in agony I would, as gently as possible, stick the needle into his arm and inject the pain-releasing insulin.

A weird and frightening thing happened on the day he died. I was into my fourth year at Oak Hall and was walking through the school grounds when I heard my father's voice. It was as clear as if he were walking beside me. He was crying and calling out my name. When I got back to the schoolhouse about an hour later the headmaster summoned me to his study. He put an arm gently around my shoulder as he gave me the news I was dreading.

'I'm sorry to have to tell you, Frank,' he said, 'that your father has died. You must look on it as a merciful release from his suffering. We have arranged for you to catch the next bus so that you can go home and help comfort your mother.'

When I arrived home two hours later my Mum was sitting in an armchair weeping. 'I'm sorry, Franklyn,' she said, 'but the good Lord has taken your father. He is out of his pain now and in the arms of our Lord.'

Mum and Dad had come over from the West Indies four years before I was born, and they were among the first black immigrant families to move into Wandsworth, which is a borough of London that sits on the south side of the river Thames close to Putney and Battersea. South West 18 to be exact. It's a tough district where you need your wits about you to keep ahead of the young Frank Brunos running wild, but most of the people will show you hearts of gold once you have earned their trust. I grew up in Wandsworth with my three lovely sisters, Faye, Angela and Joan, and my big brother Michael. Another brother, Eddie, lives in Jamaica, which is the West Indian paradise island on which Mum grew up. Michael is twelve years older and two inches taller than me, and I have often been grateful for his brotherly love and advice on the way up the mountain.

My Dad was born on the Windward Island of Dominica, and he had come to England in search of the dream that was peddled to West Indians back in the 1940s and 1950s. Because of the breakdown of his health he found only broken dreams. I just wish he had been alive to see that I managed to achieve something with my life, which I almost certainly would not have done but for he and my mother having the courage to make that adventurous trip from the Caribbean in search of a dream.

In the days before Oak Hall I was constantly in trouble for throwing my weight around. I was always head and shoulders above other kids my age at Swaffield Primary School, and I used to find it quicker and easier to use my fists rather than my tongue to settle arguments. I ran with the young tearaways who were turning the streets of Wandsworth into a violent playground, and while at Swaffield I was called into the headmaster's office so many times that I wore a hole in his carpet. He used to shake his head and wonder what was to become of me.

Away from school I was more of a rascal than a villain. Some of the mates I used to mix with later got themselves into heavy trouble with the law, and their fate brings it home to me that but for boxing I could easily have slipped into a life of serious crime. Wandsworth Prison was just a few minutes from our home, and I often used to walk past the outside wondering what it was like on the inside. I once filled in one of those magazine questionnaires that asked what I would have been if I had not been a boxer. I jokingly wrote 'a black Ronnie Biggs'. But it could easily have been true if the discipline and demands of boxing had not pointed me in the right direction.

Later in life I was to meet the really heavy villains. On a visit to Broadmoor with Sir Jimmy Savile in the summer of 1991 I opened a new gymnasium at Britain's notorious top-security hospital, and among the inmates introduced to me was Ronnie Kray. He and his twin brother, Reggie, are looked on almost as folk heroes in the East End, and what we had in common was that, like them, I started my professional boxing career in East London. The twins had been good class fighters before devoting their time and energy to other matters. I had an interesting chat with Ronnie, and he told me how several of his old boxing chums regularly call in to see him and talk about old times. It was difficult to believe that the mild-mannered man facing me was once feared as the boss of London's underworld. Even more fascinating, or frightening – however you want to look at it – was the fact that standing alongside Ronnie Kray was none other than the infamous Yorkshire Ripper Peter Sutcliffe. He was much plumper than he looked in old newspaper photographs, and as I shook his hand I looked into his eyes expecting them to be really scary. But he just seemed an ordinary bloke, and it was mind-blowing to think that this was the man serving life for the murder of thirteen women.

Seeing so many men locked up in Broadmoor was one of the most disturbing experiences of my life, and it made me more appreciative of all the freedoms that I enjoy yet take for granted. The worst sort of crime I used to get involved in was the occasional bit of shoplifting, and I stupidly followed the lead of my older pals by considering it my right to travel on the London Underground without paying the fare.

I once got caught with some pals who were preparing to nick something from a counter at Selfridge's in London's West End, and the store detective was called. I nearly died of fright and I never did it again after I had been let off with a severe warning. Luckily the detective came from Wandsworth and was married in my local church. He knew that reporting me to my Mum would be punishment enough. My mother gave me the full length of her tongue over that incident and a whack to go with it, and from then on I always used to keep my hands in my pockets whenever I was in a store. If any of my younger fans are reading this please take it from me that life is a lot easier to lead if you go by the book and do what is right. They say cheats never prosper – and they're right. (You can tell that a lot of my Mum's preaching has rubbed off on me!)

I pulled the gloves on for the first time when I was nine. In a roundabout way it was Mum who launched my boxing career. I had got myself in trouble yet again for bullying other kids, and my mother told me: 'Franklyn, you have been blessed with great strength, and you should make it work *for* rather than *against* you. Why not take up a sport in which you can put your strength to good use?' I think Mum had meant something like discus throwing, but my imagination had been fired by the comeback of Muhammad Ali for his 1970 'Fight of the Century' against Smokin' Joe Frazier and I chose boxing. I joined the local Wandsworth Boys' Club and my first painful experience of climbing into the ring is a bruise on my memory.

One of the trainers, Keith Leverton, had been tipped off about my bullying manner and he decided I needed a short, sharp lesson. There was only one boy my size who could spar with me – his son, Gary, who was five years older than me and a relatively experienced amateur. Gary was a southpaw, meaning that he led with his right fist and right foot forward. This completely threw me and I had no idea how to stop his unorthodox punches that rained in on me. As his gloves thudded against my nose my eyes watered like Niagara Falls. It was enough to turn me off boxing for life, but I surprised Mr Leverton – and myself – by returning the next night, and I became a regular at the training sessions. I had been bitten by the boxing bug.

I used to get a reminder of that first taste of leather whacking into my lips while living in London early in my professional career. I would spot a certain policeman walking his beat. It was Gary Leverton, who made a successful life for himself with the Old Bill and regularly won the Open Police Boxing Championships.

The major problem I had as an enthusiastic member of the Wandsworth Boys' Club boxing squad was finding opponents. There was hardly anybody around at my weight and in my age group. I had just three contests while at Wandsworth, and all of them were against the same opponent – Gary Hill, a heftily built white boy who was a good banger but about as raw as me. I won two of the contests and he won one. I collected a coveted National Association of Boys' Clubs championship, but it was a paper crown because I got a bye in every round including the final. That was the sum total of my junior boxing experience. I then got involved in a fight outside the ring that was to change my life.

There was a particular teacher at Swaffield Primary who, I believe, had it in for me. We gave each other bad vibes, and he seemed to pick on me at the least excuse. One day while on a school visit to the Houses of Parliament I tried to borrow a camera from a girl in my class. She did not want me to have it and told the teacher. By then I had hold of the camera and the teacher came gunning for me. We got involved in a silly tug-of-war that finished with the camera on the floor. The tug-of-war had now given way to a wrestling match and I was getting much the better of it when I realised what an idiotic thing I was doing. I ran off as fast as my legs would take me, across Westminster Bridge and all the way home to Wandsworth. As the teacher got up off the ground he shouted, 'You're in real trouble this time, Bruno. I'm reporting you to the headmaster.'

My mother dragged me to school the next day for a confrontation with the headmaster. He had the teacher's written report in front of him, and shook his head gravely as he read it. The teacher reported that I had hit him, but I reckon I had only pushed him around a bit. 'No matter what you claim, Bruno, I cannot have pupils going around laying hands on members of my staff,' said the headmaster. 'It seems that all the warnings I have given you in the past have fallen on deaf ears. I have no alternative but to expel you.'

I was in tears as I left his study. None of us – the headmaster, my Mum or I – would have believed it in a million years if somebody had said that I would one day be invited back as guest of honour to present the school prizes. I hope all the youngsters now at my old school realise that I was a stupid pupil who deserved to be expelled. It seemed as if my brains were in my fists.

My Mum, who had her hands full coping with my bedridden Dad, organised a place for me at Oak Hall. I cried my eyes out when I realised it was a boarding school, and I begged Mum to change her mind. But she said with that conviction in her voice that you hear when she is praising the Lord: 'Franklyn, this is for your own good. You need saving from the devil that's inside you.'

So off I went to deepest Sussex.

Oak Hall was not quite Harrow or Eton. In fact it was a school for young scoundrels, and it came as a shock to my system. It was funded by the Greater London Council, and the one subject in which everybody was expected to pass their examination was *discipline*. The all-boys school was a world away from the hustle and bustle (particularly the hustle) of Wandsworth. The school was full of young hustlers who had been sent to Oak Hall to have the rebellious attitude ironed out of them. I hated my first few days there and used to cry myself to sleep, wondering how my Mum could have landed me in such a hellish place. One evening, after I had been bullied by a couple of older boys, I made up my mind that I was going home. I waited until it was dark and then crept out of the dormitory. With the branches of the giant trees moving in the wind it was really scary as I made the half-mile walk up the drive towards the school gates. As I prepared to clamber over the gates I was spotted by a teacher, who gently talked me into returning. 'Give it a chance and I'll promise you that you'll enjoy it here at Oak Hall,' she said. And she was right.

Once I adopted the attitude that I had to make the best of it I found I began to like the life at Oak Hall. It was very regimented, and most of the teachers had been hand-picked for their ability to deal with troublemakers. One wrong move and they could have snapped you in half. They were armed with slippers, and if you broke the strict school rules you got a stinging whack across the backside. In my first year I felt the full weight of the slipper a dozen times, but the behave-or-else message slowly got through my thick hide and I settled down to become what our headmaster Alan Lawrence has since described as 'a model pupil'. Mr Lawrence was a tough disciplinarian but he was also a gentleman with great charm and, provided you did things his way, he treated you fairly and with almost fatherly feelings. But God help any boy who decided to buck the system.

About fifty of London's wildest and most unruly problem kids were housed at Oak Hall, and Mr Lawrence and his staff had their hands full making sure we all followed the correct code of conduct. There were small gangs operating among the boys, and some bullying and terrorising went on out of sight and sound of the teachers. I knew how to defend myself, and few boys tried to take liberties with me once I had shown in the first couple of weeks that I could give much better than they could dish out. In my first term I remember one older bully threatening me with a good hiding if I didn't go into the local sweet shop and nick him some sweets and cigarettes. Maybe he thought he was the leader of the Quality Street Gang. Anyway, I took another boy with me and made him do the dirty deed. So my first lesson at Oak Hall was learning the art of delegating. Or ducking and diving as I would have called it then.

One boy we kept a particularly close eye on had been sent to Oak Hall because he had set fire to his previous school. Another was caught with a handgun in his possession. Discipline was so strict that there was no chance of any of the boys smuggling in drugs. A couple of them wanting to look big used to talk about things like marijuana, but it was all talk. I don't want to make myself sound like a goody two-shoes, but I have never wanted to have anything to do with the drug scene. My mother got through to me with her continual advice to say no to drugs. At the first sniff of cannabis I would run a mile rather than get involved. Gradually the school staff were able to sort out the worst of the troublemakers among us, and some of the boys took terrible beatings in the battle to make them conform. Thrashings seemed to be the only thing they understood.

We were encouraged to be independent, and went on hikes across the Sussex Downs and took regular camping breaks where we were taught to look after ourselves even to the point of cooking our own food. It was quite military at times, and everything had to be done with clockwork precision. Anybody stepping out of line had privileges taken away from them, and any boys consistently getting into trouble were delegated to punishment work parties. I got to enjoy the discipline (well almost), and it has helped me in later life when I have had to be single-minded and concentrate on getting myself physically and mentally fit for fighting at the highest level. The foundation for this self-discipline was laid at Oak Hall where the exercising of the mind took second place to physical education.

There was another vitally important development for me while I was at Oak Hall. My mother had given up trying to push her religious beliefs on me, but she was convinced that I would find God in my own good time, and she was, as usual, proved right. I converted to Roman Catholicism in my second term at school and started taking confirmation classes. I have remained a practising Roman Catholic, and my Bible is a well-thumbed book that is never far out of reach. There are a surprising number of current professional boxers who are born-again Christians, and all of us pray for God to be in our corner. I get enormous comfort and strength from my faith in God, but I doubt if I will ever follow my mother as a preacher. She has the God-given drive and desire to put across the sort of deepest thoughts and feelings that I prefer to keep private.

It was at Oak Hall that sport became a way of life for me. Among the sports I tried and enjoyed were basketball, canoeing, horse-riding, swimming, gymnastics, weightlifting, judo, tennis, athletics, cross-country running, water-skiing and roller-skating. The objective of all this activity was to burn off our surplus energy and make us more pliable and easier to manage. Most of us were hyperactive and it was only sport that could be guaranteed to hold our attention for any reasonable span of time. My favourites were cricket in the summer and football in the winter, and I daydreamed about making a career as a Michael Holding-style fast bowler or as a Peter Osgood type of centre-forward. I could bowl fast but without real accuracy. I was more accomplished at football and led the Sussex Schools attack, but I applied too much muscle for the taste of opponents and referees and I doubt whether I would have made it as a professional.

I played the game more like John Fashanu than Peter Osgood, who was all silken skills. It was crash-bash stuff when I was chasing the ball, and more than one centre-half wanted to knock my block off after feeling the weight of one of my challenges. I was not deliberately dirty, but what I lacked in skill I tried to make up for with strength. I once partnered that master athlete Steve Cram, a real football nut, in a charity match in the north-east. Neither of us could understand why we didn't get a call from the then England manager Bobby Robson after our performance together. We were just like Barnes and Rush − Carol Barnes and Jennifer Rush!

The one sport I did not try at Oak Hall was boxing, which was banned by the GLC because it was considered too violent. That was a daft decision, particularly for a place like Oak Hall where boxing would have been the ideal sport in which to get rid of our hang-ups and to release our aggression. There is no sport to touch boxing for character-building and for making you have respect and humility. I had just a few unofficial bouts, using training gloves in the gymnasium which became like a second home to me. Headmaster Alan Lawrence realised I was hooked on boxing, and he did his best to get me a taste of ring action. I was sent to the local Heathfield youth club where the leader, Mike Hannington, tried to get other boys to spar with me but nobody was interested. Then they arranged a contest for me at Alan Minter's club over at Crawley, but when I arrived my proposed opponent took one look at me and decided to get changed and go home. In those days at Oak Hall I was a shy boy and used to prefer my own company, spending hours alone working out with weights and following a general fitness programme that provided the first muscle-building steps for the physique I have today.

To help give us confidence in our last term they used to hold mock job interviews. My interview was conducted by Harold Becker, one of the school governors. 'And what job do you want to do young man?' he asked. 'I want to be a professional boxer, sir,' I said. Mr Becker told me that I should get myself a career to fall back on just in case my boxing plans did not work out. He added: 'To be a professional boxer you will need to be totally dedicated and determined. That is not a sport to approach with anything less than 100 per cent dedication.' They were wise words of advice that I have never ever forgotten.

I have often returned to Oak Hall since leaving in 1978, the year in which I was proud to be appointed head boy and school sports captain. It was only after my schooldays were over that I appreciated just what a beautiful place Oak Hall is, and I have since been fascinated by its history. The impressive oak-panelled manor had been built in the late 1920s by millionaire Sir Harry Oakes, who was a friend of the Prince of Wales (not Charles, but Edward). Sir Harry somehow managed to get himself murdered in Bermuda in 1941 in mysterious circumstances, and a few years later the manor was converted into a special school to help stop London kids who were running on the wild side from becoming villains (and, dare I say it . . . murderers!). The dormitory and dining room at Oak Hall are in the manor house which is set in delightful grounds. The actual school building is a half-mile walk away down a leafy country lane past a home for old ladies. I wonder what they would have thought if they had known that every day some of London's roughest, toughest young rebels were walking by to and from the school house. Headmaster Alan Lawrence and I greet each other like old friends rather than master and pupil when I make my return visits, and I want to take this opportunity to place on record my thanks to Alan, his wife, Joan, and the staff for all that they did to help shape me into a reasonable human being. I tell the current pupils that they, too, can be successful when they leave Oak Hall provided they are prepared to listen and learn. (There I go, preaching again.)

When I left Oak Hall I was a tremendous advertisement for the school's fitness programme and their ability to turn a brute of a boy into a responsible young man who could look after himself. But I had neglected the academic side of my work, and it is only since leaving school and with the help of a lady called Laura and a lot of hard work that I have been able to conquer a complex I had about two of the three Rs – reading and writing (I was okay at arithmetic, certainly bright enough to add up my purses and fees). I am not ashamed to say that Laura has helped me catch up on my education since leaving school. I urge anybody who, like me, did not give proper concentration to their lessons at school not to be too proud to find somebody who can help you put together some of the missing pieces. The older I get the more I enjoy learning, and words that used to frighten me now fascinate me. If anybody had told me when I left Oak Hall that I would one day be able to learn and memorise an entire script for a pantomime I would have thought they were barking mad. I have still got a long way to go before I can consider myself properly educated, but I am working at it, know what I mean?

My lack of academic qualifications meant there was not exactly a rush of offers for me to become a trainee banker, solicitor or doctor when I almost sadly walked out of Oak Hall for the last time as a pupil. It would have been easy for me to sign on the dole, but I wanted to earn my own living and my hunt for a job led me into a metal-polishing factory. I was paid a weekly wage of £43 to slave away in a small room in which the heat and the metallic smell was enough to suffocate an elephant. I stood it for a year before escaping to a more physically demanding job as a labourer for a plumber.

If they ever make a *Carry On Plumbing* film they can hire me as a consultant to show how to plan funny situations. All the houses we used to work in were terraced with cramped hallways and narrow staircases. Getting a bath up six flights of stairs was the biggest challenge. I used to get more bruised and bloodied knuckles doing that than I've ever got in the ring. I've been trapped on landings with a bath sticking into my ribs, have tripped over pipes and flooded rooms, and I once carted a bath to the top of a terraced house only to find I was at the wrong address. Our adventures could have come right out of a script featuring Del Boy Trotter, who did all of his televised ducking and diving just up the road at Peckham.

I parted company with the plumber to avoid drowning him, and had a spell as a warehouseman before starting work on a building site as a labourer. As the newcomer to the gang I was treated as the 'boy'. It was all Bruno do this, Bruno do that, Bruno go here, Bruno go there. 'Yes, suh, boss,' I used to say in my best slave accent. I have never worked so hard in my life as on that building site, and when the going got tough in my apprenticeship days as a professional boxer I used to remind myself of how lousy life could be away from the ring. Boxing was a doddle compared with the world of bricks and cement. It was only when I later got a cushy job serving behind the counter in the famous Lonsdale Sports Shop that I discovered that work did not have to be all sweat and strain.

By then I had started out on my journey as a professional boxer, but not without losing my way a couple of times.

Chapter Two

A Hot Property

It was in my last term at Oak Hall that I got my boxing career under way. There was a lot of talk about a sixteen-year-old heavyweight called Paul McDonald, who was reckoned to be the hottest young prospect around. At six foot tall and thirteen stone he was, understandably, finding it hard to get opponents in his age group. I read that he would take on anybody, and so – with the support of the staff at Oak Hall – I travelled to his club in Claygate, Surrey, to challenge him. I was very much the novice, but I managed to outjab him in the first round before bloodying his nose in the second to force a stoppage. This winning start strengthened my appetite for boxing, but I could not find any other boys my size to box.

I want to be upfront here and admit that I was frightened to death of getting into the ring that first time, and I can tell you that the fear gets no less with experience. But conquering that fear is a victory that every boxer has as he climbs through the ropes, and that is why you will never catch me slagging off another boxer. Just getting into the ring is a victory in itself.

Once I had left Oak Hall I decided to make a serious attempt at becoming an amateur boxer. Al Hamilton, a sports journalist and would-be entrepreneur, was going out with my sister Faye, and I asked him if he knew where I could train. He was friendly with an outstanding amateur called Frankie Lucas and helped me enrol in his club, the Sir Philip Game Club in Croydon. Hamilton hung around me throughout most of my amateur career, but it was only in later years that I realised his interest in me went in a different direction to friendship. I now want to zap forward in time to 1988 and to a case that was heard in the High Court. The same Al Hamilton was claiming a percentage of my earnings from manager Terry Lawless. So that I don't cross any legal barriers I shall reveal what happened in the case just as it was reported in a cross-section of newspapers, starting with how *The Times* recorded the first day of the trial:

Frank Bruno was at the centre of a High Court battle for his cash yesterday. Al Hamilton, who claims to have launched Bruno's career as a teenager, said the heavyweight's manager, Terry Lawless, owes him a share of the profits, thought to be around £250,000.

Hamilton claims he guided Bruno to the ABA heavyweight title in May 1980 before persuading him to turn professional. According to Hamilton, he first met Bruno as a fifteen-year-old living at the Bruno family home in Barmouth Road, Wandsworth. His counsel, Mark Strachan QC, told Mr Justice Brooke that Bruno said to him: 'I want to be a boxer. Can you help me?'

Hamilton took him to a club in Croydon, fixed him up with a trainer and was 'in some sense his mentor, public relations man and manager'. He said: 'Bruno was like a younger brother to me. He was special to me.'

Continuing, the QC said Hamilton guided Bruno through his eighteen-bout amateur career and was involved in all of them by which time Bruno was a 'potentially hot commercial property'.

Hamilton claims that in June 1980 he had a meeting with Lawless at La Trattoria restaurant in Leytonstone and it was agreed that he would get 5 per cent of the boxer's earnings if, as happened, he persuaded him to sign for Lawless. The 5 per cent was to come out of the manager's 25 per cent.

'Mr Lawless said there was substantial money to be made. I did not need to be told that. I knew I was holding on to the hottest property in British boxing.'

But Hamilton said that he had had just three payments totalling £800 between 1982 and 1984 and was now asking for an account of Frank Bruno's ring earnings so that his share could be worked out. He said he had invested hours into Bruno's career, wiping the sweat from him and spending hours in gymnasiums on cold nights. He said he was 'calling the shots' and persuaded Bruno to sign for Lawless even though he wanted to sign for Burt McCarthy. He said Bruno was 'besotted' by the millionaire manager and after riding in McCarthy's new Rolls-Royce 'he was like a kid who had never seen a toy before. He kept saying "I want to be a millionaire." '

Bruno, sitting with his manager, muttered angrily when Hamilton said that if he told him to jump off Nelson's Column he would because: 'I was the boss. I was the guvnor.'

Lawless admits the restaurant meeting but denies any oral agreement. He claims the £800 was a loan and is counter claiming for its return plus interest. Hamilton's claim is described as 'fictitious and unfounded'. It is claimed the loans were only made because Hamilton made himself out to be broke and in need of the money.

The judge was told how Bruno eventually signed for Lawless in February 1982 after a battle for his signature with McCarthy, who reached a secret settlement with the boxer in 1985 over a signed agreement.

This was how Gill Swain reported it in the *Daily Mail* when I was called as a witness:

It would have taken one quick forehand jab and the barrister would have hit the deck. But Frank Bruno was involved in sparring of a different kind yesterday. The Big Man, a sort of giant cheeky chappie, delivered some of the longest speeches he has ever made in public. And he had the judge, lawyers, reporters, relatives and even the opposing sides in his court battle all rolling in the aisles.

The former European heavyweight champion was giving evidence on behalf of his manager Terry Lawless who is defending a claim by former boxing journalist Albert Hamilton for 5 per cent of Bruno's earnings.

The venue could hardly have been more different from a sweaty, noisy boxing ring surrounded by overheated crowds gathered to watch bruising and blood. This was a small, modern, light-oak panelled courtroom in St Dunstan's House, an annexe to the High Court, presided over by a judge who peered over his reading glasses at Bruno and obviously enjoyed learning all about the wheelings and dealings of the boxing world.

The Big Man, whose best-known utterance up to now has been 'Know what I mean, 'Arry?' answered questions for twenty-five minutes before he said 'Know what I mean?'

He wore a blue striped suit, a red tie and a red handkerchief in his breast pocket. He stood by a laminated top desk covered in legal papers in front of three rows of lawyers in the small courtroom, which seemed to dwarf his six-feet-three-inch frame. Only his enormous shoulders reminded you of his power.

When Mark Strachan QC stood up to cross-examine him he realised he was just three feet away from those immense hands.

'Obviously I am very close to you,' said Mr Strachan, a man with a habit of rocking back on his heels as if he was afraid of the Big Man invading his space, never mind clocking him one.

'If we differ about any topic, will you make sure your responses are verbal and not physical?'

Bruno the joker told the court: 'I always wanted to get on in life but I didn't have the education to be a barrister or a solicitor or anything like that, so I had to use my strength to do something constructive.'

When he was asked if he would like to sit down, he replied: 'No. I'll stand up. This is sort of training for me.'

Asked by Mr Strachan if he had been disappointed in the purse he received for fighting Joe Bugner, he said everyone was always disappointed with his pay.

'You will probably be just as dissatisfied when you get your cheque after all this,' said Bruno and Mr Strachan replied amid gales of laughter: 'I believe the word for that must be "touché".'

The ex-champ talked about his devoutly Christian mother and said she was a 'wise, wise lady' who directed him towards boxing by telling him when he was an eight-year-old bully that he should put what he had to good use.

Bruno told the court that he had signed up with his first manager, Burt McCarthy, because he had driven up in a yellow Rolls-Royce carrying suitcases full of money, but his brother, Michael, had told him money wasn't everything in life and he knew that now.

He said that he was first attracted to Terry

Lawless because the highly respected manager came 'humbly' to his home when he was a young amateur, and he treated his mother, brother and sisters with respect.

'Certain people can go on an ego-trip, can go on a rave and think they are bigger than anyone else,' said Frank. 'But they are not because they can be right up there surrounded by the Press one day, but the next day they are right down with nothing. You come into this world with nothing, and you go out of this world with nothing.'

This was Robin Young's account in *The Times* when I returned to continue my evidence:

In the absence of Mike Tyson, Frank Bruno, Britain's top heavyweight, amused himself yesterday with a little sparring against Mr Mark Strachan, QC, a legal adversary.

He was continuing his evidence at the High Court, where Mr Al Hamilton is suing Mr Terry Lawless, the boxer's manager, for 5 per cent of Mr Bruno's earnings. That, as the boxer observed, is 'serious corn'.

Mr Strachan's position was not an enviable one. The case is being heard in Court 2, St Dunstan's House, which does not have a witness box in which Mr Bruno's six-feet-three-inch frame might safely be contained. Instead, witness and cross-examining barrister stood eyeball to eyeball across a desk. Nothing Mr Strachan could throw troubled the boxer.

'You're building up to something,' Mr Bruno said during a series of questions, 'so okay, fire away.'

When the barrister suggested that Mr Hamilton, who formerly lived with the boxer's sister, had influenced his early career, Mr Bruno retorted: 'Are you crazy? You wouldn't get cowboys in from outside to run your business for you, would you?'

Immaculate in a double-breasted blue blazer, rocking gently as he flexed his leg muscles, Mr Bruno gave his measured opinion that Mr Hamilton was 'trying to live off my back'.

Had Mr Hamilton not been 'enthusiastic for his career'? inquired the QC.

'Enthusiastic for my pocket, you mean,' parried Mr Bruno. 'I had definite vibes for this man. He was not really my cup of tea.'

When he heard Mr Hamilton asking for a 5 per cent share in his contract, Bruno said that he felt 'gutted'.

Mr Bruno admitted he had once been a 'bit of a rockhead' and had signed a management agreement with Mr Burt McCarthy that he had regretted immediately.

His evidence flowed as easily as combination punches in the gym. Mr Justice Brooke told the boxer: 'You are doing very well, Mr Bruno.'

The case continues, but on this day Mr Bruno had clearly earned a victory on points.

This was how Terence Shaw recorded the verdict in the *Daily Telegraph*:

Frank Bruno, in training for his delayed world heavyweight title fight with Mike Tyson, learned yesterday that a claim by a freelance boxing journalist for 5 per cent of his earnings had been rejected by the High Court.

The claim brought by Albert Hamilton against Bruno's manager, Terry Lawless, alleged that the money was owed under a verbal agreement reached in a London restaurant in 1980 in return for Mr Hamilton's help in persuading the boxer to join Lawless.

Mr Justice Brooke ruled that there had been no such agreement and that Hamilton, forty-six, of Manor Park, East London, had 'overstated his case'.

But he added that Hamilton, who claimed to be Bruno's mentor during his amateur career, was 'fully entitled to recognition' for the part he played in the development of the boxer's career.

'Mr Hamilton had far more influence on Frank Bruno's early life than Mr Bruno is at present willing to give him credit for,' said the judge.

Hamilton was ordered to pay the costs of the case, estimated at up to £50,000. However, the judge said that, as he was legally aided, the order should not be enforced without leave of the court.

This means that Lawless faces his own costs for successfully defending the action.

I have deliberately given a full account of the court case to illustrate how boxers are considered little more than 'properties'. In my opinion both Al Hamilton and Burt McCarthy wanted me for the money they could make out of me, not because they liked or respected me as a person. Boxers – all professional sportsmen – want people around them who look past the pound notes and see the human being. We don't deserve to be treated like lumps of meat. I have quoted the court case newspaper reports because to talk too openly about certain matters could get me into a legal tangle. I have had enough of courtrooms to last me a lifetime, thank you very much. I am going to carefully watch and weigh every word I say in this book. The legal eagles are not going to feed off me, know what I mean?

When you go into the world of boxing you walk a political minefield. The unwritten rules are that if you do business with one person there is somebody else from another faction you should never speak to, let alone consider working with. I like to try to be open and friendly with everybody, but you have to be on red alert against the many harbour sharks waiting to feed off you. I advise any young boxer thinking about becoming a professional to do his homework on the man trying to sign him before putting pen to paper. Ask yourself: 'Is this man interested in me or only in the money he can make out of me?' Find out how he has treated previous boxers that he has managed. Remember, it's *you* who will be taking the punches while he is taking the percentages.

I was lucky to find in Terry Lawless a man who genuinely cares about the boxers he manages. In nearly ten years together he was always conscientious, and he dedicated himself to getting me to a position where I was respected for my boxing inside the ring and my behaviour outside the ring. We went as far as we could together, and our relationship finally ended because we had lost the early spark between us. More of that later, but first back to my early days as an amateur with the Sir Philip Game Club.

I came close to quitting boxing almost before my career had started. In only my third amateur contest I was matched way over my head against Irish international Joe Christle. It was a ridiculous match to make when I was still in the novice class, and I was given a mummy and a daddy of a hiding. I hardly landed a punch as Joe skipped and danced out of range, picking me off with thumping blows that bloodied my nose and made me wonder what I was doing in the ring. My pride was hurt more than my body, and it was several days before I sheepishly returned to the gym where trainer Freddie Rix pumped up my enthusiasm by telling me that, even in defeat, I had shown a lot of potential.

Two years later I represented London in an inter-city match in Dublin, and in the opposite corner was my old tormentor Joe Christle. I had the satisfaction of stopping him in two rounds, and so wiped out the only defeat of my amateur record. I have since met Joe working at the ringside as a commentator. He is a lovely warm Irishman with a great wit and charm, and he told me: 'The night you beat me I knew you were going to make a name for yourself in the ring.

The improvement you had made from our first meeting was just phenomenal.'

The highlight of my amateur career was winning the ABA heavyweight championship at Wembley Arena in 1980. I had to dig really deep to outpoint Welshman Rudi Pika. There was a lot of pressure on me that night because managers were already sweet-talking me and telling me about the fortunes I could make. I knew that winning the title would be like a passport into the professional ring, and when I fought Pika nervous tension drained me of much of my strength and stamina. I did enough in the first two rounds to snatch a narrow points win, and we were both so exhausted in the third and final round that we could hardly throw a telling punch. A secret I kept to myself was that I went through with the contest despite a broken knuckle on my left hand. It hurt like hell every time I threw a jab, but I was determined that nothing was going to stop me winning that title. At eighteen I was the youngest ever ABA heavyweight champion, and I was really proud when I looked at some of the names of the outstanding boxers who had won the title before me. They included Jack Gardner, Joe Erskine and Brian London, all of whom had gone on to become British professional champions; and Henry Cooper won two ABA titles at light-heavyweight.

Now I was all ready for the professional ring. My brother, Michael, shared my dream that I would one day challenge for the world title and he had written on the wall in our kitchen at our Wandsworth home:

FRANK BRUNO HEAVYWEIGHT CHAMPION OF THE WORLD 1986.

After some dithering and second thoughts, I selected Terry Lawless ahead of Burt McCarthy as the man I wanted as my manager. During a weak moment of indecision I signed a piece of paper with McCarthy that was to prove an expensive mistake. Remember, I was only a naive teenager with pennies in my pocket and dreams in my head. I admit that I allowed McCarthy to turn my head with his flashy yellow Rolls Royce and his trappings of wealth, but which youngster in my position would not have been sucked in by it all? McCarthy later described me as a confused young man, but no wonder I was confused when so many different promises were being whispered in my ear. Could all those managers hot on my trail see pound notes for me or pound notes for themselves? I leave you to draw your own conclusions rather than risk an opinion that could land me back in court.

McCarthy, a likeable character who could charm the birds down out of the trees and then get them to sing his tune, lodged the piece of paper that I had signed with the British Boxing Board of Control, claiming that it was an agreement by me that he should be my manager.

Just two days before my professional debut there was a High Court ruling that refused an injunction by McCarthy aimed at stopping me from taking the fight under the management of Terry Lawless. The judge ruled that Terry was the holder of the only valid contract, but added that McCarthy might well recover 'substantial damages'.

I wonder how many kids in the situation in which I was placed, with wealth and fame being promised to them, would have been tempted to do exactly the same as me? I was earning less than £50 a week, and when you are hungry it is easy to make misjudgements. It taught me a lesson about diving in and making hurried decisions. I have now learned to weigh things up before putting my signature to any contract.

To add to the pressure I was under I got a phone call about the time of the court case warning me that I was going to have my kneecaps blown off. I never found out who was making the threat, but for weeks I went around in fear of my life. The call was probably just made to scare me. If so, it did the trick.

Five years later, on the eve of my European title challenge against Anders Eklund, Terry settled out of court with McCarthy to end a long-running dispute caused by my signature on that piece of paper. Including legal expenses, signing it had cost something in the region of £100,000. Having learned the hard way, my advice to any sportsman is don't sign your name to anything without first getting legal advice. You have to learn to protect yourself in and out of the ring. Boxing is a hard and dangerous sport, and sometimes you will find the most menacing opponents are on the outside of the ropes. Remember boxing's number one rule: *Defend yourself at all times*.

Within days of agreeing to join the Terry Lawless stable I got the shock of my life. Following a medical check by Dr Adrian Whiteson, the British Boxing Board of Control medical officer informed me they were refusing my application for a licence to box as a professional because I was short-sighted in the right eye.

I nose-dived into a deep depression when the Board told me my boxing career was over before I had thrown a single punch as a professional. It was beyond my understanding as to why not being able to clearly see the letters on an eye chart had any bearing on my being able to box for a living. All that mattered as far as I was concerned was that I could see across the ring. It was patiently explained to me that I had a rare form of short-sightedness called keratomileusis, a weakness of the eye retina that could be further weakened by the force of punches landing in the region of the eye.

Terry took me to see David McLeod − now Professor McLeod − at Moorfields eye hospital in London. He is the surgeon whose skill a year earlier had saved the career of my stablemate, former world light-middleweight champion Maurice Hope, when a damaged retina threatened to force his retirement. Mr McLeod suddenly pumped me full of hope by telling me that an operation had recently been perfected that could cure short-sightedness.

'That's the good news,' he said. 'The bad news is that there are only two surgeons in the world who can perform the operation. One is in Moscow, the other in Bogotá.'

Moscow? Bogotá? I would have gone to Mars if

it had meant that I could get a professional boxing licence.

It was eventually decided that I should go to Bogotá where, in February 1981, I was booked into the clinic run by Professor Jose Ignacio Barraquer, a pioneer of the sort of operation that is now performed in many countries, including England. Terry – and, I believe, Mickey Duff and Jarvis Astaire – footed the £5,000 bill, and I hope they feel they have since got a good return for their money.

I did not have a clue where Bogotá was, and I gulped when I was shown a map that revealed that it was 7,000 miles away in Colombia. The farthest I had ever travelled before was across the Irish Sea to Dublin when I represented London in an inter-city match, and making the trip on my own to far-off Colombia was a challenge in itself. All that most people seemed to know about Bogotá was that it was the city where England football captain Bobby Moore was arrested on the eve of the 1970 World Cup on a trumped-up charge of stealing a bracelet. I vowed to stay away from all jewellery shops.

I have never known loneliness like I experienced during my six week stay in Bogotá. It seemed more like six months. Few people at the clinic or in the nearby hotel where I stayed spoke a word of English and my Spanish did not go much further than *muchas gracias*. I passed the time watching programmes on television like *Bonanza* and *Ironside* dubbed in Spanish, and with two other patients I played a lot of chess, which I had been taught at good old Oak Hall. To keep fit I went for early-morning runs, and I walked miles until one afternoon I passed a house where a man with a revolver in his hand was giving me a distinctly funny look, and I don't mean funny hah-hah. I raced away from him as if I was Ben Johnson on steroids and from then on I decided to stay close to the hotel which was on the outskirts of Bogotá. The only time I went into the heart of the city the bus I was travelling on broke down and I finished up helping the other passengers push it. It seemed that people in the city were either fabulously rich or on the poverty line. There were a lot of raggedly-dressed kids begging in the streets, and it made me appreciate that Wandsworth wasn't such a bad place to live after all.

I had a scary experience on the way back to the hotel when I decided to get a taxi. I had just sat down in the back when three men wearing masks dived in as I was about to close the door. Just as I thought I had got caught up in a bank robbery the men pulled down from their faces what turned out to be handkerchiefs and paid their fares. I discovered that the taxi was known as a 'colectivo' which meant that the driver could pick up as many fares as he liked for one journey. They had been wearing the handkerchiefs over their mouths because of the pollution in the city. I had a good laugh to myself once I realised what it was all about, but for one moment I honestly believed I was about to get involved in a cops-and-robbers shootout in a city where there were lots of guns being flourished.

During all the boring hours I spent alone I tried to keep positive thoughts in my mind, but I was worried

about the operation and whether it would be successful. In my second week Professor Barraquer gave me
a local anaesthetic and then operated for about twenty
minutes during which he scored the surface of my
right eye and made minute incisions. It was explained
to me that the Professor was making the incisions in
the cornea to alter its shape. I spent the next week
with a patch covering my right eye. There was no
real pain but the eye felt very sore. When the patch
was removed the Professor beamed different streng-
ths of light into my eye while making a thorough
examination. After about half an hour, he slapped me
on the back and said in broken English: 'Everything
is fine, young man. In just a few months you will be
able to return to the boxing ring.'

In fact it was just over a year before the Board
of Control finally gave me the go-ahead to start my
professional career, and on March 17 – St Patrick's
Day – 1982 I made my debut with a first round knock
out victory at the Royal Albert Hall over American-
based Mexican Lupe Guerra.

Chapter Three

Jumbo and the Bonecrusher

An unfunny thing happened to me on my way to the first of my challenges for the world heavyweight title. I got crushed by the Bonecrusher. Everything – well, almost everything – had gone smoothly with my carefully planned climb up the championship ladder. Then, on the nightmare night of Sunday (bloody Sunday), 13 May 1984, my world fell apart.

As long as I live, I will never forget that defeat by James 'Bonecrusher' Smith. I had won my previous twenty-one fights as a professional, surviving just one major scare in my nineteenth contest when an ex-convict called Floyd 'Jumbo' Cummings knocked me senseless with the last punch of the first round. I give detailed reports of all my contests in the 'Fight File' at the end of this book, but the battles with Cummings and Smith were important landmarks in my career.

Cummings had been released on parole after starting his professional boxing career in prison where he served twelve years of a fifty-to-seventy-five-year jail sentence for his part in the shooting of a grocer during a robbery in 1967. While in prison he had spent every spare minute on a body-building programme that had given him a physique like a bull elephant, which explains his 'Jumbo' nickname. He hit me so hard with a thundering overarm right to the chin that I was literally out on my feet as the bell rang to end the round. Terry Lawless and trainer Jimmy Tibbs got to me as I swayed on my feet like a tree in a high wind, and they steered me back to the corner. I didn't know whether I was in London or Timbuktu, and I was still in a daze when I went out for the second round. For the first time in my career I had to fight by instinct. All I knew was that I had to avoid the clubbing right from Cummings, and every time he shaped to throw it I pulled him into a clinch. I was lucky that he was so desperate to knock me out that he was telegraphing his big punch, and even with my mind still in a mist I was able to dodge it.

At least a minute of the round had gone before I started to regain my senses. Then I began to knock Cummings off balance with the ramrod left jab I had practised and perfected during hundreds of rounds of sparring in the gymnasium. By the time the fight was halfway through I was in full control. Cummings had worn himself out trying to repeat his first-round success, and his right-hand punches were now clumsy rather than dangerous. In round seven I started to shorten my punches and the referee rescued a confused Cummings after I had sent him reeling with a right of my own.

It was immediately after this fight that I innocently started what was to become almost a double act with commentator Harry Carpenter. The contest was shown 'live' on BBC television, and when Harry climbed into the ring to interview me he asked me what I thought of the Cummings punch in the first round. I replied, 'What punch was that, 'Arry?' It was not meant to be funny, but everybody fell about laughing and from then on Harry and I were continually linked together like, well, Little and Large!

The fans gave me a standing ovation when I left the ring after my victory over Cummings. It had not been easy to win their acceptance. There had been a lot of fierce criticism of the standard of my opponents, and Terry Lawless used to get really uptight over some of the things that were written and said about the careful way I was being brought along. Even I started to get impatient and wanted to step up in class, but Terry is famous for his caution and patience and insisted on keeping me on a tight rein. The fight against Cummings proved I still had a lot to learn, but the way I had battled back from the edge of defeat at least showed my critics that I had what is known in the trade as 'plenty of balls'.

Then – three fights and seven months later – came that night of Sunday (bloody Sunday), the 13th. Unlucky for me. James 'Bonecrusher' Smith, a winner of fourteen of his fifteen professional fights, was the man waiting for me in the opposite corner at Wembley Arena. Smith, a college graduate and former army sergeant and prison guard from Magnolia, North Carolina, had been hand-picked by Terry and matchmaker Mickey Duff as the ideal opponent for my debut on NBC's 'live' coast-to-coast boxing programme in the United States. For nine rounds it seemed as if their judgement was 100 per cent right as I jabbed my way into a commanding points lead against an opponent who was always threatening danger but was never able to get his timing quite right because of the accuracy of my left-hand work. For the first time in my life I allowed the tension of the occasion to get to me, and by the sixth round I was feeling tired and my gloves seemed to weigh a ton. Adding to the pressure was the fact that Mickey Duff had announced before the fight that if I won my next opponent would be former world champion Mike Weaver. As I slumped on to my stool at the end of the sixth round Terry gave me a terrible tongue-lashing that was picked up by the television microphones. 'If you're tired, how d'you think the other feller feels?' he shouted. 'Stop feeling sorry for yourself and get out there and do your job.'

It was the motivation I needed and I regained my self-control and composure. I knew in my heart that, although I was winning with reasonable ease, I had not really done enough to impress the fans at Wembley and the American television audience. As the bell rang for the tenth and final round I made up my mind to go for a spectacular finish. And I provided it, but not quite in the way I intended!

I went looking for an opening for a right-hand

knock-out punch, and it meant leaving holes in my defence. This suited Smith – six-feet four inches tall and built like a brick outhouse – because he knew his only chance of winning was by a knockout or a stoppage, and my change of tactics was giving him unexpected hope. It was stupid of me because suddenly I was reducing a fight that I had all but won to a gamble. We were like Wild West gunmen in a duel, and it was Smith who was proved to be the fastest on the draw. As I shaped to throw a right he whipped over a cracking left hook to the side of my jaw. I fell back on to the ropes in a daze, just as I had against 'Jumbo' Cummings. This time there was no bell to save me. If I had been more experienced in this sort of situation I would have gone down for a head-clearing count, but my pride would not let me and I took the daft option of trying to duck out of trouble while backed on to the ropes. Smith then whacked me with a cluster of fourteen punches before a final big swinging right sent me toppling sideways to the canvas like a torpedoed ship going down at sea. I have since seen on video how I tried to clamber back up by clinging on to the ropes as referee Harry Gibbs counted me out for the only time in my career, but at that moment I had little idea of who or where I was.

My critics claimed that this knockout defeat proved that I could not take a punch, but I am convinced that most heavyweights would have gone down and out to the first left hook. I was devastated by the defeat. Smith's final volley of punches had opened a gash inside my mouth that needed eight stitches, but

I could not have cared less about the pain. It was my pride that had been hurt most of all.

What I did not realise until the next morning was that Terry had taken the defeat even harder than me. Just before I had climbed into the ring at Wembley on that unlucky Sunday the 13th his middleweight hope Mark Kaylor had been blasted to a seventh-round defeat by Philadelphia's Buster Drayton. The double blow had knocked the fight out of Terry, and he told me that the pressure had got too much for him and that he was going to quit boxing. We were due at a post-fight press conference, and it took me more than an hour to persuade him that there was still all to fight for.

'If you quit, I'll quit,' I told him, 'but we've come too far to give it all up now.'

Terry is a master at motivating other people, but this time I was having to do all the persuasive talking. He finally agreed to go to the press conference where he revealed that I had bullied him into attending. 'Frank has convinced me that it is worthwhile carrying on,' he said. 'The show goes on, folks, but at *my* pace. I am not going to allow Frank to be rushed.'

There were some terrible stand-up screaming matches between Terry and Mickey Duff, who sometimes wanted to put me in with higher quality opponents than Terry would allow. It was often alleged that Terry was manipulated by Mickey, but when it came to the crunch I have to say that Terry was very much his own man.

I have since often thought back to that morning when I talked Terry into carrying on, and I know

now that if he had quit boxing I would have returned to the ring. In my view, I had lost to Bonecrusher only because of stupidity on my part. He had not proved himself the better man, and just six months later he gave Larry Holmes a lot of problems before being stopped in the twelfth round of a world title fight. It further convinced me that I could still develop into a contender for the world heavyweight championship.

It was Harry Carpenter, a walking record book on boxing, who gave me a confidence booster when he reminded me that the great Joe Louis had suffered his first defeat (a twelfth-round knockout by Max Schmeling) in his twenty-second fight. The set-back against Bonecrusher had come in the last round of my twenty-second fight and on what would have been the Brown Bomber's seventieth birthday. Knowing what Louis had achieved after that defeat, including a crushing first-round victory over Schmeling in a return match, I looked forward to the future with new hope and inspiration.

Most of my fans were tremendously supportive after my defeat by Bonecrusher, but I sensed a nasty turn among a section of the public. I had to put up with a lot of insulting things being shouted at me as I walked down the street, and even kids were giving me stick – imitating my *Spitting Image* dummy and yelling things like: 'I've been Bonecrushed, know what I mean 'Arry.'

But I pretended I couldn't hear them. When you're near the top of the ladder you've got to expect people in this country to want you to fall off. I don't know why it is, but in Britain we seem to take a great delight in building up heroes and then knocking them down just as quickly. I'm not talking about myself so much, but you see it happening all the time with sports and showbiz stars. I consider myself lucky because the vast majority of my supporters have stuck with me through thick and thin.

While Bonecrusher – a real charmer of a character outside the ring – was deservedly getting on the gravy train, I restored my credibility with four more victories that set me up for a European title challenge against champion Anders Eklund, a giant Swede who stood a towering six feet six inches and weighed more than seventeen stone. It was while I was waiting for this first chance to win a professional championship that Terry was put under more pressure by a story leaked in a Sunday newspaper that he was a member of a cartel along with Mickey Duff, Mike Barrett and Jarvis Astaire. The allegation was that their partnership – in which they shared profits from promotions – was against the interest of boxers and the sport. Fleet Street had found out about the agreement after a contract signed by the four of them had been stolen from Mickey Duff's home. It was suggested that the boxers in the Lawless camp were paid smaller purses so that the takings would be bigger for the cartel.

Terry called a meeting of all his boxers and explained that he had joined forces with Duff, Barrett and Astaire to benefit his fighters, and I was happy to take his word for it. We all gave him a vote of confidence after he had said that we were free to walk away from him if we thought he was cheating us. The British Boxing Board of Control later ruled that they did not operate a cartel against the interest of boxers, but a lot of damage had been done by the story. I would be less than honest if I did not say that at the back of my mind I began to wonder if the agreement was in my best interests. But I kept my doubts buried and got on with trying to bring true my dream of becoming the first British-born world heavyweight champion of the century.

I knew that a European title would be a passport to a world heavyweight championship contest, but I had to suffer months of frustration before I could get at Eklund. A fight that was first scheduled to take place in the early spring of 1985 was continually postponed because of bitter political and financial disputes with the Eklund camp, and it was 1 October before I finally climbed into the ring at Wembley Arena to face the man mountain from Sweden.

During the months of hanging about waiting for Eklund I had literally taken steps to improve my balance and movement in the ring. There was no question that I was too stiff and upright, and Terry arranged for me to have dancing lessons with the master of tap, Roy Castle. I needed to become more supple and to bend my knees so that I could get more leverage for my punches. Terry Downes, former world middleweight champion who is never short of an opinion or three, described me in that no-nonsense way of his as being 'as stiff as a bleedin' lamppost.' Roy Castle's lessons certainly helped me become more relaxed and lighter on my feet, and they gave me a head – or a foot – start in later years when I had to learn dance routines in pantomime.

Eklund had led me a dance before I finally got him into the ring, and I was in the mood to take a quick step to my first professional title. Before the fight I had my punching power measured by scientists at Loughborough University of Technology. Watched by a group of researchers and computer experts and under the eye of a high-speed camera I took right-hand swipes at a specially-built instrumented pendulum that was suspended on four 500-pound strain-taking strands. The target I aimed at was heavily padded, and after three hours of tests the scientists went off into a huddle to judge the results. Reporter Fred Burcombe later revealed in the *News of the World* that my strongest punches had landed with the force of a ten-pound hammer, with a rate of acceleration equal to 0 to 200 miles an hour in one second. What I didn't tell the scientists is that I held back a little on my punches because I did not want to risk damaging my hand with a major contest coming up.

But I did not hold back against Eklund. They say that the bigger they are the harder they fall. In the giant Swede's case, it was the bigger they are the easier they are to hit. I could hardly miss him with my left jab, and after I had spent three rounds softening him up I knocked him out with a combination of four successive rights to the head. He sank slowly to the canvas like a giant balloon that had been deflated and took the count in a squatting position. In fact he looked like a man who had been hit by a ten-pound hammer.

The victory lifted me into the world ratings, and I comfortably won a warm-up fight against Larry Frazier before I was matched with South African Gerrie Coetzee in a final eliminator for the world championship. Coetzee had been to the top of the mountain already, and had held the WBA version of the world title three years earlier. The Anti-Apartheid Movement put me under enormous pressure to pull out of the fight. Terry and Laura did their best to protect me from the shower of hate mail that poured my way, and I put my head down and tried to ignore the distractions. This was a subject for politicians, not sportsmen.

The Anti-Apartheid Movement used John Conteh, former world light-heavyweight champion, to try to get to me. A letter signed by him put the Movement's case for why I should not go into the ring with a white South African who had grown up under apartheid laws. My former stablemate Maurice Hope also had his name on the letter, but he later denied any knowledge of it and claimed that he had been used. The letter pointed out: 'There are other ways to get to the top, and these are very noble ways without the scar of apartheid.'

Conteh, a fighter I had hero-worshipped as a youngster, was entitled to his views, and he had put action where his mouth was during his days as world champion when he turned down a six-figure purse for a title defence in South Africa. I am not a political animal, but I too, would have refused to box out there. On the other hand, I could not see how fighting Coetzee in England would either harm or help the battle against apartheid.

If I had thought my not going through with the fight would have made a jot of difference to the black struggle for equality in South Africa I would, without any hesitation, have pulled out. But in Coetzee the protesters had picked on the wrong target. Mickey Duff knew Coetzee well and he assured me that he was anti-apartheid and had dozens of black friends. His black sparring partner, Randy Stephens, was best man at his wedding, and he had often had the courage to go on record criticising the poisonous political system in South Africa. He had also adopted a young black boxer, whose parents had died. Boxing was the first sport out there to go genuinely multi-racial, and Coetzee had earned his rating as the WBA's number one contender by beating white and black opponents alike. I have always believed that – in boxing and in life – it is a man's ability and attitude that should be judged, *not* the colour of his skin.

I weighed up everything very carefully before deciding to go through with the fight. If I had refused to box Coetzee it would not have caused the slightest change of heart in South Africa (where P.W. Botha was still in charge before the rise of F.W. de Klerk). In the end I took what could be interpreted as the selfish decision of agreeing to box. The way I saw it, if the protesters had got their way and had the fight cancelled it would have been me who was being punished because of the colour of *my* skin. I had fought my heart out to get to within punching distance of a world championship fight, and it would have set me back a year if I had refused to take part in this vital eliminator. As a professional sportsman, I knew I owed it to my family – their future security – to go ahead with the fight despite all the hateful criticism being aimed at me.

Coetzee unintentionally had his audience of British media men falling about laughing at a press conference a week before the fight when he said: 'I detest the apartheid system, and I have made this clear time and again because I believe in calling a spade a spade.'

It was quietly pointed out to Gerrie that in this country 'spade' is a derogatory slang term for a black person.

At a meeting of anti-apartheid protesters I was described as a traitor who had betrayed his brothers. As far as I was concerned, I would have been betraying my family if I had not gone through with the contest.

I had never been so keyed up for a fight as for this title eliminator at Wembley Arena on 4 March 1986, and I took out all my pent-up anger and frustration on poor old Coetzee. The contest – all one minute fifty seconds of it – is reported in depth in the 'Fight File'. All I know is that I had never hit anybody as hard as with the final right that sent the thirty-one-year-old former WBA heavyweight champion sprawling unconscious through the ropes at the end of our brief, violent encounter.

It was several minutes before Coetzee recovered sufficiently to be helped back to his corner, and for a while we were concerned about the damage I had done with that final blockbusting punch. It was unnerving, and I was relieved when Coetzee was able to leave the ring under his own steam. Just a few days later the dangers of boxing were further underlined when poor Steve Watt, Scottish welterweight champion, died after being stopped in ten rounds by Rocky Kelly in a fight at London's West Hotel. The abolitionists were out in force demanding that boxing be banned, but I turned a deaf ear to their arguments – not because I am stupid, but because I am fully aware of the risks I take every time I climb into the ring. *And I am happy to take those risks.* Nobody holds a gun to my head and demands that I box. I fight because I enjoy it and the element of danger adds to the attraction of the sport. When Nigel Mansel is behind the wheel of a racing car, Chris Bonnington is scaling a mountain peak, Peter Scudamore is approaching a national hunt fence or Rory Underwood is going headlong into a tackle they are not thinking about the dangers involved. They are fired by the challenge of their sport, and the same goes for me when I climb through the ropes. I know and accept that there are medical reasons why boxing is not exactly good for your health, but it's a risk every time you drive on a motorway or even step across the road. Boxing has given me a standing in life as well as a healthy bank balance, and I don't think there is a sport to match it for character-building and teaching self-discipline. All those critics who want to see boxing banned on medical grounds should try to balance their view by taking into consideration the good the sport does by helping people – the boxers *and* their families – to escape the poverty trap. Thanks to the rewards from boxing I am able to offer my wife and daughters a far better future than they could ever have hoped for had I still been stuck as a labourer on the building site. Obviously if there were not the huge financial incentives I would not be so keen to take the risks, but I would hate to think where I would be today if it was not for boxing. Locked up, I would imagine.

I went to see Coetzee in the dressing room to check that he was all right, and I did not choose my words very carefully when I told him: 'Sorry that I disgraced you in front of your family.'

Cabinet Minister Kenneth Baker, a keen boxing fan, was standing behind me. 'I don't think Frank will make a politician or a diplomat,' he said with a laugh.

Gerrie, a real sportsman in and out of the ring, took no offence at what I said, and told me: 'I have been boxing for more than twenty years and nobody, but nobody, has hit me as hard as you did tonight. I considered myself the best fighter in the world. Now I recognise you as the number one man, and I'm sure you will prove it in your next contest.'

By knocking Coetzee out of my path I had opened the way to a dream fight for the world heavyweight championship, and the man waiting for me in the opposite corner was a Philadelphian by the name of Tim Witherspoon.

Chapter Four

A Dream Too Far

The promoters made one major mistake during the build-up to my world championship challenge against Tim Witherspoon. They hired a publicity director who seemed to think he was Barnum and Bailey rolled into one and was more interested in selling himself than the show. He set up camp – along with his portable computer, mobile telephone and fax machine – in the Royal Oak gymnasium six weeks before the fight, and he managed to put me under more pressure than any of my sparring partners.

I know that professional boxing is about box office – or 'bums on seats' as it is known in the trade – and I have always done my best to help with the necessary publicity build-up before fights. The one thing I have never gone in for is the public insulting of opponents because I find that too degrading and undignified. I have respect for any boxer who is courageous enough to climb into the ring, and will never get involved in bad-mouthing or mocking him for the sake of selling tickets.

The publicity man for the Witherspoon fight had what he thought was the bright idea of holding a 'Bruno Hour' at the gymnasium after every training session. It meant that every day I was at the beck and call of any media person who cared to drop into the gym, and I was continually having to answer the same tired questions in dozens of interviews while photographers snapped away at me and radio and television microphones were stuck under my nose. The toughest questions were aimed at me by the women reporters from the magazines and tabloids, most of whom seemed more interested in asking about bonking rather than boxing. I lost count of the number of times I was asked whether I was still having 'it' during my training build-up, and I had to lean on my old reply of, 'No, I have to keep telling Laura that I've got a headache.' When a woman reporter from one of the posher papers kept on at me about whether I have sex before a fight, I tried to be witty in answering what had become a tedious question. 'I've been away from Laura for so long that I don't know if I've still got lead in my pencil,' I said. In her article the next day she made it seem as if I was obsessed with the subject, and that I had made her blush. If anybody was blushing it was me. Believe me, those female reporters don't pull punches and you have to be really careful that you don't give them the ammunition to do a hatchet job on you.

When these 'Bruno Hours' finally finished the publicist boasted that he had arranged a total of 165 personal newspaper, television, radio and magazine interviews. What he forgot to mention is that, as he had turned it into a free-for-all, the established boxing writers stayed away because they expected – as in the United States – special access to the champion and challenger. I talked myself almost hoarse giving interviews, yet finished up accused of being unco-operative because Terry and I decided we would not hold my sparring sessions in front of the press. It would have been too much of a distraction to have television and newspaper cameras trained on me while trainer Jimmy Tibbs was taking me through my fight strategy as I sparred in the Royal Oak ring. This was interpreted by several critics as a sign that I was cracking up under the pressure, and one reporter went so far as to suggest I was on the verge of a nervous breakdown. This, of course, was nonsense. I just wanted to be single-minded and I did not feel that I could work out naturally if the gym was crawl-ing with media men hungry for stories. How would they like it if I kept looking over their shoulder every time they tried to write a sentence?

My main sparring partners were former world title challenger David Bey, unbeaten Detroit heavyweight prospect Rufus 'Hurricane' Hadley – a bubbling per-sonality who brought life and laughter to the gym – and my stablemates Horace Notice and Gary Mason, both of whom were scheduled to box on the world championship show that had been arranged for Wem-bley Stadium on the night of 19 July, 1986. My chal-lenge against Witherspoon was scheduled to start at midnight to allow for 'live' television coverage in the

United States by Home Box Office. Boxing would be dead on its feet without the injection of cash from television, but it was a row over television that at one stage threatened to cause a postponement of the fight. Both the BBC – who had covered all my professional fights – and ITV – who had an agreement with joint promoter Don King – claimed the right to screen the championship contest. Just as it looked as if they would take their argument to court they agreed on a compromise deal, with both companies showing the fight the next day.

The publicist managed to get Fleet Street interested in one story when he revealed that David Bey had been forced to return suddenly to the United States with a broken nose and two broken ribs. 'It just shows how hard Bruno is punching,' the press release said. What the publicity man failed to include in his story is that Bey had been involved in a fracas in a London nightclub. I think the bouncers had punched harder than me!

The saddest moment for me during the build-up to the fight came when we had to bar the one and only Muhammad Ali from watching me in a training session. It was just ten days before the showdown and Don King wanted to bring Ali to the Royal Oak. I knew it was just a publicity gimmick, and did not want my training workout being turned into a circus. There are few bigger fans of Ali than me. I idolised him when I was a kid, and I still consider him 'The Greatest'. But it's sad and upsetting to see him as he is today, a shambling shadow of the magnificent athlete he used to be. The boxing abolitionists jump at the chance to point at him as an advertisement for what boxing can do to a man, and they always somehow manage to forget to mention that the form of Parkinson's Disease from which he suffers afflicts thousands of people who have never laced on a glove in their lives. I have never been able to match Ali as a showman or as a boxer, but I have always considered it wisest to try to be myself rather than a copycat. I was told that our publicist made a big thing of introducing himself to Ali while he was in London for the fight. 'Hello, champ,' he said. 'Remember me – I worked with you as one of the publicists for your title fight with Richard Dunn in Munich.'

'So you did,' said Ali. 'You sure did well because that fight drew the smallest crowd in the history of heavyweight boxing!'

Ali had not lost his ability to cut with his tongue. He said of my fight with Witherspoon: 'If Bruno can't dance, he ain't got no chance. I nicknamed Tim "Terrible Tim" when he used to be my sparring partner, and only somebody who is smart on his feet can beat him. So tell Bruno to get his dancing shoes on.'

Sweet-as-a-lollypop dancing has never been my style in the ring. I like to plant my feet to get full power for my punches. When Ali's advice was passed on to me, I said: 'The only dancing I'll do at Wembley is a war dance.' Even my publicist was impressed with that reply.

One of my idols who *did* come along to the gymnasium was Sugar Ray Leonard, who was covering the fight as a television commentator. We chatted for an hour, and he told me all about the eye problems that had forced him to retire from the ring. He confided in me that he was itching to make a comeback and that he thought the risk was worthwhile. It was a conversation I was to recall five years later when I was faced with a similar dilemma, although my torn retina was nowhere near as serious as Ray's detached retinas.

The biggest laugh I had during the preparation for the fight was when the publicist made the naive mistake of visiting the Tim Witherspoon camp in Basildon, Essex, while carrying a box crammed with special zip-up championship-fight jackets that were to be presented as a memento to each media man covering the contest. He was no match for the dozen giant Philadelphians from Witherspoon's entourage who descended on him, and he finished up running out of the hotel with just half the jackets left.

I can get very moody in the week before a major contest. I like to channel all my concentration on the fight, and I prefer my own company as I prepare myself mentally for the challenge ahead. The one thing I insist on every day during the build-up is an hour-long massage that gets my muscles nicely loosened. Yet despite the magic fingerwork of East London masseur Rupert Doaries – who incidentally, is related to Lennox Lewis – I admit that I tensed up too much before the fight with Witherspoon. I am not for one moment trying to make excuses, but I have to say that nothing could have prepared me for the enormous pressure I felt in the final hours before climbing into the ring. I had no fear of Witherspoon, but I was frightened of letting everybody down. An extra burden had been placed on me by the dramatic defeat of Ireland's featherweight idol Barry McGuigan by Steve Cruz in a world title defence in Las Vegas just a few weeks earlier. It had been a bitter blow for British boxing, and I knew a lot rested on me to try to restore some pride to our sport.

As I sat in the same Wembley dressing-room that the England footballers had occupied when winning the World Cup exactly twenty years before I could hear the thirty thousand fans booming out their 'Brun-o, Brun-o' chants. I wondered how my Mum was coping with it all as she waited to see me fight for the first time in her life. She was sitting at ringside with Laura, my sisters Faye, Angela and Joan and my brother Michael. I knew Mum would be praying for me, and folded into the back of the Bible that I was reading in the dressing-room was a special prayer that had been written for me and which would be the last thing I would read before starting the long walk to the ring:

Dear Lord God, Father Almighty,

I know that with so much want and misery in the world it is selfish and remiss of me to ask for something that is for me alone. But on this one occasion, oh Lord, I ask you to give me the strength, the courage and the willpower to become the heavyweight boxing champion of the world. In so doing I would be better able to spread your Word and give an example of Christian beliefs and attitudes to the young people that I am fortunate enough to have following my lead. More than ever, oh mighty Father, I need you in my corner when I make my challenge for the world title and I ask you to help make me a winner of whom everybody can be proud. I appreciate and understand that there are many more vital things to concern you, but this is the most important moment of my life and I pray that you can fill me with the fire and determination that will be needed to win that championship. Win or lose, please let me conduct myself with dignity and grace and make it so that neither I nor my opponent suffer any serious injury. I hope and pray that I get the opportunity to be your spokesman as heavyweight champion of the world, but regardless of the result I will remain your humble and obedient servant. Through Jesus Christ Our Lord, Amen.

As I did my final warm-up in the dressing-room with twenty minutes of shadow boxing, Terry quietly went through the strategy that we had worked out. It was wrongly assumed by many from Witherspoon's appearance at the weigh-in that he was not in the absolute peak of condition. He weighed in at a couple of ounces under sixteen stone eleven pounds, a stone above what was considered his best fighting weight and this led strength to the stories that he had not been giving 100 per cent concentration to his training. Terry warned me: 'Take no notice of what people are saying about the way Witherspoon has prepared for the fight. He's the sort of tough character who can come in off the street and fight fifteen rounds. Be sure that once the bell goes he'll prove himself good and ready. But both you and I know that you are a stronger puncher, fitter and more determined. This is going to be *your* night.'

I felt that I knew Witherspoon almost as well as he knew himself. Ever since I had earned the fight with him by beating Coetzee I had made a special study of him on a collection of videos. I admired and respected him as a boxer who was a fine all-round technician with a clubbing right hand that he liked to swing over the top of an opponent's defence almost in the style of a cricketer bowling a ball. I knew I had to be careful of that punch. He would be seven pounds heavier than me, but – with a reach of eighty-two inches – I had a five-inch reach advantage and I planned to make full use of it by getting behind a long left jab, which I would use as a foundation-builder for the heavier blows to come from my follow-through rights and left hooks. Witherspoon had won twenty-four of his twenty-six professional fights, and one of his defeats – a points loss to Larry Holmes in a WBC world title fight in 1983 – had been loudly disputed. He had won the vacant WBC championship in 1984 by outpointing Greg Page, and had then lost it in his first defence against Pinklon Thomas. In January 1986 he captured the WBA version of the world title by outpointing Tony Tubbs, and now I was plotting to take the crown away from him. One thing of which I was convinced is that I was fitter and more dedicated than Tim, who earlier in the year had been ordered by the boxing authorities to go to group therapy to help him beat a drug problem. Without wishing to boast, I knew there was no fitter boxer in the world than me. In fact my fanaticism for training had reached the point where during the final weeks of the build-up for the fight trainer Jimmy Tibbs had to order me out of the gym because I was working too hard.

I had a clear picture in my mind of what I had to do to win, and as I shadow-boxed to work up a sweat I felt quietly confident that my dream of becoming heavyweight champion of the world was about to come true.

In the course of my two hours in the vast Wembley dressing-room I had watched my stablemates Mark Kaylor, Jimmy McDonnell and Gary Mason return triumphant after their supporting contests, and now it was my turn to try to make it four-in-a-row for the Royal Oak gym. As I stepped out into the corridor at just after midnight to walk to the ring behind the Union Jack there was a column either side of me of uniformed policemen and security guards. We had walked the fifty yards up the slope on the route that the cup final teams take when I suddenly realised why the security cordon was so necessary. As the spotlight picked us out and the fanfare blared across the stadium it sounded as if all hell had let loose. The crowd were screaming their support and as we reached the pitch area – the grass covered with boards – dozens of fans tried to break through the cordon as if they thought that a slap on the back was what I needed to motivate me. Gary Mason, all seventeen and a half stone of him, was at the head of the procession and he later told me that he knocked at least ten people out of the way with his enormous bulk.

'I worked harder than in my fight,' he said (he had knocked out Mark Young in the fifth round).

To be honest, the journey from the dressing room was really scary and I vowed that if I ever fought at Wembley again I would find a more sensible way to get to the ring. A cameraman with a hand-held television camera walked backwards directly ahead of us, and deserved a bonus for not falling over as he was buffeted from side to side while doing his best to train his camera on me. The publicity man had wriggled his way inside the cordon. I was just surprised he had not arranged for me to be interviewed on the way to the ring. I had the hood of my red dressing-gown up over my head and my bandaged hands were resting on the shoulders of Terry, who was pushing ahead of me flanked by trainers Jimmy Tibbs and Frank Black. As I climbed the corner steps, ducked under the top rope and stepped into the ring the roar of the crowd almost took my head off. All the voices were shouting almost as one for me, and I now just wanted to get on and win the fight for them. I looked down to the ringside seats nearest my corner from where Laura blew me a kiss. Mum, my sisters and Michael were standing waving at me. I crossed myself as I acknowledged them with a nod. I knew their prayers were with me. Alongside them, Terry's close friends Les Eyres, Ken Gilliland, his wife Jean, and Eileen Giller sat with Sylvia Lawless – all of them rooting for me and giving me added strength.

Witherspoon tried the oldest trick in the book of keeping me waiting for ten minutes before he deigned to join me in the ring, but I had mentally prepared myself for the delay. He arrived surrounded by an entourage of at least twenty supporters, all of them in jazzy tracksuits and waving miniature Stars and Stripes. I was wearing mental blinkers and deliberately made myself oblivious to all the trappings. I did not even take much notice when Muhammad Ali and Henry Cooper were brought back together in the ring where they had their famous fight in 1963 in which Henry knocked down the then Cassius Clay with his left hook. By the time the national anthems had been sung and referee Isidro Rodriguez had given his final instructions I was fired up for the fight of my life.

My fight strategy, worked out with Terry and Jimmy Tibbs, was to keep nice and tight for the opening rounds and operate behind a solid left jab. It was clear from Witherspoon's record that he had a strong chin and he had never taken a count throughout his amateur and professional career. I knew it would be unwise to launch a nuclear attack in the first round as I had against Coetzee. I needed to conserve my energy for what would almost certainly be a long journey, and I had steeled myself for having to go fifteen rounds for the first time. When I came back at the end of the first round well satisfied with my performance I was surprised to find that Terry was several seconds late getting into the ring to give his instructions. He is famous throughout boxing for getting through the ropes like a whippet, and he later explained that his delay was caused by an American TV cameraman who was standing on the ring apron right in front of him. Terry wasted little time kicking him out of the way, and the cameraman apparently went on strike for the rest of the fight in protest. Nothing and nobody is allowed to come between Terry and his boxers on fight night.

As I went out for the second round I was reminded to keep my chin tucked into my shoulder because Witherspoon had a looping right that could take out anybody if given the opening. For the first five rounds I was in charge of the fight, keeping Tim on the end of my left jab and getting out of clinches as quickly as possible. He was doing his best to turn it into a rough-house fight, but I stuck to my boxing plan because I knew that in a free-for-all I would come off second best. Don't ask me why, but Americans are better brawlers than the Brits. Having been to the States on many occasions and visited the ghettos, I guess the reason is that they have to fight harder in the streets to survive. The mean streets of New York, Los Angeles and Philadelphia make Wandsworth seem about as rough as a school playground.

I didn't manage to hit Witherspoon with my best combinations, but I landed the sort of single punches that would have blasted out virtually any other heavyweight in the world. Each time Tim just took a step backwards and then closed up on me before I could follow up with the combination punches I had practised for hours on end in the gym. He had an exceptionally strong chin, yet I know that I had him worried several times during the early stages of the fight. Whenever I pinned him with a good punch he would smother and cover and duck and dive until his head had cleared, and then he would come back with those crude but effective swings of his. He clubs you with his fists and I have to admit that he was a much harder puncher than I had imagined.

The turning point of the fight came midway through the sixth round when I stupidly allowed Witherspoon to kid me into following him to the ropes, and as I went to throw a right he caught me on the side of the jaw with a swinging left and then a clumping right to the left side of my head. For the first time I had to seek the safety of a clinch as I waited for the mist to clear from my eyes. Tim's swollen left eye was beginning to close and he had been breathing heavily for the last couple of rounds, but he now knew that he had hurt me and this did wonders for his confidence.

My stamina started to drain away from me at an alarming rate, and I could only imagine that all the tension during the build-up to the fight had started to take its toll. I felt as if I was just in front going into the tenth round, but the fact that there was still a third of the fight to go was playing on my mind. I got Witherspoon angry with a couple of rights that drifted off target on to the back of his neck and he complained bitterly to the referee. I interpreted this as showing that he was beginning to run out of steam himself and as I went out for the eleventh round I decided to unload some heavy ammunition in a bid to get the fight over. I thought I was just getting the better of the round and I remember whacking him with a right cross that would have dropped most heavyweights.

I was ready to follow up with a left hook but he managed to catch me with a right of his own on the side of my jaw. From then on everything is hazy in my memory. I can just recall trying desperately to hold on to him while I got my senses back together, and I later saw on video how he started to hurl those cricket bowler's punches at me. Two more clubbing rights sent me reeling across the ring. I remember bashing backwards against Witherspoon's cornerpost and I knew my dream of winning the world title had disappeared as I went down in a daze. They later told me that Witherspoon had hit me three times while I was down but I was not aware of it. I was lost in a world of mists and mazes as the referee waved the fight over and then, for some reason, hauled me up and started levering me towards my corner like a removal man. By rights he should have left me where I was until I had received a medical check. The next I knew Terry Lawless had me in his arms and was saying: 'All right, Frank. We've got you.'

I came fully to my senses once I was back in my corner and I briefly cuddled Witherspoon and we kissed each other – one warrior respecting another. The trip back to the dressing-room was even tougher than our entrance, particularly as my legs felt like jelly. I found out later that it was even more harrowing for Witherspoon. A mob of mindless morons hurled chairs in his direction, and police made twenty-seven arrests during the mini-riot that followed the finish of the contest. I know my fans were disappointed, but there was no need to take it out on Tim, who had proved himself a magnificent champion.

I wanted to see him straight after the fight but the corridor separating our dressing-rooms was jammed tight with journalists, photographers and television crews. I telephoned the Witherspoon camp the day after the fight and gave this message to the Champ: 'You have earned my full respect, know what I mean? You confirmed what I always thought . . . that you are far and away the best of the three champions. I know you'll now go on to become the unified champion. I hope you didn't take those nasty words that were put into my mouth by my publicist before the fight seriously. It was all part of the ticket-selling hype. Safe journey home and I hope you have some good thoughts about me and your stay in Britain.'

Tim told me: 'You gave me the shock of my life. You were far better than I thought you would be and in eighteen months you could be world champion. You hurt me more than I have ever been hurt in the ring before and even now I can feel your punches. Stick at it. You're young yet.'

He said he had been overwhelmed by the welcome he got in Britain and was big enough to say that he knew that the trouble after the fight at Wembley was caused by just a stupid minority.

I really liked Tim, and it was sad to see his career temporarily come off the rails after his victory over me. He was not in the right mental or physical shape when he met late substitute Bonecrusher Smith in a title defence five months later, and amazingly he was bombed to defeat in the first round. There followed a long and bitter legal dispute with promoter Don King, and Tim was making all sorts of allegations about his purses not being anything like he had been promised. I am among those British boxers who have had a moan about money, but we tend to be well looked after when compared with the way some of the American fighters are ripped off.

When I was sitting in the Wembley dressing-room after the fight nursing a jaw that was swollen to twice its normal size I insisted against the wishes of Terry that I should give a press conference. I was determined to show that I could take defeat with dignity.

Terry felt that I needed a complete rest but I wanted to help all those journalists who had kindly supported me on the way up. So coming up to four o'clock in the morning the publicist ushered in a posse of photographers and reporters who trooped into the dressing-room where I was sitting with an icepack jammed to my puffed-up jaw. Monty Fresco, the *Daily Mail's* legendary cameraman from a famous family of Fleet Street sports photographers, was the first through the door and I told him: 'Do us a favour, Mont, only take a picture of my good side.'

As the photographers snapped away Terry suddenly called for hush. 'Just listen to these words, Frank . . . just listen . . .'

Whitney Houston was singing on a tape on my ghetto-blaster in the corner of the dressing-room. The song was 'The Greatest Love Of All' and she was just delivering the line, 'Oh no . . . no matter what they take from me, they cannot take away my dignity . . .'

The reporters asked about the fight, which was fine

by me. 'Tim beat me good and proper,' I told them through my swollen lips. 'He is a magnificent champion, and has got a chin like granite. I hit him with some really heavy punches, but he just took a deep breath and came back at me. Sorry about the way I'm talking to you. It's only my mouth. I haven't turned poofy or anything.'

That got them laughing and lightened the morgue-like atmosphere of the Wembley dressing-room. There is nothing worse than a loser's dressing-room, and I wondered how many footballers had sat close to tears exactly where I was sitting with runners-up medals in their hands. Coming second ain't no fun. At Wembley it hurts more than ever.

The press conference was going along nicely until it was spoilt by a news reporter – and remember this was after the hardest fight of my life and with me not feeling exactly on top of the world. 'When are you going to end all the speculation and marry your girlfriend?' he asked.

How would you have reacted to a question like that considering the circumstances? I managed to contain myself and just snapped: 'My private life is my private life. Mind your own business.' I then added with heavy sarcasm: 'You'll be the first to know.'

Laura, sitting quietly in a corner of the dressing-room with my Mum, made us all fall about laughing by asking: 'What, before me?'

The greatest thing that happened to me following the fight was the response of the public. I was feeling sorry for myself after the defeat but I got some indication of how people felt when I was taken by car from Wembley Stadium to Northwick Park Hospital in the early hours of Sunday morning for a precautionary X-ray on my swollen jaw.

It was at the hospital that I met the real heroes of the night, and of all times: the doctors, nurses, specialists and general staff who work all hours. The place was buzzing with business, mainly dealing with patients admitted after accidents on the way to or from Wembley. I was lying on a bed in a side ward having my pulse and blood pressure checked when I heard applause. The curtains were drawn back to show a line of patients queuing up to see me.

One chap with his leg in plaster was pushed forward in his wheelchair to meet me. He shook my hand and told me: 'I fell down the steps at Wembley and broke my leg before you got into the ring and didn't even see the fight. At least you had the consolation of being paid for the state you're in!'

I handed out more than thirty autographed photographs to the patients and staff and their cheerfulness almost made my hospital visit enjoyable. As I lay waiting for an X-ray that revealed no broken bone I looked up to find the publicist standing alongside me looking genuinely concerned.

'Give it a couple of days and I'll call a press conference to announce your retirement,' he said. 'You don't want to go through this sort of thing any more.'

I nodded in agreement, although deep down in my heart I knew I would have to fight again. The dream of one day becoming world heavyweight champion was still with me.

The publicist was big enough to apologise for the

pressure he had heaped on me in the month leading up to the fight, and admitted that he had demanded too much of me. He had somehow managed to get under my skin, and even to this day he hangs around helping me out with PR and with such chores as after-dinner speeches and with putting articles and books together.

When Terry Lawless and his pal Les Eyres dropped me off at home just after 5.30 on Sunday morning there were already notes and letters stuck in my letterbox from people commiserating with me. It was the first time I had been home for a month. I had escaped the comforts and distractions of home life to live at Terry's house where his wife, Sylvia, looked after me like a VIP guest. Terry got home to find a dozen supportive letters on his hall mat. That was just the start.

The count of letters, Telemessages and telephone calls in the next week shot up past the 5,000 mark. The Post Office did a great job getting the letters to me because some of them were addressed simply: 'Frank Bruno Gymnasium, London' or 'Frank Bruno, Essex'. All but a few of the messages were wishing me luck and praising my performance. A handful of nutters wasted money on stamps to send me insulting letters, aimed at my colour, my performance or both. But I shrugged them off. From the first day that I started getting publicity as a professional I have had to put up with insults from bigots and people envious of my achievements. I always adopt the attitude that they are entitled to their warped opinions (but I would be happier if they kept them to themselves).

Jimmy Tarbuck was among a load of show-business people kind enough to contact me and he told me: 'Put it all down to experience. You will be all the better for it. Thank you for doing us all proud.'

King athlete Seb Coe, who had been at the ringside, rang to say: 'You have no need to apologise to anybody. You performed with pride and courage and we all love you.'

That really moved me, and just ten days later I was in Edinburgh for the Commonwealth Games cheering him on the track just like he cheered me on in the ring. I had gone to Scotland to outline my future plans at a press conference, and this brought accusations that I was hijacking the Commonwealth Games and using them as a platform for commercialism. What my critics failed to point out was that it was the idea of sports journalists that I should make my announcement in Edinburgh because that was where most of the established boxing writers were operating in their double-up roles as athletics correspondents. I kicked off the conference by announcing that I was giving up boxing and moving into a monastery. When asked if I felt I had made any mistakes in the fight against Witherspoon I said: 'Just one. I came out for the eleventh round.'

The joking over I got down to the serious business of announcing – despite all the advice that I should hang up my gloves – that I was fighting on.

'In heavyweight terms I am, at twenty-four, still a baby,' I told the press. 'I am too young to think of retiring. I still have the dream of winning the world heavyweight championship. I am sure I have plenty more to give you to write about . . .'

Chapter Five

Enter George the Dragon

George Francis came back into my life breathing fire like a dragon and promising to turn me into the 'Mr Nasty' of boxing. I had first become acquainted with George during my amateur days when I used to work out in the gymnasium where he was training world light-heavyweight champion John Conteh. He was known as a sergeant-major of a trainer, bullying his boxers into super-fitness, and – as I was to find out – his bite was every bit as bad as his bark.

Terry and I had decided that George was the ideal trainer for me after Jimmy Tibbs had crossed the political minefield to the rival Frank Warren camp soon after my defeat by Witherspoon. Faithful Frank Black was still at the Royal Oak to help out with my general fitness work. 'This is the end of the gentle giant,' George told the press after taking over as my trainer early in 1987 as I prepared for a testing comeback contest against former WBA world champion Greg Page. 'Frank has been too mollycoddled. I'm going to be like a Royal Marines sergeant with him, and I don't care if he ends up hating me. I'm going to make him nasty and spiteful.'

It was not all talk. George toughened my training routine, taking me on exhausting runs across Hampstead Heath which ended with brisk swims in the icy waters of Highgate pond. In the gymnasium he introduced me to his murderous medicine-ball exercises, hammering my stomach muscles until they were like a wall of iron. He climbed into the ring with me and, calling on his forty years of experience as a trainer, introduced me to all the old-pro tricks that you will not find in any boxing textbook. George showed how to unbalance opponents by a nudge to the shoulder, how to push down on the opponent's neck at close quarters (a Muhammad Ali speciality) and how to hold, particularly on the blind side of the ref. It was the sort of education I had needed when Bonecrusher and Witherspoon were taking free whacks at me. If I had been more ring-wise I would have grabbed them and held on the moment the first of their bombshell punches landed.

I have owned up to having been too stiff and rigid. Now George was teaching me to relax, to conserve energy and to get that all-important bend in the knees for full leverage of my punches, and he was also stressing the importance of getting my head down in the clinches.

'You're great at sportsmanship but useless at gamesmanship,' George told me. 'At the level you are now fighting you must know all the tricks in the book, and a lot more that never quite found their way into print. Heavyweight championship boxing is not for choirboys. Just watch the likes of Mike Tyson. He is evil in the ring, and would hit you with the stool if he thought he could get away with it.'

Tyson had become the undisputed champion of the world since my punch-up with Witherspoon. It was no surprise to me. I had first come across him during a learning-and-earning trip to the United States back in 1983 during which I had one fight, knocking out Mike Jameson in two rounds in Chicago (I finished him off with a left hook and a right uppercut, the best combination I had ever thrown). During my training I had worked out with boxers of the quality of Mike Weaver and Michael Spinks, but it was sixteen-year-old Tyson who made the biggest impression. Just a handful of spectators watched us work out at the famous Grossinger's training camp in the Catskill Mountains. We sparred for three rounds, and I like to think I got the better of it with my left jab but Mike, five years my junior and with that bull neck of his already a feature of his muscular physique, impressed me with his hand speed and his determination. Mickey Duff was among the onlookers and he commented at the time: 'One day you two could be fighting each other in front of a worldwide audience and with millions of dollars at stake.' It was quite a bold and prophetic statement considering that Tyson was still an unknown amateur.

Another highlight of that trip to the States was visiting the palatial Pennsylvania home of Larry

Holmes, who was then the undefeated heavyweight champion of the world. I went to him hoping for some advice on boxing, but he was more interested in warning me to look after my money, to beware of hangers-on and to 'stay off the coke'. I listened open-mouthed as Holmes told me: 'The evil drug pushers have infiltrated the world of boxing over here in the States. The game is full of cocaine sniffers. It makes me want to weep to see so many kids getting into the stuff.'

He raised a forefinger and jabbed it at me to emphasise the point he was making. 'Now I'm telling you for your own good,' he said, 'don't have anything to do with it. It's no use me, Mickey Duff or Terry Lawless advising you how to block a left lead or throw a right cross if you're going to go off and ruin it all by sniffing coke. Remember, you've gotta leave the stuff alone.'

Holmes was preaching to the converted. I had long ago decided to have nothing to do with the drugs scene, and I had a slogan printed that read: *ONLY MUGS TOUCH DRUGS*.

While training in the States I noticed that many of the top fighters worked out to a background of rock and soul music blaring from their ghetto-blasters. This appealed to me, but Terry – an opera lover and all-round music fanatic away from the gym – decided it was too much of a distraction. 'You have to be able to hear the trainer's commands and the music breaks your concentration,' he said. But, happily, George Francis believed the opposite and he talked Terry into allowing me to have music playing while I trained. It was George's belief that the music would help me to relax and to get extra rhythm into my movement.

I found a surprising gentler side to George once our punishing training sessions were over. A former Covent Garden fruit porter with a quick Cockney humour, he had 'got religion' while training Cornelius Boza-Edwards for his world title fights in Las Vegas. 'I had no real religious belief until Boza kept on at me about how wonderful it was to have faith,' George told me. 'I used to run Boza and other fighters to church and would wait outside in the car. Then I started to go in, more out of curiosity than anything. Once inside I started to listen and to learn. I then studied to become a Roman Catholic and now feel more contented than at any time in my life. I was always a hard bastard, but now I have mellowed and am sympathetic to others.'

He saw my eyes opening wide as I listened, and he quickly got back into his sergeant-major's disguise. 'But don't you think that means I'm going to be soft on you,' he added. 'It's all very well being a gentleman outside the ring, Frank, but once that bell goes you've got to bring out the animal in you. The ring is a jungle where only the toughest survive.'

Soon after George and I had started working together Greg Page pulled out of our scheduled fight at Wembley on 24 March 1987, with a cut eye and James 'Quick' Tillis was called in as a substitute. Tillis was a cowboy from Oklahoma, whose chief claim to fame was that he had been the first opponent to take Tyson the distance. During my ten-day stay at Grossingers training camp in 1983 I lodged in a log cabin alongside one that was occupied by Tillis and an unforgettable character called Jeff Sims. We used to spar together every day, and the two American heavyweights just did not know what to make of me. I was the same size, the same colour but I talked with what to them was a strange accent. Every day we would all have lunch together at a large table in the communal kitchen, and I was aware that both Tillis and Sims were giving me some strange looks during my first couple of days at the training camp. Since my Oak Hall days I had always prided myself on my manners and made a point of saying 'please' and 'thank you'. My politeness obviously had an unsettling effect on Sims, who took Terry Lawless on one side and said: 'This guy Bruno, is he a faggot?'

Terry laughed out loud and replied: 'He's about as big a poof as Sylvester Stallone.'

That helped them accept me and for the rest of the stay they treated me with more respect, particularly as I gave better than I got in our tough sparring sessions. Tillis, who always wore a ten-gallon cowboy's hat outside the ring, was a strong, upright boxer whose style was not unlike my own. But Sims was unconventional and a law unto himself. I never tire of telling the following story of Sims, who remains one of the most incredible people I have ever met.

I knew that he was something different from the first minute of our opening sparring session. I dropped him on the seat of his pants with the first right hand that I threw. He sat on the canvas and said in a deep drawl: 'S-h-e-e-t. That chain gang done slowed me down more than I thought.'

Later on over dinner I asked him what he meant about the chain gang. It turned out that he had four bullets still wedged in him from two shooting incidents plus scars from forty stitches following knife fights. He had served seven years in jail – most of them on a chain gang – for shooting dead a man who had previously shot him. Sims had never known his father and from the age of seven had travelled the South with his mother and ten brothers and sisters, all of them working for a sharecropping gang. He started boxing while in jail and became prison champion of the State of Florida. It was boxing that got him remission from a fifteen-year sentence, and he turned professional on his release and won his first nineteen fights by knockout and was ranked number eleven in the world ratings.

This was how twenty-nine-year-old Sims, talking in a Deep South drawl, described how he lost his place as a title contender: 'I'd got myself noticed and, man, I was living high on self-respect for the first time in my life. Then my manager goes and matches me with another young world title contender. To save on expenses, the manager got both of us to live together while training. I ain't kiddin' you, man. The most important fight of my life and I'm having to sleep in the same room as my opponent. S-h-e-e-t, man, it was like putting a lion and a tiger in the same cage, and sure enough we were soon at each other's throats.

'Anyways, one night we got to arguing over who

should do the dishes and who should shift the garbage. We start to fight and the next thing I knows he's pulled a gun and is pointing it right at me. As I dived for my life he shot six times and I got hit by three of the bullets − in the shoulder, the ribs and the thigh. As I lay on the floor I heard him re-loading and I thought, s-h-e-e-t, the son of a bitch is gonna finish me off. I dragged myself up and jumped two storeys out of the window. When I got outta hospital three weeks later I still had them slugs buried in me, plus another from when I got shot years earlier.'

I decided not to tell him the story of my days growing up in Wandsworth and going to Oak Hall because it might have convinced him that I really was a faggot!

Late one night during our second week at the camp we had one of the worst storms I've ever known in my life. Lightning hit a tree right outside our window and set it on fire, and a power cut plunged the entire camp into darkness. It rained so hard I thought we were all going to get washed away down to the foot of the Catskills. When the rain stopped I followed Terry on a stumbling journey through the pitch-black grounds to our cabin. It was really frightening, I can tell you. As I passed Jeff's cabin I noticed that his door was wide open. I peered into the darkened cabin and found him lying stark naked on his bunk, staring dreamily into space as if he didn't have a care in the world. 'Ain't you scared being in there on your own, Jeff?' I asked, only half joking.

He didn't blink an eyelid as he replied: 'It don't worry me none, man. I done used to solitary.'

There was a definite unhinged side to Sims, who

had a favourite word that he kept using. At first I thought it was four words. It sounded like 'wreck a car ration'. It then dawned on me that it was one word, recreation. In the middle of one night he came banging on the door of my log cabin shouting: 'Come out, Bruno, you no-good Limey. It's time for our showdown. Let's get it on right here and now.'

I ignored him but was really angry to have my sleep interrupted. I gave him a right earful of choice Wandsworth street language the next morning and he found out that there were times when I could forget to be polite. He put two big arms around me and hugged me. 'Sh-e-e-t, man,' he said, 'I was only having a little rec-a-re-ation.'

I wondered what the Fleet Street reporters would have made of him if he had been my substitute opponent instead of James Tillis, who had earned his 'Quick' nickname because of his fast fists and speedy footwork. He also had a quick tongue, as he proved at the press conference before our fight in March 1987 when asked how he had come to be outpointed by Joe Bugner in Australia six months earlier. 'Man that was a home-town decision,' he said. 'I beat him by such a wide margin that I can only guess the judges must have included Stevie Wonder and Ray Charles.'

Tillis, wearing his cowboy hat, added: 'I've not come here as a stepping stone for Bruno. I'm gonna rustle him, ride him, rope him, brand him and corral him.'

I arrived at the conference with a few days' growth of beard, and several of the reporters wrote that this was my deliberate new, mean, 'Mr Nasty' look. In actual fact I had a skin rash and had not been able to shave. The press also misjudged my mood at the conference. They thought the fact that I virtually ignored Tillis was all part of the new 'big bad Bruno' act, while the truth was that I was uptight and feeling the pressure.

I knew that if I lost I would be going nowhere with my career. There was the added burden of knowing that the winner would almost certainly be a future title-fight opponent for Mike Tyson, who was due at Wembley to watch the contest as a co-commentator alongside my old pal, Harry Carpenter. A lot of people had written me off as finished after the defeat by Witherspoon. Now, eight months later, I was determined to prove them wrong.

By the time of fight night at Wembley I had shrugged off all my doubts and fears. George and Terry between them got me nicely motivated, and I gave poor old Jimmy Tillis quite a going over. I shook off my ring rust and took command of the fight from the first bell, forcing Tillis on to his back foot with two-handed combinations that I had been sharpening under the gaze of George the Dragon.

I had just one critical moment in the second round when Tillis landed a cracking right counter to my jaw. I went into a clinch, held on the blind side of the referee Francis-style until my head had cleared and then regained control with a barrage of lefts and rights to the head. I could sense the resistance draining out of the cowboy who had now become 'Slow' Tillis. Midway through the fifth round he waved a glove in surrender and turned his back on me after a sequence of lefts and rights had ripped gashes on his nose and eyebrow. As referee John Coyle waved the fight over Mike Tyson told BBC viewers: 'I'm very impressed. That's a tremendous job by Frank. He will be a very good opponent for me, and I look forward to fighting him.'

I was just glad to get the job over and done with. There would have been nowhere for me to run and hide if I had lost. Now I had Tyson in my sights, but I knew I needed at least two more fights before I would be ready to challenge him, and when Terry suggested a warm-up contest down in Cannes I jumped at the idea. I was not to know that it was going to develop into a French farce and the most embarrassing evening of my life.

The opponent lined up for me in the Palais des Festivals in Cannes was an American called Chuck Gardner, who I had been billed to fight in my fourth contest until Ron Gibbs was brought in as a substitute. The alarm bells should have rung when American-inspired reports started appearing in the newspapers more than a week before the fight dismissing Gardner as – and I quote – 'a washed-up bum'.

Rival promoter Frank Warren tossed in his two-pennyworth when he described the fight as 'a sham' and claimed that his gardener could do better against me than Gardner.

It was all worrying stuff, and with the benefit of hindsight I wish we had called the whole thing off before I was dragged into what was described by one newspaper as 'the biggest boxing scandal for years'.

I have to be honest and say that I could not believe it when I first clapped eyes on Gardner before the fight. He was supposed to have been thirty-three but looked at least ten years older. At seventeen stone four pounds he seemed to be carrying about two stone surplus weight, and most of it was draped around his waist in great rolls of fat. I wondered what the viewers at home would make of him when they watched the fight 'live' on BBC.

Mind you, they did not see him for long. He collapsed as if he had been shot when I connected with the first solid punch that I threw, a half jab, half hook to the side of the face. It was all over in fifty-nine seconds, most of it spent with me stalking Gardner as he almost galloped backwards around the ring.

Gardner slipped under the bottom rope and lay perfectly still with his head resting on the apron. The referee did not bother to count him out, but bent down to remove his gumshield. As he did so, it looked as if Gardner's set of upper dentures came out at the same time. It was like something out of a Monty Python sketch and just about put the cap on a perfect evening.

For more than a week there was uproar in the press, with the BBC getting much of the flak for screening the event. The whole world suddenly seemed full of people screaming: 'We told you so.' One newspaper printed the story that Gardner's true age was nearer fifty than thirty, and there were reports that he had not trained for a month before the promotion after twisting a knee while working as a bricklayer.

I said as little as possible about the affair because as far as I was concerned I had just done my job as a professional boxer. My opponents were always selected for me. I never had a say in the matter. It was the job of Terry and matchmaker Mickey Duff to find the opponent, and on this occasion even they had to admit they had made a big mistake.

It brought a major showdown within the cartel, with Mike Barrett going on record as saying that it was 'like a sick joke'. He told reporters: 'I have to be frank and say that this was one of the most disgraceful mismatches in boxing history and those involved have to take responsibility. It gives boxing such a bad image. I was only relieved that Frank did not connect with more force when he knocked him out. He could have killed him. We could have had a fatality on our hands. What would that have done for boxing?'

These outspoken comments brought to a head the ill feeling that had been simmering just beneath the surface between Terry and Mike, and it was not long after that Barrett ended his links with the cartel.

I wanted to get back to the ring as quickly as possible to try to bury the memory of the Gardner fiasco, and my wish was granted two months later. This time I travelled to the holiday resort of Marbella in Spain where, waiting in the bullring to meet me, was another American opponent: Reggie Gross, who was substituting for Greg Page, a man I seemed destined not to meet in the ring.

Gross had been knocked out in the first round by Mike Tyson, but had a reasonable record before then. His career had been brought to an abrupt halt when he was arrested on a charge of murdering a man with a gun. He spent seven months in prison before being cleared of the charge, and now he was looking to relaunch his career – with me as his stepping stone back towards the top.

Our fight was to be the chief supporting contest to the world welterweight championship defence by Lloyd Honeyghan against Texan Gene Hatcher. After a twenty-four-hour delay caused by nonstop rain (the rain in Spain was a pain) Lloyd wasted no more time, bombing out Hatcher in just forty-five seconds.

I took quite a bit longer against an opponent who seemed more interested in ducking and diving than fighting. Gross was allowed to take my punches for eight of the scheduled ten rounds before the Spanish referee at last stopped what was one-way traffic to save the man from Baltimore soaking up any more punishment.

I have never known Terry as angry as he was during this one-sided fight. For at least three rounds I had been whacking solid punches through the defence of Gross without him trying to reply, and I could hear Terry yelling at the referee to stop the contest. When he finally stepped in, Terry jumped up on the ring apron and shouted: 'You are a bloody disgrace, referee.'

We tend to take British referees for granted, but after the experience I had in Marbella I reckon they are as good as any in the world apart from a handful of exceptional refs in the United States. The referee in Spain must have been watching too many bull-fights. It was as if he wanted us to fight to the finish, and it was poor old Reggie Gross whose ears I was going to have.

I was beginning to feel the benefit of the new George Francis training routine, and I believed the time had come for me to step up in the quality of opposition. Terry agreed, and I was excited when I was told that my next opponent would be former WBC world heavyweight champion Trevor Berbick at Wembley in September 1987. It would be considered as a virtual final eliminator for a world title fight against Tyson. I had sparred many rounds with Berbick when he had been based in London and I strongly fancied my chances against him. Tyson had become the youngest world heavyweight title-holder when he stopped Berbick in two rounds in November 1986.

George was getting me nicely tuned up for the fight when, with just two weeks to go, I was given the frustrating news that Berbick was pulling out because of a back injury. A search for yet another top-line substitute failed and the show was cancelled. I was just sinking into a deep depression when a name was whispered in my ear that brought all my fighting instincts to the surface.

The name: Joe Bugner. And doing the whispering: Barry Hearn.

Chapter Six

Laying the Bugner Ghost

Almost from the moment I threw my first punch as a professional I was haunted by the name of Joe Bugner. He was just beginning to make a name for himself in the ring when I first laced on the gloves as a skinny nine-year-old schoolboy. In 1971, the year before I was sent to Oak Hall, he was adjudged to have outpointed great heavyweight hero Henry Cooper in a triple title fight for the British, European and Commonwealth championships. It was a disputed decision and Hungarian-born Joe, then just twenty-one, was never really forgiven for beating 'Our 'Enery', who bowed out at the age of thirty-seven with the fans still very much on his side.

Eleven years later when I launched my professional career Joe was in the United States flirting with the third of several comebacks, and ringside reporters were making comparisons between Bugner and me almost from my first fight. By the time I had got thirteen wins under my belt Joe had returned to Britain to resume his comeback and he made no secret of the fact that he had me in his sights.

Much of the fighting talk was being done by Joe's wife and business manager, Marlene, a tough Australian journalist who was a match for even the most hard bitten boxing impresario. Joe would have been world champion if he could have fought half as aggressively as she talked.

I was ready to fight Joe. Any time, any place. But Terry was still preaching the virtue of patience. There was also a political barrier between Joe and me. He was fighting under the banner of Frank Warren, who was just starting to challenge the dominance of the Duff-Barrett-Astaire-Lawless cartel.

I have to admit that Bugner was bugging me. There could be no disputing that he was one of the best defensive boxers in the world. He had twice gone the distance with Muhammad Ali, had outpointed Henry Cooper, had given Joe Frazier a tough time in a distance fight and was noted for the toughness of his chin. But there was also little doubt that he was one of the most boring of all heavyweights to watch because his style was so negative. I would have jumped at the chance to test Joe's chin with my right hand, but – despite several attempts to get us together, including a proposed open-air fight in Vienna – the political mountains were always too high to climb. Joe got sick of hanging around waiting for us to be brought together and he emigrated to

Australia in 1985. That it seemed was the end of any chance of a Bugner-Bruno showdown.

At about the time that I was preparing for my world title challenge against Tim Witherspoon news came through from Down Under that Joe – now 'Aussie Joe' – was getting himself in shape for a fourth come-back campaign. And also round about that time a new face started popping up on the British boxing scene – millionaire snooker entrepreneur Barry Hearn.

Barry was from our manor in Essex, to where I had moved soon after the start of my professional career. He was the supremo of the enormously successful Romford Matchroom Snooker club that had produced a diamond of a player in Steve Davis, and was largely responsible for turning snooker into a television mega-sport. He and near-neighbour Terry became quite friendly, and when I travelled to Brentwood for a face-to-face meeting with Witherspoon to publicise the fight it was Barry who drove us there in his Rolls-Royce; and it was noted that he took a seat on the stage for the press conference, drinking in the atmos-phere and taking a keen interest in every aspect of the fight.

He later revealed to Terry that his big ambition was to promote boxing with the same sort of style and flair that he had brought to the world of snooker. They agreed in the summer of 1987 to form a partner-ship, concentrating at first on small-hall shows where Terry's stable of boxers could get much-needed work and projection. It seemed the new partnership had hardly been going five minutes when Barry kept quietly asking my opinion of Joe Bugner. 'Do you think you could beat him?' he asked.

'I've never doubted it,' I said, truthfully.

When he told us that he was going to try to bring Bugner over from Australia to fight me Terry burst out laughing. 'You can forget that one,' he said. 'There's no chance.' Mickey Duff, who had cut his close ties with Bugner, agreed that it was a waste of time trying to get us together in the ring.

That was just the challenge that Hearn needed. In the short time that I've known him I have discovered that he likes nothing better than to try to prove the impossible is possible.

Everything seemed to be against Barry. He was talking about an autumn open-air fight, which would be a gamble with the weather, and he had to get past perhaps the toughest barrier of them all – Joe's wife, Marlene. Then there was the little matter that Joe faced the threat of arrest if he stepped foot in Britain because of alleged non-payment of alimony to his first wife.

Marlene gave Barry more aggravation than he had experienced in hundreds of snooker promotion negotiations, and it took him a total of more than seventy telephone calls to Australia – and several increases in the purse offer – before he finally clinched the 'impossible' fight. Working closely with Dennis Roach and David Shapland of the PRO international management agency, he booked Tottenham's ground at White Hart Lane for the fight everybody said could not be made. Roach and Shapland, a former deputy editor of the *Sun*, were best known in the world of football. They, along with Hearn, had the advantage of not knowing anything about the politics of boxing (take it from me that Barry has since found out all about them).

Mickey Duff was brought in on the promotion, but – to the best of my knowledge – Jarvis Astaire and Mike Barrett were not involved. Terry's partnership with the high-powered Mr Hearn was causing eruptions within the cartel, and I could see that Terry was beginning to feel distinctly uncomfortable with the new direction he was taking.

Melody, Joe's first wife, was paid her alimony, but still almost sank the fight by giving a series of interviews to a newspaper in which she alleged that Bugner had knocked her about. Joe dismissed it as lies, and said that this was the sort of aggravation he could do without. He threatened not to come back to London, but the lure of the purse and the prospect of at last getting into the ring with me persuaded him to get on the plane to Heathrow.

From the moment he landed, Joe's mouth worked overtime. He spilled even more words than Muhammad Ali at his peak, and the wall-to-wall publicity made it just about the most talked-about fight in British boxing history. You could hardly turn on a television chat show, listen to the radio or open a newspaper without finding either Joe and/or Marlene in full flow. The more the Bugners talked the more I liked it because I was on a percentage of the takings. Joe grumbled that he was doing all the banging of the drum, but it suited me. I have never been one for shooting off my mouth before a fight, and he was doing enough talking for both of us.

The strange thing about Joe and me was that despite the way we had been linked for so many years we had never really met. I had no idea what he was like behind the loud-mouthed braggart that he presented for the publicity machine. His scripts at times seemed to have come from those rubbishy spaghetti westerns in which he had featured during his various retirements from the ring. Some of the stupid things he said made me wonder about his sanity, but I was assured by people who knew him well that it was all an act, and that underneath the blarney he was a likeable big softie with a good sense of fun. Leading up to the fight I did not want to know about the 'nice guy' side of Joe. He had got me wound up with many of his insults, and I fed on this as my motivation to give him a good hiding.

When I at last came face to face with Bugner at the pre-fight press conference I could hardly believe the size of the man. He looked huge, and I wondered if he was exercising his body as much as his tongue. Joe was certainly bigger than in his three impressive comeback victories Down Under where he had out-pointed James 'Quick' Tillis, David Bey and the man I found so elusive, Greg Page. He said that he wanted the extra weight so that he would be able to push me around.

Joe followed his usual silly script at the conference, saying things like: 'Frank is stepping out of his class. He's strictly "C" class while I'm A-plus. He is going to get a real bashing.'

He added: 'The tension is going to get to him. He'll be a bag of nerves when the first bell goes, and long before the twelve rounds are over, only one man is going to finish on his feet. The other won't be – and I know who that will be – . . .'

It was the perfect feed line and I dived in and said: 'You!'

There was a lot of tension between Joe and me, and it was not manufactured for the press. He was trying to do an Ali-style psyching job on me, and I was not going to stand for it. I lightened the mood when somebody asked if we would have to fight barefoot if the heavy rain that was around continued.

'I don't think the man who supplies my Nike boxing boots will be very pleased with that idea,' I said.

As it turned out the Saturday evening weather was kind to us. There was an autumn chill in the air, but both Joe and I were well wrapped up going to the ring. I was all in red, while 'Aussie Joe' wore a fancy dressing-gown in the gold and green colours of Australia. As I stared across the ring at him clutching the flag of his adopted country in his right glove during the playing of the national anthems I felt as if I was looking at one of the Australian Alps. At the weigh-in I was amazed to find Joe stepping on the scales at a massive eighteen stone four pounds, the heaviest of his career. I weighed in at a trim sixteen stone four pounds, deliberately light so that I could pu' into practice the tactics I had agreed with Terry and George of a jab-and-move campaign.

You will find a full ringside report in the 'Fight

File', but as far as I was concerned it was the most satisfying performance of my career. Joe came out swinging, trying to land a quick knockout. He had obviously believed all that rubbish about me having a weak chin, but his punches were of the flappy sort, not nuclear blows like Bonecrusher and Witherspoon had thrown. It had worked for him ten years earlier when he had bombed out Richard Dunn in the first round, but he found me a much tougher and more elusive opponent. I pulled him up in his tracks with a couple of left hooks and then started to dominate the fight with a stiff left jab that kept snapping back his head.

From the second round I concentrated on switching my attack, first banging away with both fists to the huge expanse of Bugner's belly and then going to long range to launch jabs and hooks through his high guard to his face. Joe was always trying to wrestle me to the ropes, using his enormous bulk to push me back. But I kept pulling away, claiming the centre of the ring from where I was able to pick my punches.

I could sense Joe tiring as I stepped up the pressure in the middle rounds. You know before anybody else when you have your opponent on the slide. You hear it in his grunts as you land to the body, and you see it in his eyes that are suddenly dulled and anxious. The sparkle had gone out of Joe, and every time I ripped punches into his ribs he sucked in deep mouthfuls of air like a winded bull. I knew it was only a question of time before I put him out of his misery.

We were into the last minute of the eighth round

when I shook Joe with a right cross to the temple. He wobbled like a giant jelly, reeled across the ring and then fell slowly backwards into the ropes. There was some criticism later that I had been allowed to hit him while he was down, but the bottom rope was holding him up and referee John Coyle did nothing to stop me as I unleashed a volley of about eight punches before brave old Joe went down for a count of eight.

As he got up looking like a man in a trance I went gunning for him, but this time Mr Coyle pulled me off just as the white towel of surrender came fluttering in from Bugner's corner. The bell went at the same time, but it was too late to save poor old Joe.

I had at last laid the ghost of Joe Bugner. There were the inevitable cynics who claimed that I could not have beaten him in his prime, but I could do no more than I had done. Joe, announcing his retirement yet again, was sporting enough to say: 'Frank did a good job on me. He punches much harder than I gave him credit for before the fight and is a better all-round boxer than I imagined. I gave out a lot of bullshit before the fight to sell tickets, but Frank has earned my full respect. He will give Mike Tyson a lot of trouble.'

So old Joe wasn't such a bad guy after all. He went into his final final retirement with my best wishes. I don't think either of us really meant the nasty things we had said about each other over the years, and he can proudly tell his grandchildren that he was one of the greatest defensive heavyweight boxers ever to climb into the ring. I will tell my grandchildren that

I beat a proud man who − unfortunately for him − talked a better fight than he could produce. Would I have beaten him in his prime? I think so. But I would say that, wouldn't I!

Joe and I have something in common − we have both had to take a lot of stick from Henry Cooper over the years. The few times I have met 'Our 'Enery' for any length of time I have always found him a likeable, down-to-earth bloke. But all the things he says about me − that I'm too stiff, can't take a punch and struggle against the top Americans − are criticisms that could have been levelled at him during his career, that is judging him by old film I've seen of him in action. I hope when I've hung up my gloves I don't go in front of a microphone or into print knocking young prospects. I always try to see the best in people, and prefer to say encouraging things. But who knows, perhaps once you are retired you start getting bitter. I hope I won't find out yet awhile.

Bugner's reference in the after-fight interview to me meeting Tyson was because the champion's manager, Jim Jacobs, was at the ringside, and early negotiations were already under way for me to challenge for Iron Mike's world title in London the following summer. I shall save all my breath about Mr Tyson for a later chapter.

There was a funny postscript to the fight with Bugner when Jim Rosenthal climbed into the ring to interview me for ITV. I looked around and asked: 'Where's 'Arry?' I was not meaning to be rude to Jim, but I was so used to Harry Carpenter being the man with the mike in the ring after my fights. Mind you,

you could easily mistake his old chum Reg Gutteridge for Harry. They are rival commentators, but good pals away from the microphone. As former Fleet Street colleagues and television commentators they have between them seen just about every champion of note over the past forty years and I have a tremendous respect for both of them. The ITV combination of Reg and my old stablemate Jim Watt is a winning partnership, and they go together like fish and chips. There are few people around who can match Watt for reading a fight. His views are respected throughout the world of boxing.

An interesting sequel to my victory over Bugner came at Tower Bridge a few days later when former world light-welterweight champion Terry Marsh got wet on my behalf. He had sworn in a newspaper article that if I beat old Joe he would throw himself off Tower Bridge. Not for the last time, Terry made a big splash.

I was hailed as a hero, but some weeks later I became a very bitter man when I found out what my night's work had earned for me. Bugner had reportedly settled for a guarantee of a quarter of a million pounds plus the Australian television rights. After discussing it with Terry and Barry, I agreed to gamble on taking a percentage. Barry Hearn was widely quoted as saying that I would earn anything between £550,000 and £750,000. I did not get anything like those figures and I was desperately upset. Estimates of the attendance for a fight that was one of the most publicised of all time swung between 30,000 and 40,000.

The last thing I want is any legal hassle, and I am making it clear here and now that I am not pointing the finger at anybody. I am not saying that Terry, Barry, Mickey or anybody was responsible. I just wish my hopes of a really big pay day had not been built up, and in the circumstances I could not help feeling that I had been ripped off.

Most people I have spoken to who were at the Tottenham ground that night felt there was a near-capacity crowd, certainly over 30,000. I was told that the attendance was only 25,000, and Barry Hearn later said there was a crowd of nearly 27,000. The last thing people want to read about is me moaning and groaning about my pay packet because I have done very nicely out of boxing, thank you, but this experience filled me with a determination never to get taken by anybody again. I was the man going into the ring to give and take the punches. For the sort of risks I was taking and the attention that I was drawing I knew that I deserved top rewards. I decided that in future I would ask for my money upfront.

I conveyed my feelings about the Bugner fight purse to Terry, and he said I should not have believed the figures that Barry was giving to the newspapers. 'It's all newspaper talk,' he said. 'They often tend to exaggerate for the sake of headlines.'

The Lawless-Hearn partnership was already on its last legs, and their friendship was being stretched to breaking-point. Terry did not like some of the outspoken statements that Barry was making to the press, and I know that he had been getting hassle from Mickey Duff and Jarvis Astaire over his association with Hearn.

Barry and Terry soon decided to go their separate ways, and they have been the best of enemies ever since. Once again the poison of boxing politics had caused the problems.

Hearn used his experience in promoting my fight with Bugner as the foundation for his rise to a place of power in British boxing. His Matchroom promotions are now well established thanks to regular projection on satellite television.

I thought he and I had a mutual respect for each other, but I was to find out that I was wrong.

Chapter Seven

A Hurricane Called Gilbert

I needed to wind down after the Bugner fight, and I decided to trace my roots by visiting for the first time my mother's home island of Jamaica. Just to top up my tan, you understand. A lady called Laura and our two lovely daughters – Nicola and Rachel – came with us, and we found something close to paradise. When you first see the island, set like a jewel in the shimmering Caribbean with its Blue Mountains and its spotless white sands, you wonder how anybody could be mad enough to leave it for the greyness of Wandsworth. But on closer inspection, away from the polished tourist beauty spots, you find pockets of poverty, with islanders living in tumbledown shacks and their kids running around with bare feet and in ragged clothes. Man, I tell you, that can really hurt your insides when you realise it could be your kids.

I had an emotional meeting with my elder brother,

Eddie, who prefers to live in Jamaica. We got on famously – well, like brothers. He doesn't look unlike me except that he's about two inches taller and a stone or two heavier. Believe me, they build 'em big in Jamaica and I found that I was only just above average size. Knockabout games of cricket were being played by boys all over the island, and I saw some gigantic young bowlers who will give England nightmares in the near future.

The highlight of the holiday – which brought me to tears – was meeting my grandma for the first time: my Mum's Mum, eighty-four-year-old Grandma Henrietta Brown. I wept when I realised that she was virtually blind. She had lost the sight of her left eye and had a cataract in her right eye. Grandma was overjoyed to at last meet me, Laura and her two great-grand-daughters. Quietly and without fuss I contacted that genius of an eye surgeon David McLeod on my return to England, and I was able to arrange for Grandma to fly for the first time in her life to London where I paid for her to have an operation at Moorfields eye hospital that restored her sight. I am not telling this story to win any brownie points, but just to underline what I was saying a few chapters ago about boxing not only helping hungry fighters but also their families. It was only because I was making sufficient money in the boxing ring that I was able to literally bring some light into my Grandma's life. If you think this is too sugary, I'm sorry. But this is as it is, know what I mean.

A year later, in September 1988, we returned to Jamaica for another holiday that this time turned into a nightmare and threatened to cost us our lives. We got caught up in the middle of a hurricane called Gilbert.

I have never been so frightened in my life as when the hurricane started to whip through the island at 200 miles an hour. If you experienced the hurricane that hit England in the autumn of 1987 then imagine that terrifying wind at twice the power and speed and you'll get the picture. The beach-side holiday hotel in which we were staying was shifting in the wind as if it was made of cardboard, and as ceiling tiles fell and light fittings came tumbling to the ground I did my best to protect Laura and our two terrified daughters by gathering my arms around them and shielding them with my body. There was a load of junk written about me being a hero, but any husband and father would have tried to do the same thing. We were all in fear of our lives.

It seemed hours before the storm passed, and the sight of the trail of havoc and death that it left behind will haunt me into old age. More than forty people were killed, and nearly half a million made homeless. It was not just the wind but ten inches of rain that did the damage. Because the telephone lines were torn down, we could not make contact with the outside world and the story got back to England that my family and I were missing, feared dead. Thank God, this was nonsense, but it could easily have been that bad.

Jamaican Prime Minister Edward Seaga was not exaggerating when he described the island as 'looking like Hiroshima after the atom bomb'. He estimated the damage at nearly £5,000 million, a staggering figure when you realise the population of the island is only 2.3 million. Nearly 80 per cent of the homes on the island suffered damage. The rain washed out the banana crop, wrecked the poultry industry and thousands of coconuts were blown into the sea. I toured the island the day after the hurricane and saw whole villages where not a single building was left standing.

What amazed me was the spirit and courage of the island people who had seen just about everything they owned literally blown away. They were still managing to charm me with their sunny smiles as I wandered among them trying to see if there was anything I could do to help.

Days after the hurricane the capital, Kingston, was still littered with toppled trees, ripped-off advertising hoardings and masses of assorted debris. I joined in with troops and civilian volunteers at work in virtually every street, pulling down collapsed roofs, clearing wreckage and taking food and clothing to the homeless. The lads from HMS *Active*, a Royal Navy frigate that had been on exercises in the Caribbean, came ashore and did a marvellous job helping out with the mopping-up and rescue operations.

I can honestly say that I have never been so frightened in my life as when the hurricane was at its peak. Man, did I get through some prayers. It was the sort of experience that makes you appreciate just how precious life is, and I realised how much Laura and my two girls meant to me. As soon as I could I got to my grandma's house on the outskirts of Kingston, and was relieved to find she had come through the hurricane unharmed.

When the press tracked me down I told them: 'Nothing will scare me now. Mike Tyson will be a breeze after this.'

A month later I was honoured to get the chance to take part in a live TV show in England to boost the emergency funds to help ease the burden in Jamaica. Pop stars like Keith Richards and Boy George and the cast of *EastEnders* were among a host of celebrities who willingly gave of their time and their talent and thousands of viewers telephoned pledges. I know my 'brothers and sisters' in my mother's homeland of Jamaica would like me to say a big thank you.

I might easily have got caught up in a storm of a different kind when I went to Wembley in 1988 to watch the FA Cup Final between Wimbledon and Liverpool. I was making my way out of the ground after seeing Wimbledon cause an amazing upset by beating Liverpool when a drunken fan started giving me aggravation. 'You're a w – – ker, Bruno,' he shouted in a thick Merseyside accent. 'You couldn't knock my old granny over.'

He was entitled to his opinion, and I did my best to ignore him as I shuffled along with the crowd filling out of the stadium. Who knows, perhaps his nan was Supergran.

'So you're deaf as well, Bruno,' he yelled.

Again I ignored him, and his reaction this time was to charge at me like an angry bull. I sidestepped and the punch that he was aiming at my head glanced off my shoulder.

I tensed ready to hit back in self-defence, but thought better of it. 'Leave it out,' I said, as his mates hustled him away. 'It's not my fault Liverpool were beaten.'

It was all over in seconds, and – amazingly – Fleet Street missed what could have developed into a nasty incident. Can you imagine the headlines if I had lashed out? I could also have been in big trouble with the police because in a court of law a professional boxer's fists are considered lethal weapons. I had the self-control to contain myself, but I can understand how the likes of Paul Gascoigne can get drawn into trouble by idiots trying to make a name for themselves. I can also understand why so many celebrities these days have a minder or two with them when they go out. There are a lot of nutters around looking for the chance to get into the headlines.

If it had not been for boxing, I might easily have tried to make a career for myself as a professional footballer. But I would not have fancied the sort of attention a player like Gazza gets on and off the pitch. I've had more than my fair share of media exposure, but I have always managed to keep my family life fairly private. At least when I close my door behind me I know that my time and my space is my own. But from the moment Gazza captured the nation's hearts with his talent and his tears in the 1990 World Cup his privacy was kicked into touch. I've been in Gazza's company and have seen the way the press hound him. It's not fair. He should be judged purely on what he does on the football field. His private life should be his own.

I know how difficult it must be for him, but he must try to cock a deaf 'un to people who attempt to wind him up in the street or when he's trying to relax in a restaurant or any public place. When he loses his temper and responds he is giving these tiny-minded people some sort of victory.

One of the biggest aggravations can be when you are having a quiet meal or a private conversation and somebody you have never met in your life before comes up and thrusts a piece of paper in front of you, demanding an autograph. Terry taught me very early on in my career that I should look on this as a privilege rather than a pain. 'The time to start worrying, Frank,' he used to say, 'is when they stop asking for your autograph.'

Once my boxing career had really taken off I found that when going out I could not have two minutes of peace without the autograph hunters descending on me. This is going to sound conceited . . . I decided to get myself some small portrait photographs printed, and each week I put an hour aside while I sign them. I am always armed with them when I go out, and when fans politely ask me for my autograph I give them a photograph. It costs a lot of money over the course of a year, but I feel it is more satisfactory than signing a torn piece of paper.

In the spring of 1986 I was flying to Las Vegas to be at the ringside for the world middleweight championship clash between Marvin Hagler and John Mugabi. I was relaxing in my seat while we were cruising when Terry said, 'Frank, there's somebody here wants to meet you.'

Instinctively, I reached into my pocket and produced a signed photograph of myself and thrust it into the outstretched hand of the person bending over me. When I looked up I found myself staring into the surprised face of pop superstar George Michael. He was nice enough to laugh off my gaffe, and we sat down together and talked about our two worlds of sport and music. If I had not become a professional sportsman I would have liked to have had a go at singing for a living. Mind you, as anybody who has heard me in panto will confirm, it would have meant searching deep down for my voice which is somewhere in my boots. My brother Michael is the musical one of the family and is an excellent keyboards player; and all my sisters can sing beautifully. I wonder if George Michael has still got my autographed picture? That was one of the more embarrassing moments of my life.

The drunken fan who tried to whack me one at Wembley wanted his picture in the paper rather than a signed photograph from me. There is always somebody around who wants to show off to his friends and to try to prove that they are macho. It's like being the fastest gun in the west, and they want to prove they are quicker on the draw. I am determined that these sort of people will never get famous off my back, and whenever I sense there is a troublemaker around I am extra careful about watching what I do and say.

I watched the Cup Final at Wembley with my Cockney mate Jimmy Greaves, who has the headlines to prove that he knows a thing or three about being hassled by idiots looking to make mischief. Jimmy has always encouraged me to build up my career outside the boxing ring, and it was he who, in 1983, gave me my first chance to appear in front of the television cameras away from conventional boxing press conferences. He was presenting a series called *The Greaves Report* for Central Television, and he invited me to go to Birmingham for an offbeat, light-hearted interview.

We did some sparring in front of the cameras in a local gymnasium and that in itself was hilarious. I'm six inches taller than Jim and he was having trouble getting past my long arms to ask his questions. The plan was that Jimmy would 'fight' his way inside my reach and then interview me as he held on.

It was the idea of Gary Newbon, now head of sport at Central and a terrier of an after-fight interviewer. I don't think Gary quite appreciated the effort and energy you use when sparring. Each time Jimmy fought his way close enough to ask his questions he was breathing like a winded carthorse. He'd start the interview and the soundman would interrupt and say: 'All I can hear is heavy breathing.'

'You could sell the soundtrack for a bleedin' blue movie,' said Greavsie, with that cutting tongue of his that has made him such a popular television personality.

After about six tries, Jim finally fixed it. 'I'll tell you what, Frank,' he said. 'You lean back on the ropes and I'll interview you there.'

A pity the camera didn't follow us down the motorway when we left the Birmingham studios, with Jimmy giving me a lift back to Essex where we both live. We stopped off at a service station for a bite to eat and Jimmy had the place in uproar by going up to the biggest, toughest looking lorry drivers he could find and jokingly challenging them to a fight. Then he'd point at me and say: 'I should let you know that I'll be bringing on a sub.'

I don't think Jimmy has yet recovered from the fact that my food order filled three trays. And he was paying.

Jimmy and I had a return match a year later, and that was even funnier – although Jim says that his eyes water at the memory. Greavsie was doing a regular stint on *The Saturday Show*, a kids' programme presented by Tommy Boyd and Isla St Clair. Jimmy had learned from our first meeting in front of the cameras, and this time he rehearsed his interview with me before our 'live' sparring session in a ring that had been set up in the studio.

He worked it out with me that he would ask a question and then lightly hit me with three pulled punches. Bang, bang, bang. Then I was to reply and hit him with three light punches. Bang, bang, bang.

We got a nice rhythm going at rehearsal. Question – bang, bang, bang. Answer – bang, bang, bang.

Then we went 'live' with the interview in the middle of the studio ring – and I suddenly got the sort of blank that all television performers fear.

Jimmy asked his first question and lightly hit me with three punches. I replied and lightly hit him with three punches. He asked his second question and I replied, gradually getting into the rhythm. But I was concentrating so hard on getting my answers right that I managed to get out of synchronisation with my punches. Jimmy asked his next question − bang, bang, bang. Instead of replying as we had agreed, I instinctively threw three punches that were twice as hard as we had rehearsed and they caught poor old Greavsie completely unawares. His knees buckled and he fell forward into my arms with his head spinning and water streaming from his eyes.

The studio crew were all falling about laughing off camera as Jimmy somehow managed to get through the interview. He got himself locked into a close-quarter clinch and hung on for dear life rather than risk taking any more out-of-time punches.

I had the honour of playing alongside Jimmy in his very last appearance on a football pitch. His son, Danny, was sadly forced into early retirement by a leg injury, and I was invited to play in a testimonial match that Southend United staged for Danny. Jimmy came out of retirement at the age of fifty for one last performance, and though he was carrying a couple of stone extra than in his prime he still managed to move like the thoroughbred footballer that he is.

There is a whole generation growing up who think of Jimmy purely as a television personality, not realising that he was one of the greatest goal-scoring geniuses ever to set foot on a football pitch. I used to support Chelsea when I was a kid − before I was turned off by hooligans threatening to kick my f − − − ing head in because of the colour of my skin. I was not going to play the brave man by challenging them, and decided I was best off staying away. I used to walk to Stamford Bridge from my Wandsworth home to see the likes of Peter Osgood, Alan Hudson, 'Chopper' Harris, Charlie Cooke and John Hollins playing beautiful football that brought them the FA Cup and European Cup Winners' Cup in the early 1970s. In the Danny Greaves testimonial match I had the thrill of playing in the same team as two of my heroes from that Chelsea era, goalkeeper Peter Bonetti and defender David Webb. The cup-winning team was managed by a good friend of Terry's, Dave Sexton, whose father, Archie, fought for the British middleweight title in the 1930s before a detached retina cost him the sight of an eye. That was in the days when there was very little medical supervision in boxing.

Greavsie was just winding down his career with West Ham in the days when I was a terrace fan at Chelsea, but he was still a legend at Stamford Bridge where he had started out as a professional in the 1950s. It will always be a treasured memory of mine that I played alongside him and fed off his passes in his very last match. I always choose to play at centre-forward in the charity matches in which I appear, and Jimmy was kind enough to say that with a little more polish I could have been a handful for any defence. He was too polite to mention the fact that the way I go charging in for the ball I would not last five minutes without getting a yellow card. Strength rather than skill was always my main feature when I was dreaming about a career as a professional footballer in my days at Oak Hall when I won representative honours with Sussex schools.

Greavsie and I also appeared alongside each other several times on the quiz show *Sporting Triangles*. I have to be honest and admit that my all-round sports knowledge is pretty weak. I know quite a lot about all sports, but when it comes to statistics and dates I go blank. I was like that when studying history at school. I'm the one who thought the Battle of Hastings was something to do with the mods and the rockers.

It was while I was recording *Sporting Triangles* with Greavsie in November 1987 that Gary Newbon secretly arranged to mark my twenty-sixth birthday with the presentation of a huge cake. Greavsie, a keen horse-racing fan, pointed out that jockey Willie Carson, also a guest on the show, shared my birthday and Gary had to get one of his assistants to dash out and buy a second cake. Jimmy, of course, had a crack to make about it all. I towered more than a foot taller than Willie as we stood side by side receiving our cakes from Greavsie, who said: 'It's a lovely coincidence that you both share the same birthday, but I don't think anybody will mistake you for twins!'

Greavsie and I were lined up to appear together again on 'live' television when he had his chat show on Central in 1988. The show's producer, Roy Bottomley, best known as the chief scriptwriter for *This Is Your Life*, booked me to appear in the role of a general handyman who was going to keep popping up during the show that was supposed to be based in Jimmy's kitchen. I was to be the resident straight man.

At the last moment I had to pull out of the 'live' appearances because I was in training for a big show of my own with Mike Tyson. So I filmed a series of telephone calls, giving pre-recorded answers to questions from Jimmy. But it did not work, and when the Tyson fight was called off the spot was dropped from the chat show after just a few weeks. It was so stiff and stilted that one critic wrote: 'I thought I had tuned into a repeat of *The Woodentops*.' Jimmy, with that savage sense of humour of his, said that we looked like our *Spitting Image* dummies! I didn't think we were that good.

Jimmy flew out to the United States to interview Mike Tyson for the *Saint and Greavsie* show. It was an exclusive insert in their special preview programme for the FA Cup Final between Liverpool and Wimbledon. Jimmy met Mike in the gymnasium in the Catskill Mountains, and was immensely impressed as he watched him training for his world title defence against Michael Spinks. 'The man is awesome,' Jimmy told viewers. 'There is an electricity that comes out of him. I am sure that if I put a naked light bulb against his chest it would light up.'

Winding up his report, Jimmy passed on this personal message to me from Tyson: 'Give my best wishes to Frank and tell him to look after himself. After Spinks, he is next. I like Frank, but you'd better warn him that I will be full of bad intentions once we are in the ring together.'

Greavsie, genuinely concerned for my welfare, was

later honest enough to say to my face: 'If I were you, Frank, I'd give Tyson a miss. The man's from another planet.'

We were watching Wimbledon cause one of the football shocks of the century against Liverpool in the FA Cup Final at Wembley at the time. As the final whistle blew I said to Jimmy: 'See, Jim – it's the year of the underdogs at Wembley. I can do to Tyson exactly what Wimbledon have done to Liverpool.'

The plan at that time was that I would be returning to Wembley Stadium to fight Tyson. But I finished up having to face him in Las Vegas after a succession of frustrating postponements.

I can truthfully say that it was a world championship fight that had me hypnotised.

Chapter Eight

A Typhoon Called Tyson

My reward for beating Joe Bugner was to be named number one contender for the world heavyweight title held by Mike Tyson. That was the easy part. Actually getting him into the ring with me was to prove something of a nightmare, and there were a couple of occasions when I wondered whether Tyson would be alive to defend the championship.

The contest was first of all pencilled in for 24 June 1988, at Wembley, and it had the blessing of Tyson's dynamic manager Jim Jacobs, a former world handball champion and a boxing historian who was the owner of the greatest fight-film collection ever assembled. A close friend of both Jarvis Astaire and Mickey Duff, Jacobs left a message on Terry's answering machine during a visit to London in which he said: 'Would your big boy like to come out and play with my little boy?' This was his way of saying that he was ready to negotiate a deal for the fight.

Sadly, before the nitty-gritty details could be finalised, in the spring of 1988 Jacobs died and Tyson was distraught. He had looked on Jacobs like a father after his mentor and guardian, Cus D'Amato, had passed on three years earlier, and now he had lost the two major influences in his life. There was a hint of the turmoil into which Tyson had been pitched when he announced that he did not wish to be managed by Bill Cayton, Jacobs's partner, and they started hitting each other with writs.

Meantime, my date at Wembley with Tyson was put back to 3 September 1988 to make way for his mega-money defence against Michael Spinks in Atlantic City on 27 June 1988. I went with Terry to see the fight, and wish I had stayed at home. It was all over in ninety-one seconds, and all I learned was that you must not forget to duck when Tyson is throwing his big bombs. Spinks, a blown-up light-heavyweight, forgot and went down and out in less time than it takes to boil an egg.

I sat in on the after-fight press conference, and could hardly believe my ears when Tyson dismissed the entire media as 'assholes' and then revealed that he was quitting the ring. He said that he was sick to death of the way the press were insulting him, his wife – actress Robin Givens – and his mother-in-law. As Tyson stormed off, the press looked to me to give them some quotes after their short shrift from the champion.

'D'you think you'll last longer than Spinks?' was

the straight-to-the-chin opening question from a grizzled American reporter (they don't believe in taking any prisoners with their interviews over in the States).

'Spinks is a cruiserweight who has pumped himself up to be a heavyweight,' I said. 'I'm a natural heavyweight and Tyson will know I'm in there with him.'

'But do you have the power to handle an animal like Tyson?' was the next shot.

'You'll see on the night,' I said. 'I wouldn't be getting into the ring with him if I didn't think I could beat him.'

'Bonecrusher and Witherspoon whupped you,' said the grizzly bear. 'What makes you so confident you can stand up to Tyson's ferocious punches?'

'He's not King Kong,' I said. 'He's a human being with two arms and two legs. I was a baby when Bonecrusher beat me, and I learned a lot from my defeat by Witherspoon. Let's see if Tyson can stand up to *my* punches.'

'Ain't you frightened after you've seen what he did to Spinks tonight?'

'I won't be like so many of Tyson's opponents who are beaten before the first bell because of their fear,' I said. 'I refuse to be intimidated by him. I've sparred with him and I know that he is not the monster you all make him out to be. I'm honestly confident that I can take the title from him. Come to Wembley in September, gentlemen, and you'll see for yourselves.'

I was pleased with the way I had handled myself under interrogation from the American pressmen, but they were obviously unimpressed. In their reports the next day they completely dismissed my chances of beating Tyson and said I would be just another horizontal British heavyweight. One went so far as to write: 'My prediction is that Bruno will not last as long as Spinks.'

It was all good stuff to motivate me for the showdown, but a couple of weeks later Tyson – having decided to forget his threat to retire – said he was calling off the fight. Flanked by his wife, mother-in-law and new adviser, the billionaire businessman Donald Trump, he announced: 'I just don't feel like fighting. Frank Bruno is not in my immediate future. I don't want to fly 3,000 miles for a fight. I want to stay here in the States, and I'm going to take six to eight weeks off.'

Just twenty-four hours earlier he had said: 'I'll be going to London to defend against Bruno. I have sparred with him and had no problems. I would be crazy to pass up this chance of picking up about eight million dollars. It's just too easy.'

His somersault just a day later followed an out-of-court settlement with Bill Cayton, with Cayton remaining as his manager until February 1992, but having to take a drop in his share of Tyson's boxing earnings from 33 per cent to 20 per cent.

I blew my top when I heard Tyson's about-turn decision, and I told the British press: 'Tyson's been saying what an easy touch I am. Now he seems to have changed his mind. I can't understand why he is screwing me around like this. But I'm the number one challenger and he had better get used to the idea that he has got to fight me at some time.'

Jarvis Astaire, a master at the negotiating game, made a second flight to New York in four days and turned the whole thing around again. He came back triumphant with the fight clinched and a new date for Wembley: 8 October. Within a matter of days of the announcement being made at a packed press conference at Wembley Stadium in August the date had to be shifted to 22 October to give Tyson time to recover from a hairline fracture of his right wrist. He had collected the injury in such a bizarre way that I was honestly forced to wonder if he was beginning to crack up.

Tyson had got involved in a street fight with a former opponent, Mitch 'Blood' Green, who had once been jailed for leading a gang in New York's notorious South Bronx area where the streets are so mean they say even the birdies are armed. What made the whole episode so crazy is that they had their rumble outside an all-night Harlem boutique at four o'clock in the morning – this just six weeks before he was supposed to be defending his world title against me.

I have a halo over my head as I make the point that from day one of my career as a professional boxer – thanks largely to the influence of Terry Lawless and a lady called Laura – I have always attempted to present myself in a dignified manner. It is important, in my view, that sportsmen in the public eye should set the right example, both with their behaviour and their appearance. So many kids look up to us that we have a responsibility to give them the right lead. I know that this sounds wimpish and pious, but that's the way I see it. Terry drummed it into me from the first day that we got together that a smart man out-side the ring is a smart man inside the ring.

Tyson was hardly being smart getting himself caught up in such a stupid incident. I wondered to myself how solid his heavily publicised marriage could be if he was cruising round the streets of Harlem in the middle of the night. A few weeks later he was photographed with his glamorous wife in, of all places, Moscow where he was visiting her 'on location' during an episode she was shooting of the TV comedy series *Head of the Class*, in which she had a starring role.

It hardly seemed the ideal sort of preparation for his title defence at Wembley, and this fight finally went out of the window in September when he crashed his car into a tree and was knocked uncon-scious for the first time in his life. There were all sorts of rumours that he had tried to commit suicide following an argument with his wife, but I have no knowledge of what was going on in his private life. All I know is that there was no way he was mentally right to climb into the ring, and I was not all that surprised when our fight was put off yet again. What with his marriage problems making the headlines and his reported rows with his mother-in-law and now this dramatic car smash I was beginning to feel as if I had a supporting role in a television soap opera. All it needed was a J.R. Ewing type of character to com-plete the script, and he duly arrived in the enormous shape of Don King.

Suddenly it emerged that he was the new man pulling the boxing strings for Tyson, and we had a fresh set of rules to follow. King is the man who wears his shock hair like a crown and brags – with some justification – that he is the 'King' of boxing. A loud, flashy, larger-than-life character who stands way over six feet tall, he talks as if he has swallowed a dictionary and adds quite a few invented tongue-twisting words of his own. King educated himself while serving time in jail on a manslaughter charge, and since his release his influence on world boxing has grown to such an extent that it is considered by many people to be unhealthy for the sport. Anyway, he was now the man who was the main guiding influence for Tyson, acting for this fight in an advisory capacity. Jarvis Astaire had to once again go to the States for renewed negotiations with Bill Cayton and the Las Vegas Hilton owners, who were the official promoters. This time – consoled by an increase in my purse money – I had to give up 'home' advantage, and the fight was arranged for the Las Vegas Hilton on 14 January 1989, later shifted for promotional purposes to 25 February.

This was the sixth date for the fight in eight months. I cannot believe that any challenger in the history of heavyweight boxing has been so messed about in the build-up to a championship contest. There again, I shouldn't think a champion has ever had such a stormy, muddled and confused preparation for a title defence. The difference was that Tyson's troubles were self-inflicted, while I was the innocent party on the receiving end. When you are getting ready for a contest of this magnitude you need single-minded concentration and tunnel vision, centring all your thoughts and effort on getting yourself physically and psychologically fit for the fight. I kept pumping myself up mentally for what was going to be the challenge of my life, and then had the frustration of having to let myself down. It made me miserable and morose, and for at least six of the eight months that I was kept waiting, Terry, trainer George Francis and Laura found me a difficult man to live with.

On top of everything else I now had the disappointment of having to surrender the enormous benefit of fighting Tyson in front of my own fans at Wembley. That was a real body blow. I would willingly have given up the extra money (well, some of it!) to have had my own supporters behind me. It is not only the sound and the sense of their support on the night of the fight that is important, but also the comfort of being able to go through your preparations in familiar surroundings and without unnecessary distractions.

I was unhappy to have to go to the United States for my final training work, and I think this had an effect on my performance. But before I got into the ring there were still more astonishing events involving Tyson, who had seemed to be almost on a course of self-destruction. He had two women accusing him of sexual harassment, escaped unhurt from another car crash, this time in Las Vegas, and then took time off at the peak of his training programme to dash up to Vancouver to see his wife, who was making a film in Canada. While in her hotel he got caught up in a skirmish with some media people, and he managed to smash a photographer's camera and to throw a hand-held TV camera to the ground in a fierce show of temper. He also sat through a two-day appearance in a Las Vegas courtroom where he gave a deposition under oath in another bid to break from Bill Cayton so that he could be promoted exclusively by Don King.

All these pressures piled up together were enough to drive most people to a sickbed. I certainly could not have handled such hassle, and in other circumstances I would have felt sorry for Tyson, who was showing all the signs of being on the verge of some sort of a nervous breakdown. But I was too near the most important fight of my life to soften my attitude by showing sympathy. It's a sad but true fact that in this hard game you have to work up a hatred for your opponent.

Just eleven days before the fight – on Valentine's Day – Tyson performed the unromantic act of flying down to the Dominican Republic to get a 'quickie' divorce from his wife due to what were described as 'irreconcilable differences'. You would have thought that by now he had exhausted all ways that a boxer could get into the headlines, but three days later there he was again – this time on the receiving end of a $10 million writ from his ex-trainer Kevin Rooney, who had been as close to him as a brother during his astonishing rush to the world championship. Everybody in boxing thought that they were inseparable, and now it seemed that Tyson had surrounded himself with relative strangers.

Meantime, I had arrived in Arizona via New York for my final training sessions, and I was in less than a contented frame of mind. All the postponements and distractions had got to Terry as well as to me, and for one of the few times in our ten years together we had trouble communicating with each other. He would say the moods were mine. I would say they were his. I suppose we were both feeling uptight, and there was not the best of atmospheres in our camp. We did not have rows; just silences.

Our tempers were not helped by the reception we received when we arrived at the Club Mirage in Arizona that housed my training quarters. We had a lousy time getting there, being diverted to Los Angeles after heavy snowfalls had delayed us for twenty-four hours in New York, where I gave what I believed would be my last press conference for at least a couple of weeks. Yet when we arrived at the Club Mirage there was a small contingent of pressmen camped on the doorstep, and I angrily told them to get lost. It was out of character for me, and a sign of the edgy mood into which I had slipped. After I had reluctantly posed for photographs, Terry told them I would not be giving interviews and we got some stick from the newspapers over this non-cooperation. This was not the best of starts, and it did not get much better when Terry ordered an American television crew to stop filming one of my early sparring sessions. It finished with him jamming a hand over the camera lens so that they could not film. We were really on edge, and convinced that every American just wanted to see me fall flat on my face. Tyson is not the best loved sportsman in the States, but the one thing they never want to see leave their country is the treasured world heavyweight title.

I had been given a great send-off from London with a farewell bash in the swish Voltaire Suite of the Grosvenor Hotel where there was a bottle of good old HP Sauce on every table to remind everybody that HP were going to be the sponsors of my training camp. Everything is big business in boxing these days, and I was very HP with this arrangement. There was one prickly moment in the final press conference in London before I boarded Concorde for the flight to New York. Jarvis Astaire – whose patient negotiating had clinched the fight – started to reveal that my purse from the contest, including British TV and closed circuit rights, would be in excess of £2 million (I can assure you that my final take-home pay was not in that league, particularly after I had cleared all my overheads and the taxman had taken his massive bite). As Astaire outlined the financial details Terry suddenly angrily interrupted and said: 'Please don't keep going on about the purse. It's not your business and it's not the business of the press. If anybody asks me about it they won't get an answer.'

He clearly did not want a repeat of what happened before my fight with Bugner when I chose to believe all the figures that were being bandied about, only to discover that the final amount was nothing like as high as I had expected.

A newspaperman would not let the subject drop, and this time it was me who snapped. 'How much do you earn?' I asked. 'What are your wages?'

The British TV rights for the fight had been sold to

Sky, the new satellite television company, who were going to screen it 'live' only a couple of weeks after starting transmissions. The BBC had got the rights to screen it twice within twenty-four hours after the fight, and a closed circuit network was being organised. ITV started to cut up nasty because they had been left out of it after showing all of Tyson's major fights. They threatened legal action, and I pleaded with them not to give me any hassle or distractions before this vital contest. The last thing I wanted was court proceedings causing another postponement.

The Club Mirage – where we were looked after with great care and affection – was a beautiful new leisure and fitness holiday complex about thirty miles drive from Phoenix. It had been selected as my training base because the average temperatures were very close to those at Las Vegas. We would be staying clear of the pressures and diversions of that crazy city until two weeks before the fight.

I did most of my training in a huge tent specially erected for my workouts. Letting go all my pent-up frustration, I was really cutting loose in my sparring sessions and we were having trouble getting sparring partners to stay the course. George – or 'Gorgeous George' as I introduced him to everybody – was breathing his hottest dragon's fire for this one, and as we worked out tactics for the fight he kept reminding me that Tyson was a bullying street fighter who would, if necessary, resort to gutter tactics to win. 'He'll hit you in the balls, with his elbows, in the kidneys, on the back of your neck and will really try to rough you up,' he said. 'You can't expect protection from the referee because this sort of thing is accepted in the States, particularly from an animal like Tyson. You've got to park your gentleman's manners at the front gate and get ready to give as good as you get. When he hits you low, you hit him low. When he elbows you, you elbow him. When he whacks you after the bell, you whack him after the bell. This is not going to be a vicarage tea party. You've got to be prepared to fight as rough and as dirty as him.'

George spent long sessions out of sight of the press pushing me around the ring as though he were Tyson while I clamped his neck with one hand and hit with the other. I wanted to be good and ready to 'hit him and hold him' so that he could not settle into his usual quick-fire rhythm. This was not cheating, but simply doing things the Tyson way.

I used the training sessions to work off the ring rust that had gathered since my fight with Bugner sixteen long months before. My critics said that I had not been risked in a fight since then because it was feared I might get beaten and blow away a fortune. There was an atom of truth in that because it would have been madness to risk losing my number one contender's position, but the major reason that I was inactive was because the Tyson fight kept getting postponed. I had spent ten months in stop-start training for it, and now finally the big day was near.

I made a big mistake in agreeing to go on a 'live' hook-up with Terry Wogan in London. He surprised me by having my lovely daughters, Nicola and

Top: Here I am lapping up the love of my Mum and Dad. That's my sister Joan looking as pretty as a picture.

Left: I hardly look the big bully here with my sisters Angela and Joan. I'm wearing my Sunday best. Mum always made sure we were a well-dressed family.

Above: The support of my family has been a hidden weapon for me. Here I am with, left to right, brother Michael, Mum and sisters Faye and Joan. *Below:* It's nice to be able to do something for your loved ones. This is my Mum's mum, Grandma Henrietta Brown, whom I was able to bring over to London from Jamaica for an operation to save her sight.

This is the lady in my life, Laura, and our two gorgeous daughters Nicola and Rachel. I don't think Rachel was too keen on having this photograph taken.

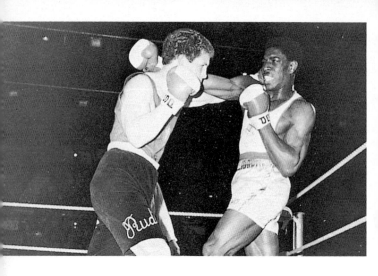

Above: The most important amateur contest of my career. I am on the way to a points victory over Welshman Rudi Pika in the ABA heavyweight final at Wembley. At eighteen I was the youngest ever winner of the title.   *Below:* My twentieth professional fight, and this is Walter Santemore on the receiving end of the punches that knocked him out in the fourth round.

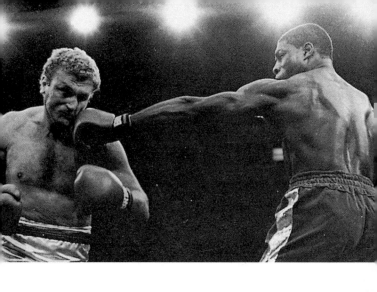

Above: The gift of the jab. This is the punch with which I softened up old Joe Bugner in our showdown in White Hart Lane.   *Below:* I have got Joe Bugner trapped in the corner in the eighth round. The end is only seconds away.

Above: Sugar Ray Leonard, one of the Greats of boxing, was a welcome visitor to my training camp before the Tyson fight. The experience he had in overcoming eye problems convinced me that I could fight on after a torn retina had been repaired. *Left:* The calm before the storm as I shake hands with mighty Mike Tyson. Later we'll be trying to shake each other in the ring at Las Vegas.

A family outing at Buckingham Palace. It's my proudest day as I show my MBE to the three lovely ladies in my life, Laura, Nicola and Rachel.

This is one of several hundred photographs that were taken of me when I collected the MBE at Buckingham Palace. I had never seen so many cameramen. I think it was the hat that attracted them. Top that!

This is me with Syd Little in the *Robin Hood and the Babes in the Wood* panto at the Bristol Hippodrome. 'Oh no it isn't!' 'Oh yes it is!'

Harry Carpenter, my favourite man with the microphone – know what I mean 'Arry!

Rachel, in the studio. I was overwhelmed with home-sickness when I saw them, and I could not stop the tears from bubbling in my eyes. When Terry told the girls to blow me a kiss goodbye, Rachel ran forward and kissed the screen on which I was appearing from Arizona. This really tore me up, and was pulling me away from the 'Mr Nasty' character I was trying to create in my training workouts. Laura came out to visit me, but she found me horrible and grumpy (and, yes, I did tell her I had a headache!).

When we moved on to Las Vegas two weeks before the fight I was disgusted by the offhand manner in which I was treated on my arrival at the Las Vegas Hilton. I got the distinct impression I was considered as little more than a walk-on extra, and I made no secret of my anger at the way I was being treated. Anybody who knows me will, I believe, vouch for the fact that there is not a lot of conceit or arrogance in my make up. I have lots of faults, but a big ego is not one of them. I told the British press: 'I am being treated like a dog. I'm just a room number to them.'

I got even angrier when the hotel publicist apparently put out a story that 'at last the fight might be getting to the Englishman and his camp'. It was nothing to do with the pressures of the fight, and once I had spoken out our treatment suddenly improved to the standard you would expect of an exceptional hotel like the Hilton.

Six days before the fight Colin Hart – the well-informed *Sun* boxing reporter who gave me my first ever write-up in a national newspaper – got hold of the story that George, Terry and I had been guarding like a state secret. I was having daily hypnosis sessions to try to ease the sort of tension that robbed me of so much strength and stamina in my first world title fight against Tim Witherspoon.

It was not a ticket-selling gimmick, which is why we tried so hard not to let anybody know what was going on. Terry had been told about the success Las Vegas hypnotist Dr David Silverman had been having in helping superstars of sport and show business to relax away from the pressures of their lives in the goldfish bowl.

I did not see what I had to lose by at least listening to what the doctor had to say, and after our first session together I was so impressed by his treatment that I had him visit me every day in the two weeks leading up to the fight. In our first meeting in my Las Vegas Hilton suite he asked me if there was anywhere in the world I had been where I had found perfect peace and tranquillity. I told him that I had found paradise when I was walking along the seven-mile beach at Montego Bay in Jamaica. He sat down in front of me and produced a large silver pin from his pocket. 'I want you to relax in your armchair and remain nice and still,' he said in a soft-as-velvet voice. 'Keep your eyes on this needle while you imagine that you are walking along the beach at Montego Bay.'

He started to describe the beach and the blue waters of the Caribbean, and I found myself going drowsy as I kept my eyes trained on the needle moving from side to side. Suddenly I was at Montego Bay, walking barefoot along the beach. I could actually feel the hot sand under my feet as I strolled in the sunshine. I walked down to where the water was lapping against the sand and happily splashed through the waves.

When Dr Silverman snapped me out of my trance – apparently after about ten minutes – I felt beautifully relaxed as if I had been on a saunter across the sands in Montego Bay for at least an hour. Terry and George had been in the room with me when I was put under and they said they too almost went into a trance even though they did not have their eyes on the needle.

Dr Silverman, who has been a respected psy-chiatrist in Las Vegas since the 1970s, told me that I was the perfect subject for hypnosis because I had such powers of concentration. In his next couple of visits he continued with the Jamaican theme, and then on the fourth day he switched to the main busi-ness of the fight against Tyson.

He made me imagine that I was in the ring with Tyson and that the bell had gone at the start of the first round. As I went into my trance I could see Tyson coming towards me almost in slow-motion, and – though I didn't know it – Dr Silverman was giving a commentary of the action. I could feel myself all loose-limbed in the ring, and I was slipping and sliding inside Tyson's bombs and unloading my own punches on him.

I got the same view of the fight at every session, and Dr Silverman's objective was to make me have a mental picture of what it would be like so that – unlike so many of Tyson's opponents – I would not freeze at the sound of the first bell.

Would it work? I was soon going to find out.

By the time of the final preparations for the fight, Terry and I had both shaken off the moods that had built a barrier between us in Phoenix. We were in Las Vegas to try to land one of the biggest gambles of all time, and Terry – true pro that he is – was, as usual, all ready to give me his full support and encouragement. In Terry and George, supported by Frank Black, I could not have had a better team working in my corner. We all knew the odds were stacked against me, but I was determined to prove that Tyson was not unbeatable.

There was an electric atmosphere in the indoor boxing hall, and the magnificent 2,000 British supporters who had come over to cheer me on managed to drown the Tyson fans in the capacity 9,000 crowd with their 'Brun-o, Brun-o' chants. I was so deep in concentration after having had a final hypnosis session in the dressing-room that I hardly gave any attention to the preliminaries. I did not take my eyes off Tyson, and locked my gaze on him almost as if I were trying to hypnotise him. I just wanted him to know that I was not in fear of him, and that he would not be able to intimidate me.

Tyson was prowling around the ring like a caged tiger as the ring announcements were being made, and he was aware that my eyes were following him as he went through his weird routine of wriggling that massively wide neck of his as if it were an extra limb. He was dressed as usual in black shorts and wore ankle-high black boots without socks. His idea was to look like a ferocious old-style ring warrior, and it was all part of his act to try to put the fear of God into his opponents. I knew his act better than anybody, and I refused to be frightened of him.

He had come in ten pounds lighter than me at fifteen stone eight pounds, his best fighting weight, which convinced me that I should forget all the stories I had heard about him not having trained properly. There is a full report of the action in the 'Fight File' section, but I have told my ghostwriter to move over while I give my version of the fight. I have bleeped myself where some of the language is strong, but – as George said – this was not a vicarage tea party. Here, in my own words, is how I saw it from the first bell . . .

Tyson gave a little skip as he came out of his corner almost at running speed. I knew he would be looking to try to land an early bomb, and I was determined to get in first. As soon as we clashed in the centre of the ring I forced his head down with my left glove and fired a right that whizzed just off target. He was throwing left and right hooks with bad intentions, but I was stepping inside them. I was biting hard on my gumshield as I braced myself to withstand the sort of punches with which he had knocked Michael Spinks cold. Then suddenly, bleeping hell, one of his overarm rights had thumped against the side of my head. My legs went from under me as if somebody had pulled the carpet away, and as I went down on one knee

Tyson clobbered me with another right. The gutter tactics.

I was more embarrassed than hurt. We had been fighting for less than twenty seconds. 'Please God,' I said in silent prayer, 'don't let me go out in the first.' I jumped up quickly at three because I did not want him to think he had hurt me. As referee Richard Steele counted the mandatory eight seconds I nodded in the direction of my corner to let them know that I was okay.

Tyson came roaring in at me for what he was convinced would be the kill, but I held him tight so that he could not get any leverage for his punches. He had his head down in front of me thumping away to my body, and I brought my right down on to the back of his neck. The ref, who had ignored Tyson's punch while I was on the canvas, shouted: 'Watch the rabbit punching, Bruno.'

When I immediately started holding and hitting again, the referee signalled to the judges that he was docking me a point. It did not bother me because I knew I had knocked Tyson out of his stride and that I had weathered the early storm. Tyson was still throwing plenty of leather and at a speed that was unbelievable, and I knew already that seeing him in slow-motion while under hypnosis had done nothing to help me. I was managing to block many of his blows on my arms and elbows, and I had the satisfaction of seeing a look of surprise on Tyson's face as I stood my ground and traded punches.

He had to back off as I got behind my left jab,

and then he jumped in at me with a big left hook.
I stepped inside it and landed with a short right
followed by as good a left hook as I have ever
thrown. It crashed against the side of Tyson's jaw
and his legs buckled under him as if he'd been
coshed. He was really body-popping, and I have
since been asked a thousand times why I did not
follow up with one more punch that could have
put him away. I did not willingly let him off the
hook. He fell against me and I could not get my
arms out to get in a punch to the head. By the time
the referee had pulled us apart Tyson had cleared
his head, and – though I did not know it then –
my chance of making history had gone.

Tyson knew that he was in a fight for his life,
and he started the rough-house stuff in a bid to
stamp his authority on the bout. Just before the bell
to end the round he caught me in the face with his
elbow, and as I blinked I was aware that blood was
running down from my nose. There was a roar
from my army of supporters as the bell rang. I had
got through the first round, which was more than
sixteen of Tyson's opponents could say. He gave
me a long hard stare at the end of the round, which
I took as a mark of respect.

I caught Tyson with a good left hook to the body
early in the second round, but he made me pay for
it with a left-right combination to the head that
made my ears ring. He was bobbing and weaving
and I found him a difficult target to pin with any
really wicked punches. I tried to claim the centre
of the ring and to keep him on the end of my left

jab, but he was brilliant at ducking under it and then firing uppercuts and hooks from close range. I attempted to get home with a similar left hook to the one that had caused him so much distress in the first round, but I was a whisker off target and as my punch whizzed past his jaw he fired in three rapid rights to the head that brought me up in my tracks. Bleep! Bleep! Watch it, Frankie. Get yourself on red alert.

In the third round I got my left hand snaking through to his head, but he came charging in at me like a bull and thumped a left hook into my face. As I held on to him in a clinch the referee again had a go at me, disregarding the fact that Tyson's head was thumping into me like a third glove. As we broke, he crashed a right over the top of my defence and I had to immediately fall back into another clinch while I waited for the spring to return to my legs. It was not the power of Tyson's punches that was causing me so much trouble as the speed of them. He's got to have the fastest bleeping hands in the business. I was so busy trying to block his attacks that I could not raise a nuclear attack of my own. I knew I was hurting him when I was getting home with my punches because I could see his eyes glazing and his mouth dropping open, but I was not landing as often as I needed to if I was going to stop his bull-charging tactics. Just before the end of the third Tyson winced as I sank a left hook into his ribs. Moments after the bell rang he threw an angry right which gave me the satisfaction of knowing that I had got him rattled. At least I knew I was proving that I was not the pushover so many people had predicted.

I made a shaky start to round four. He hammered me with a big swinging right that made me see stars, and I was forced to hold on again. I am convinced if I had used these holding tactics against Witherspoon I would have been able to withstand his eleventh round attack. But that's history . . . which is what I was trying to make against Tyson. I got my jab working in the middle of the round and was just beginning to think that I was getting on top when – after at last getting a warning for butting – he unleashed a volley of lefts and rights to the head and body that knocked the wind out of me. As the bell ended the round I have to admit that I was not feeling in control of myself.

Terry, George and Frank were all working overtime during the interval, one massaging my legs, another getting water down my neck and back and Terry holding an ice-pack to my bruised and puffy face. 'You've got to keep that left jab working,' said Terry. 'And when you're in close try to throw a right uppercut. You're doing yourself really proud, but you must get that left into his face. Make him eat it.'

These were the last instructions I was to receive. The fifth was a nightmare round during which my dream of winning the world heavyweight title died. Tyson came swarming over me, determined to carry on where he had left off at the end of the fourth. I clung on for dear life, and the ref shouted:

'Stop holding, Bruno. This is your last warning.' Bleeping hell, ref, I wanted to say, wouldn't you hold if you were in my boots! A right and a left drove me backwards to the ropes, and I could feel the strength draining out of me as Tyson launched a savage two-fisted attack. I was doing my best to defend myself as hooks and crosses rained in from the fastest fists in history, but he completely unhinged me with a right hook followed immediately by a right uppercut that nearly lifted my head off my shoulders.

I was still conscious but badly dazed when referee Steele pulled Tyson off and grabbed me in his arms before passing me over to Terry, who had been running around the ring apron preparing to throw in the towel.

I had been given a good hiding, but not before letting Mr Tyson know that I could dish out some tasty punishment of my own.

Tyson was generous in his praise of me in the after-fight interviews. 'You gave me a great fight, Frank,' he told me. 'Shit man, you really had me going there for a moment in the first round. You can have another shot anytime they can get it together. You deserve it, man.'

Dear old Harry Carpenter was in the ring interviewing me soon after the finish. I was completely recovered and in command of myself within minutes of the referee stopping the fight, and I told Harry that I hoped I had not let my fans down. I later listened to Harry's commentary when I watched a video of the contest, and I don't think I have ever heard him as excited as when I landed that left hook in the first round.

'One more punch and you might have finished it,' said Harry.

'Yeah, you're right. But that's cricket, know what I mean Harry?'

In a way I had managed to prove what I had said all along about Tyson, and that is that he is not a monster but a human being. Hit him right and he wobbles, just like the rest of us. He is allowed to get away with murder in the ring in the way he throws low punches, uses his elbows, his head and lets go punches after the bell. But I have to confess that for the one and only time in my career I fought with similar evil intent, fighting fire with fire.

In his next but one outing Tyson was sensationally knocked out by James 'Buster' Douglas. I am sure that my performance helped take the fear factor out of the fight for Douglas, who must have gained in confidence from watching what I achieved against Tyson – particularly in the first round when I was just one punch from victory.

I have played that first round over in my mind continually, and I just wish I had been able to get into a position to throw a right uppercut after my left hook had virtually knocked him out on his feet. There were several seconds when Tyson did not know where he was. Every time I watch the fight on video I am almost willing myself to throw an uppercut immediately after I have landed the left hook that made his legs wobble.

But at least I had the satisfaction of knowing that I did my best, and came close to causing what would have been one of the upsets of the century. Not one American newspaper preview that I read gave me a chance of going more than three rounds, so I made their boxing writers sit up and take notice.

The one and only Sugar Ray Leonard was kind enough to tell me that he was astonished by my improvement since the Witherspoon fight, and he told HBO viewers in America: 'Bruno hurt Tyson and gained his respect. Not many of his opponents could claim to have done that. It was a really game challenge.'

I just wish I could have challenged Tyson at Wembley, but those fans who travelled to Las Vegas did their best to make me feel at home and I am grateful to each and every one of them for the marvellous support they gave me. I was thrilled by the public response to my performance. Hundreds of fans mobbed me at the airport when I arrived back in London, and more than five thousand people wrote to me with personal words of congratulations. I wonder how many letters I would have got had I managed to bring the world heavyweight championship home with me?

I settled down into a routine of personal appearances and panto performances after my world title challenge while carefully considering my future plans. Mike Tyson, meantime, was continuing to push the self-destruct button. The explosion everybody in boxing feared was just waiting to happen finally came in February 1992 when Tyson was sensationally found guilty of raping a contestant in a Miss Black America beauty pageant.

It is not for me to pass comment on the trial. I was not a member of the jury and did not hear all of the evidence, but I would have thought that a beautiful eighteen-year-old girl visiting any man's hotel bedroom at two o'clock in the morning was inviting trouble and already leaving the door open to 'reasonable doubt' in a case like this involving somebody notorious for his sexual appetite and adventures.

If Tyson did what he was accused of, then the man is an animal. But deep down I cannot help feeling sorry for him. Everybody was looking for him to be barbaric inside the ring and then to switch off once the final bell had gone.

He is a one-off character, shaped by circumstances and an environment few of us would begin to understand. You can only take as you find, and in all my meetings with Mike – apart from in the ring – I found him to be a likeable guy who was always pleasant and amusing company. The biggest mistake I feel that he made was not choosing his friends and connections more carefully. He started to go out of control the minute his mentor Jim Jacobs died, and I feel he would have been best advised to have kept with trainer Kevin Rooney who would have helped maintain some discipline in his life.

There are people around Tyson – who had fed off him – who should be feeling guilty that they did not give him better guidance. He remains in my estimation one of the greatest heavyweight fighters ever to pull on a pair of boxing gloves, and to see what has happened to him is a tragedy both for Mike and for our sport.

Mike Tyson deserved better friends.

For months after that memorable night in Las Vegas, I clung to the hope of a return match with Tyson, but I knew in my heart that if it ever came about I would be fighting without Terry Lawless in my corner. We had gone as far as we could together. I certainly have no complaints about the way he managed me. Two cracks at the world title prove that he, along with Mickey Duff and Jarvis Astaire, did me proud. I know there will be people accusing me of being ungrateful for cutting my ties with Terry after all that he has done for me. Yes, he put corn on my table. But in return I helped to put a lot of corn on *his* table.

In all I had nearly ten years with Terry as my manager. I was a shy, nervous novice when he first signed me, and a mature, worldly man by the time we reached the end of the road. To be honest, I don't think Terry ever quite got used to the fact that I had grown up and that I was capable of making my own decisions.

Ten years is a long time for two people to be together in business. And, believe me, that is exactly what professional boxing is: business. Most of the times that we had together were successful and enjoyable, and I appreciate all that Terry (and his wife, Sylvia) did for me.

Terry helped shape me into the man − as well as the boxer − I am, and I could always recommend him to young boxers as a manager who really cares about the health and welfare of the fighters under his wing.

If anything we were *too* close, and I began to feel almost smothered. I knew after my defeat by Tyson that the time had arrived when I wanted to stand on my own two feet, and to be my own man.

My parting with Terry threw a lot of responsibility on to the shoulders of the woman in my life: a lady called Laura.

Chapter Nine

A Lady Called Laura

A lady called Laura came into my life in an unladylike way. For a dare, she pinched my bum as I was whizzing round Battersea Park roller-skating rink. I was eighteen, she was nineteen and we have been together ever since. It took me ten years to make her my wife, but I never had any doubt that we were meant for each other.

Laura is a West London girl with a strong Irish background – with a name like Mooney she must have. She can talk the ears off an elephant – I have the telephone bills to prove it – but most of what she has to say is good sense, and she has been a tower of strength in my life. Nobody can accuse Laura of having married me for my money. I was working on the building site when we first met, and she was a children's nursery assistant earning more than me. In fact for our first year or so together she supported me while I concentrated on training in preparation for my professional career.

Our early days together were not exactly easy. We put the love and feelings of both our families to a severe test because even in this enlightened age mixed relationships can cause a lot of friction. The reaction on both sides was marvellous. Laura's mother and father have never made me feel anything less than comfortable and totally accepted, and my mum treats Laura with the same affection as she shows to my three sisters. It's nice to have a chance like this to say a thank you to them for their understanding, their support and their love in difficult circumstances. A lot of parents would have struggled to handle it, but Laura and I have been given nothing but good advice and encouragement. We have climbed a mountain together, and we have had a lot of vital support on the way up.

As far as Laura and I are concerned, the colour of our skin has never mattered. If there is any problem, it is in the minds of other people − not with us. When I was at school there was a marvellous hit song by Blue Mink called 'Melting Pot' which summed up the way we think about the race issue. Its message is that a lot of the world's problems would be settled if we could all be mixed together in a great big melting pot. I feel sorry for people who get themselves worked up over the colour of skin. I won't pretend that we have not had quite a bit of hassle from extremists on both sides − black and white − but we ignore the cranks and get on with our lives. Those sick idiots who have written hateful things in letters and have shouted stupid things at us in the street have wasted their time and energy. We know they are out there, but we do not recognise them. As I say, all the problems are on their side.

Thank God, the majority of people are like Laura and me. They don't see black or white, only human beings. We judge people by their attitudes and actions, not their colour. Prejudice, I'm pleased to say, plays no part in our lives. After all, the good Lord is supposed to have created us all equal.

We decided to live together in the modern way rather than rush into marriage, and we started off in one room at my mum's and began to look for a place of our own when our first daughter, Nicola, came on the scene. Laura was never pushy and always understood that she had to take a back seat to my career while I was getting myself established. Whenever I had pressure or problems she was the one I would turn to for comfort and advice. For a long while Terry was like a father figure to me and my brother Michael has always been a good listener and wise guide, but nobody has been closer to me than Laura. She shares my secrets, my private fears and dreams, and she always fills me with good intentions. Laura is an exceptionally bright lady, who could have achieved things as a businesswoman if I had not muscled my way into her life. There are lots of things I have to thank her for, including helping me get to grips with my education after I had left school as something short of an academic genius.

Like any other couple, we have had our bust-ups. We can really roar at each other before I sink into a sullen silence, but sunshine always follows the storm. I admit to being a moody so-and-so and not the easiest person in the world to live with, particularly if I have a major fight or a demanding appointment on my mind. Laura has learned when to give me plenty of space, and she knows the time when she is best off keeping her tongue clamped. Neither of us is 'the boss' in our relationship, but I suppose that when it comes to the crunch I make the important decisions.

I try to be a good, caring father to our two daughters, Nicola and Rachel, but they have also learned that there are times when I should be given a wide berth. The fact that I am often away either training or involved in entertainment or charity work means that I do not spend as much time with them as I would like, and so they are closer to Laura than me. But that is the way it is with most families where the father has a demanding workload. It does not mean I think any the less of them, and I rate Laura, Nicola and Rachel the most important people in my life.

Thank God, our girls have inherited Laura's bright mind and both of them are showing promise at the private school to which – because of boxing – we are able to send them. Nicola has had her own moment of glory, appearing in a television advertisement for Champion bread while miming to my words in an interview with a young stand-in for Harry Carpenter. Nicola, who is a bubbly girl with a good sense of fun, was dressed in a scaled-down version of my fighting gear and wore huge boxing gloves for her debut in front of the cameras. She made a really big hit in the commercial, and we have since had lots of inquiries from advertising companies wanting to use her. But we have decided that she is best off staying cool at school and concentrating on getting the best possible education without distractions.

I think the angriest I have ever been on reading a newspaper was when, during the build-up to my fight with Joe Bugner, a reporter invented a story revolving around Laura and our daughters. He had interviewed me just once five years earlier, and before the Bugner fight wrote a disturbing article in which he described the fear that was supposed to surround me and my family. He gave the impression that – because of our mixed marriage – I was frightened to go out in the street on my own, and that I did my best to keep my children secret. If he had watched his television set he might have seen me walking hand-in-hand with Nicola and Rachel to collect a popularity award following a vote on children's BBC television. That's how secret I have kept my daughters. As for being scared to go out, my friends and neighbours where I live in Essex can vouch for the fact that this is nonsense.

Of course I'm wary of any nutters. But it is rubbish to suggest that we live in fear. We are a happy, laughing family – apart from just occasionally when Dad slips into one of his moods during the build-up to a fight. In the last year I have attended more than two hundred functions – most of them of the charity variety and quite a few in the commercial field. I am sometimes accompanied by Laura, but usually only by my driving pal, Bob. If I was so frightened of going out surely I would hire a minder like a lot of celebrities do these days as a strong-arm protection from the cranks looking to make a name for themselves. Yes, I attempt to keep my family life private. But I do not try to lock Laura and the girls away. That would be surrendering to the morons. The word 'surrender' does not belong in my vocabulary.

Laura and I have often discussed having another baby, but that is all in the hands of God. Should it be that we are lucky enough to have a third child I would dearly love it to be a boy. If we were blessed with a son, I would definitely not encourage him to become a boxer. I was a hungry fighter when I started out, and I had the motivation of trying to make enough corn to keep my family in the manner to which I wanted them to become accustomed. Any son of mine would not go hungry, and I would do all that I could to see to it that he got the best possible education so that he could become a lawyer (I know from experience that they earn fortunes!), a doctor or an accountant (another good earner!). If he were to show any sporting instincts, I would guide him towards golf, lawn tennis, athletics or football – anything but boxing. It is too hard a sport.

Since my decision to end my association with Terry Lawless, Laura has come from out of the background to help me as a sort of personal assistant, or perhaps I should say as my partner. She is a marvellous organiser and makes sure I am where I should be at the right time and in the right frame of mind. I receive literally hundreds of invitations and offers during the course of a year, the majority of them from charity organisations, and I lean on Laura to keep it all under control. I have had to learn the hardest thing of all – how to say 'no'. There are only so many things I can fit into what is already a hectic schedule, and Laura protects me by gently refusing many of the offers – simply because I am too busy.

Laura will not be involved in making any boxing career decisions, and I know she will be happiest when I have finally hung up my gloves for good. She has never stood between me and my boxing because she knows how important it is to me, and she realises the last thing she must do is sow any doubts in my mind. We are managing most things ourselves, but know where to go to for the best possible advice. I have George Francis still in my corner as a trainer, ace accountant Milton Marks looks after my money affairs and I seek the guidance of several learned gentlemen of the legal profession including David Wills, Henry Brandman and, an old friend, Chris Dixon. I shall be relying on them to read this book before publication to make sure I have not libelled anybody!

The most memorable day in our lives came when we finally tied the knot. I had wanted us to get married secretly and without fuss after the Tyson fight, and had planned a Las Vegas wedding. But the news was leaked to a newspaper, and so we postponed the big day. When we got home we discussed our wish to get married with our parish priest, Father Tony McSweeney, an energetic youth worker and a firm friend of ours who had baptised Nicola and Rachel. He is a lovely, larger-than-life character with a good sense of humour and a faith that could move mountains. 'It would give me the greatest pleasure to marry you the moment you are ready,' he said. 'You have waited ten years, so I am sure that by now you know you are right for each other!'

We had decided to get married simply because we wanted to. For a long time there had been a lot of pressure on us to marry from well-meaning people, but we were stubborn enough to want to do it when we felt like it, not just for the sake of it. My Mum had given me most stick for 'living in sin'. When I told her that we were getting married she said, 'Praise the Lord!'

It was a year after the Tyson fight before I could find the spare time for the wedding, and I had to leave all the arrangements to Laura because I was in pantomime as 'The Genie' at the Dominion Theatre. I wonder if Laura used a magic lamp because she organised a beautiful wedding that many people told us was the best they had ever attended. Everything went perfectly, and more than 5,000 lovely people brought Hornchurch to a halt as they surrounded the church to wish us good luck.

Michael was my best man, and among more than two hundred and fifty guests was, of course, Harry Carpenter – know what I mean! He had come home early from the Commonwealth Games in New Zealand just to be there on our special day. We purposely did not invite many of my celebrity friends. I wanted this to be Laura's day. She had earned it, and she rewarded all of us by looking a million dollars.

Nicola and Rachel were bridesmaids, along with Laura's sister, Jane, Jane's daughter, Louise, and my niece, Michelle. I know that everybody thinks that their wedding day is something special, but this one stood out as if it was blessed from up above. Father McSweeney told the congregation: 'Frank and Laura have come here today to make what amounts to a public statement that they intend to spend the rest of their lives together.'

A choir of fifty schoolchildren led us through 'All Things Bright and Beautiful' and 'Morning Has Broken' and Laura and I listened with tears in our eyes as Father McSweeney quoted the good book: 'Without love, I have nothing at all.'

On this wonderful day I felt like the man who has everything.

We had a police escort through the crowds to the reception at a Chigwell hotel where even I had a rare glass of champagne, and Laura and I cut a magnificent three-tier wedding cake. There were dozens of good-luck messages delivered to the hotel, and among some magnificent presents was a set of silver napkin rings from the Prince and Princess of Wales. The speeches by best man Michael and Laura's father were excellent, and mine seemed to go down all right despite me being more nervous than if I was facing Mike Tyson. Harry made a moving and humorous speech, and Terry amused us all by presenting me with a box of Kleenex and a bottle of HP Sauce – two products with which I have been happy to be associated. Then the show was stolen by my Mum, who brought just about everybody to tears with what was almost a sermon. I think that everybody there suddenly realised that I have a Mum in a million, and if I ever get half as good as her at expressing myself I shall be able to hold the attention of any audience.

My pal Monty Fresco, *Daily Mail* photographer who was there as a guest, told me: 'I'm a good Jewish boy, but the way your Mum puts her message across she could convert me!'

As Ricky Valance sang his smash-hit 'Tell Laura I Love Her' at the cabaret I danced with Laura, and wondered why we had left it ten years before taking our vows.

We repeated our vows a few weeks later at a delayed honeymoon on the beautiful sunshine island of Antigua. The ceremony was staged in a stunning hilltop gazebo decked with flowers and overlooking a deserted beach and the sparkling blue sea. Only Nicola and Rachel were there as witnesses.

As we repeated our vows there were the rumblings of a tropical storm that was blowing our way. Laura and I looked at each other and laughed nervously.

'It can't be Hurricane Gilbert coming back,' I said. 'He blew himself out last year.'

The storm blew over quickly. From then – for Laura and I – there was only sunshine on the horizon. But a cloud dropped on our lives when I went for a routine medical check-up and was told that I risked going blind if I took another punch in my right eye.

Chapter Ten

The Eyes Have It

Professor David McLeod has loomed large in my life. He was the eye specialist who arranged for me to go to Bogotá when I was eighteen for an operation to cure my short-sightedness. Eleven years on I was lying on his couch at Manchester Royal Infirmary having a routine eye check when he gave me the news that took my breath away.

'I'm afraid I've got bad tidings for you, Frank,' he said after examining me with an array of instruments. 'You have a tear in your right retina.'

I sat bolt upright as if I'd had an electric shock. 'But I've not had a glove on since I fought Tyson two years ago,' I said.

The Professor patiently explained that a torn retina is the sort of damage you can walk around with for years without realising you have it. 'It might easily have happened in your fight with Tyson,' he said. 'When a fist goes into the eye the retina gets squashed into an oval shape – something like a squash ball when it's hit − before it goes back to how it was before. The force of the blow can lift the retina from the wall of the eye, and in some instances a boxer can suffer a detached retina, which could seriously threaten the vision. A torn retina is not as serious, so the good news is that things are not as bad as they might have been.'

'Can the torn retina be repaired?' I asked, half fearing the reply.

'Yes,' said the Professor. 'It will, of course, involve an operation.'

'And would I be able to box again?' I asked. The sixty-four-thousand-dollar question. Or − if I could get my comeback under way − perhaps the four-million-dollar question.

'We'll have to wait and see,' said the Professor. 'I would say there is every chance of a successful operation.'

The newspapers got hold of the story, and suddenly everybody seemed to be an expert on eyes. I was being told by a lot of people who I am sure do not know a retina from a Cortina how I was risking going blind if I ever again laced on a glove. I cocked a deaf ear to them all. The only people whose views I was interested in were Laura's and the Professor's.

Laura and I discussed my future plans, and we agreed to wait until the outcome of the operation before making any decision. My contract with Terry had finished a few weeks before I went to have my eyes checked. It was just a routine thing before I applied to the British Boxing Board of Control to have my licence renewed.

Since it had become public knowledge that I was parting company with Terry several promoters had made contact with me to discuss future possibilities. They included the man who really interested me – Barry Hearn, who is always bouncing with ideas and enthusiasm. We did not get down to detailed planning, but Hearn excited me with his confident talk of the impact I could make in a couple of comeback contests. I was further encouraged by an article written by editor Harry Mullan in the trade paper, *Boxing News*. Harry is an honest reporter who writes it as he sees it. He has been one of my severest critics, but I have always respected his opinions and I was delighted to see him saying that a comeback by me was just the shot in the arm that British boxing needed. It was an opinion on which he somersaulted after the news broke of my torn retina.

The fight that looked a natural was for me to meet the winner of the triple championship contest between Gary Mason and Lennox Lewis. Gary, a former stablemate and sparring partner of mine, had himself undergone an operation to repair a damaged retina in March 1990 – and it was that man Professor McLeod who saved his career with his surgical skills. I was at the ringside giving a summary of the Mason – Lewis fight alongside Harry Carpenter. It was painful watching Gary eat Lewis's left hand, and after he had been stopped in seven rounds he was in even more serious trouble with another eye injury which, sadly, forced his premature retirement from the ring. Lewis, born in West Ham and raised in Canada, had won the Olympic super-heavyweight title at the 1988

Olympics. He is a classy boxer with a good dig in his right hand, and I quietly looked forward to one day climbing into the ring with him. But that was something for the future. There were a lot of bridges to be crossed before I could consider fighting Lennox – or anybody else for that matter.

Throughout my career I have rarely missed a day when I have not either worked out in the gymnasium or gone for a long stamina-building run. I cannot deny the label of 'fitness fanatic' that has been hung on me, but I take a tremendous pride in my physical condition and even after two years out of the ring following the Tyson contest I had kept in near-fighting trim. In the spring of 1991 I started stepping up my training programme ready to launch my comeback, and then I got the devastating news about my right eye. It came as a tremendous shock because I was having no problems with the eye, which is the same one on which I had the operation for shortsightedness.

It was two months before I returned to Manchester for the operation. I had a local anaesthetic and relaxed as Professor McLeod used a freezing technique to seal the tear. I was beginning to consider myself something of an expert on eye operations, and – thanks to listening to the Professor – I can tell you that the retina is a hemisphere of nervous tissue at the back of the eye which receives images from the outside world and passes these messages on to the brain to interpret them. The operation took less than an hour, and there was no pain although my eye felt quite sore.

Four weeks later I went back to the Professor for the vital test to see how the operation had worked. He was delighted and told me that the eye was as good as new.

'Does this mean I can box again?' I asked.

'As an eye specialist I would not recommend anybody to box,' he said, with an honesty I admire. 'But medically I cannot see any reason why you should not fight again.'

This was the all-clear I had been waiting for, and when the media descended on my home after the story had been revealed by Colin Hart in the *Sun* I issued this statement:

Professor David McLeod, the top eye specialist in the country, has examined me and has told me that my eye problem is completely cured. I appreciate that the Board of Control have the health and safety of boxers uppermost in their minds, and I am positive I can convince them of my fitness. I have kept in training ever since the Tyson fight, and I am raring to go. All I need is a few weeks concentrated gym work and some high-quality sparring and then I will be ready to fight again.

There need be no worry about my physical and mental fitness for a comeback. The lay-off since the Tyson fight has given me the chance to re-charge my batteries.

At twenty-nine, I am still young in terms of the heavyweight division. There is not a top heavyweight right through history who has voluntarily retired before the age of thirty. I intend to have

three or four more fights and see where they get
me.

I realised that the Board of Control would not just
rubber-stamp my request, and I took the safeguard
of getting opinions from four other leading eye
specialists to back up the written opinion I had collected from Professor McLeod. I wanted to put the
minds of the Board at rest, and to convince them that
nobody was more interested in the health of Frank
Bruno than Frank Bruno. If I had thought there had
been any risk to my eyesight I would not have been
trying so hard to make a comeback.

I became concerned at the long delay when I made
my application to the Board, and I decided to bring
in solicitor Henry Brandman to represent me so that
my case was put properly and powerfully.

Meantime I went ahead with my comeback plans,
and shocked the boxing world – and to some extent
myself – by agreeing a deal to fight on under the
promotion of the one and only Mickey Duff.

I had pretty much made up my mind to box for
Barry Hearn, but had not reached the point of agreeing anything definite with him. He had outlined
ambitious plans for my future, and I could not help
but be impressed by his enthusiasm. But now that I
was self-managed I knew I had to tug on the reins
and not dive in and take the first offer made to me.

Then, out of the blue, Mickey Duff came back into
my life. Mickey, who is in partnership with Jarvis
Astaire and Terry Lawless in National Promotions, is
without any doubt one of the most powerful men in

the world of boxing. And I do mean the world. Walk into any gym in the United States and they will know who and what Mickey is. He often bases himself in America where he is better able to make his voice heard in negotiations, and he has an encyclopedic knowledge of the world boxing scene. He is a former professional boxer who knows the game inside out and back to front. Trainer, cornerman, agent, manager, matchmaker, promoter: you name it, Mickey has done it. During the last thirty years or so there has hardly been a British champion who has not had Mickey forwarding his career in some way, and he has been a vital influence on the world title triumphs of a procession of British-based boxers including Terry Downes, Howard Winstone, John Conteh, John H. Stracey, Jim Watt, Maurice Hope, Charlie Magri, Alan Minter, Cornelius Boza-Edwards, Lloyd Honeyghan and Duke McKenzie.

Mickey was born in Poland and is the son of a rabbi. He came to Britain as a young boy one step ahead of the Nazis. He changed his name from Maurice Praeger so that his parents did not know that he was boxing as a professional, and he took the name Mickey Duff from a James Cagney character in a 1940s film. Mickey has a mind like a lawyer and the energy and enterprise of a street market hustler, another role that he has had during his incredible life that is surely worth a book or three.

This was the man who arrived unannounced on my doorstep while I was weighing up the advantages of restarting my career under the banner of Duff's greatest rival, Barry Hearn. In three hours of hard talking he convinced me that I needed his muscle and contacts on my way back into the ring. We agreed a three-fight package, starting at Wembley – later switched to the Royal Albert Hall – in November 1991 . . . provided, of course, I got the go-ahead to fight from the British Boxing Board of Control.

I know that Barry Hearn felt I had let him down, but he appreciates that professional boxing is first and foremost a business, and I owed it to myself to get the best possible deal. I might have got more money out of a comeback on a Hearn promotion, but I was swayed by Mickey's superior knowledge and understanding of the fight game.

Hearn took my decision less than graciously, and went on record with the quote that I was 'as thick as two short planks'. This led to legal fisticuffs. I don't mind people knocking me as a boxer or having an opinion about the way I handle myself either in the ring or in public. But that was a below-the-belt personal insult that was too hard to take. If I was as thick as two short planks I would have dived in and signed for Hearn when he was making all sorts of nice noises in my ear. I wonder what he would have had to say about me if I had chosen to make my comeback under his guidance? I don't think he would have made hurtful remarks about me. He claimed that he only said it as a joke. In that case I would not like to be on the receiving end if he is dishing out any *serious* insults. Anyway, I got the satisfaction of receiving a public apology and that was the end of the matter.

When the news broke that I was reapplying for my boxing licence despite the eye problem it seemed that suddenly everybody became an ophthalmic expert. People who did not know an optic nerve from an optic measure were rushing into print warning me of the dangers to my eyesight. One newspaper devoted an entire page to photographs and diagrams showing how one punch would blind me. They, along with most people drawing conclusions, made the fundamental mistake of saying that I had a *detached* retina. It was not detached. It was torn. Had it been detached I would not have given a moment's consideration to continuing my boxing career.

If you will excuse the alleged pun, I was not turning a blind eye to the risks involved. I am not so big an idiot that I would consider climbing into the ring if it endangered my sight. I went to the very best people in the eye business to get their verdicts and they all assured me that my eye – following Professor McLeod's expert surgery – was as good as new. As I kept telling people at the time, you don't get professorships in a sweetie shop. Professor McLeod is a world authority on eye problems, and he satisfied me that I was fit to box on.

A close friend of mine drew up an extensive list of 'Fors' and 'Againsts' making a comeback, and then left it for me to make a decision. I discussed it in depth with Laura, and I had her total backing in deciding to continue my career. I know that people got sick to death of hearing me say that I have boxing in the blood, but it is a fact of life. Until you have ducked through the ropes and stood up in the ring feeling an incredible buzz you will not understand what I mean. But all boxers will know what I am on about, and that is why so many of them make comebacks. Of course the money is an important part of it all, but it is not the only factor. I can earn a lot outside the ring, but it could never give me the same satisfaction and thrill as earning it with my fists. Barbaric? May be, but you must accept that there are a lot of people like me to whom boxing comes naturally. Like I say, it's in the blood.

The man who stood out as the biggest barrier to my comeback was Adrian Whiteson, the chief medical officer of the British Boxing Board of Control. I noticed that even he was being quoted on the subject of a detached rather than a torn retina.

Dr Whiteson is a Wimpole Street physician who has been the Board's chief medical officer for more than twenty years. I respect his knowledge and I am sure that he had my best interests at heart when he opposed my licence application. But I got annoyed that he was going so public with his thoughts before and after the hearing to decide whether I could go ahead with my comeback plans. It got to the point where I was having to get my solicitor to insist that Dr Whiteson should confine his comments to Board meetings.

He may be an excellent doctor, but he is not an eye specialist. If you want to know what is wrong with your feet you go to a chiropodist. If you have a heart problem, you go to a heart specialist. If you need advice about your eyes you go to an eye specialist. I went to the best in the business, and they were satisfied with the condition of my eyes.

The Board meeting was as tough an ordeal for me as a ten round fight. With my solicitor Henry Brandman beside me, I was given a three-hour grilling. It was a private meeting, and I would not consider for one moment talking about what went on behind closed doors. I was able to satisfy virtually everybody there that I was fit to box. As Leonard 'Nipper' Read, the Board's vice-chairman who in his policing days had brought down the Kray twins, said: 'Before the meeting everyone was against Bruno getting his licence back. We all love Frank and we didn't want him humiliated. But the evidence in his favour was overwhelming.'

The Board laid down the proviso that I would have to be examined by an eye specialist of their choice after each contest. I had already made arrangements of my own for regular check-ups. As I keep stressing, nobody is more concerned about the health of Frank Bruno than Frank Bruno.

Just a day after I got my licence renewed boxing was rocked to its foundations by the tragic end to the Chris Eubank–Michael Watson WBO super-middleweight title fight at White Hart Lane. Michael was taken to hospital suffering from brain damage after being stopped in the twelfth round of a brutal contest in which both boxers reached down to their boots to show the sort of courage and character that makes me proud to be associated with the sport.

As the anti-boxing brigade made a mass attack, I deliberately kept a low profile. I did not see why I should be saddled with boxing's conscience just because I was preparing to make a comeback to the ring.

Some people took my silence as a sign that I did not care about what had happened to Michael Watson. What they did not know is that I secretly slipped in the back door of the hospital where Michael was lying and said a quiet prayer at his bedside. I later issued a statement in which I made the point that all boxers are members of a close-knit family and that Michael had all our love and was in our prayers and our thoughts.

Michael is a good mate of mine. He had often trained at the same Royal Oak gymnasium as me, and was featured in a supporting contest on the Wembley Stadium bill when I challenged Tim Witherspoon for the world heavyweight championship in 1986. Michael is as nice a bloke as you could wish to meet and a fine ambassador for boxing. Like any of us who climb through the ropes, he knew and understood all the risks – just as mountain climbers and grand prix drivers do when taking part in their dangerous pursuits. I was watching a BBC television programme in which it was almost casually mentioned that during 1990 thirty-five people died in mountain-climbing accidents. That is a frightening statistic, but I would never support a call for the banning of mountaineering. If people want to climb mountains, we must let them. If people want to risk their lives behind the wheels of high-powered racing cars, we must let them. If people want to climb into the boxing ring to try to prove their superiority over an opponent, we must let them.

The answer to the dangers of boxing is not to ban the sport but to make it safer. Listening to the debates that raged for weeks after Michael's unfortunate injury, the one point I could not agree on is the compulsory wearing of headguards. For a start, I don't think it would have prevented Michael's injury because it was an uppercut that caused his distress just when he seemed on the point of victory. My experience of headguards is that they tend to make you relax and take punches that you would normally try to avoid, and you sometimes have trouble picking up hooking blows that come at you from out of your range of vision.

Headguards are now compulsory in amateur boxing, but I have seen little to fill me with confidence. The youngsters seem to me to neglect the art of self-defence because they feel the headguards offer defence against the punches coming at them. And how often do you see the boxers struggling to adjust their slipping headguards during contests? They cannot afford to have tailor-made headguards, and often they do not fit properly and cause all sorts of problems.

Mickey Duff came up with an interesting suggestion that deserves close consideration. He would like to see the setting of the lower two ropes eighteen inches or so back from the upper rope. Mickey feels that this would lessen the risk of the whiplash-type injuries that have often caused problems for boxers as they are knocked backwards.

What I do know is that to ban professional boxing would drive the sport underground, and that would be the worst possible thing to happen. There will always be people like me who want to box and there will always be promoters willing to put on fights. I am not a hungry fighter, so I would not go near a pirate promotion. But young fighters with families to feed would be willing to take all the risks involved to get money in their pockets and food on the table. In pirate promotions there would not be the tight medical supervision that you get at shows run under the jurisdiction of the British Boxing Board of Control.

The point that is never stressed enough is that it is not only the boxer but also his family who are given an improved standard of living. I repeat what I said following the tragic death of Steve Watt – thanks to boxing I have been able to give my wife and daughters a quality of life that would have been beyond my reach had I still been stuck as a labourer on the building site.

Nobody puts a gun to a boxer's head to make him get into the ring. He does it because he wants to do it, and is aware of all the risks. Let's keep trying to make boxing safer, but forget about banning it. There will always be Frank Brunos out there who have boxing in their blood.

Chapter Eleven

The Comeback

When I sat down with Mickey Duff to select an opponent for my comeback contest we knew we were on a hiding to nothing. After nearly three years out of the ring, it would have been crazy for me to consider fighting anybody in the world's top twenty. If we had brought over a journeyman American we would have had the press on our backs, so we looked around Europe. It was Mickey who came up with John Emmen, a Dutchman who had lost just two of eighteen professional contests and was the Dutch and Benelux heavyweight champion. I gave the go-ahead for Mickey to announce Emmen as my opponent after I had watched him in action on video. He looked to be a tall, stylish, upright boxer with a solid left jab and a tasty dig in his right hand. Although his early fights had been as a cruiserweight, he had developed into a genuine heavyweight and had an impressive physique.

There was no intention on our part to give the

public anything less than value for money, and to take some of the pressure off me Mickey paired hard-punching middleweights John 'The Beast' Mugabi and Gerald McClellan in a joint top-liner with the vacant WBO championship at stake.

The media interest in the fight was enormous, and I hired a media representative to try to get some protection from the nonstop flow of requests for interviews and photographs. My new spokesman lasted just seven days, and then held up his hands in surrender after fielding more than a hundred calls in less than a week and getting himself involved in slanging matches with television producers and news editors who reckoned they should have first call on me. In the end it was a lady called Laura who came to my rescue, and she handled the press with the help of Mickey Duff's office.

To get myself in the right shape both mentally and physically I spent five weeks at the magnificent Springs Hydro health farm near Ashby-de-la-Zouch in Leicestershire where trainer George Francis pushed me through a punishing programme that could not have been more demanding had I been challenging for the world championship.

Visiting journalists informed me that I was training just a few miles from where Richard III lost his crown at Bosworth in 1485. 'Really?' I said, rolling my eyes. 'In which round did he lose?'

But there were not a lot of laughs to be had during my build-up to the contest. I was taking it as seriously as any fight in my life. I had no idea what the long layoff had done to me, and I was determined to get myself in the best possible condition. Every morning I was up at first light, running across the flat local farmland for six miles, and then returning to a special marquee that had been set up in the grounds of the Springs Hydro. Here George the Dragon bullied me through a daily circuit-training schedule that included body-stretching exercises, and working out with weights and a medicine ball. I would then have a breakfast of ginseng, cornmeal porridge and grilled eggs, sausages, bacon and beans – with lashings of HP sauce, of course! At noon each day I would have an hour-long massage to get my muscles nicely loosened, and then after sessions on the heavy punchbag and speedball I would have a session of tactical sparring with George wearing target gloves. Then I would spar eight to ten rounds for real against 'opponents' flown in from the United States. This was followed by another series of exercises, five minutes at full-pace on the bike machine, fifteen minutes of speed skipping and finally a leisurely swim of up to twenty lengths of the health centre's superb swimming pool. All the time I was working out I would have upbeat music blaring out from my cassette player. It helped me relax and also to find a rhythm. Each evening at six-thirty I would polish off a huge meal – oxtail, chicken, pasta, the occasional steak – followed by lots of fruit. Be wary of me if ever I visit your home. I've been known to polish off whole bowlfuls of fruit without realising it. George and I would finish off each day with a five-mile walk during which we would discuss the tactics for the fight. John Emmen could not have got better attention had he been Mike Tyson or Evander Holyfield.

Twice a week I gave press conferences and photo-calls, and I was continually put through the mangle by reporters wanting to know my innermost thoughts about the morality of boxing and my feelings about Michael Watson. It was hardly the sort of grilling I wanted on the verge of my comeback test. I take this opportunity to apologise to those journalists who got their heads snapped off when they asked what they considered were necessary questions, but I hope they understand that I needed to keep all negative thoughts out of my head.

The most refreshing interview I had was with Helen Falkus, a twelve-year-old reporter from the *Early Times*. She gave other reporters a lesson in how to ask probing questions without being too intrusive. I was so impressed by Helen that I went out of my way to discover what she had written, and this was the article she pieced together after our head-to-head chat . . .

On Wednesday I went up to Springs Hydro Health Farm in Leicestershire to interview Frank Bruno, where he was training for his comeback in November. Just twenty-four hours before the tragic Watson v. Eubank fight, Bruno had been given the all-clear to box again after an injury to his retina two years before had threatened his own career.

Yet no doubts crossed Bruno's mind that he was doing the right thing. 'Things like this do unfortunately happen,' he said.

In between Bruno's training sessions, he is also attending rehearsals of a Christmas pantomime. With Frank in the part of Robin Hood, the show will be playing at the Bristol Hippodrome.

With Mike Watson in a critical condition and Bruno just having recovered from injury, boxing seems more than ever a vulgar and dangerous sport with its brutal aim of trying to knock the opponent out for ten seconds. So I asked Frank what he thought the attraction in the sport actually was.

'I think it is the art, the fact that it is one to one,' he said. 'You are not only trying to outpunch your opponent but also to out-think him. There is much more to boxing than just the brutal side. Of course it's a violent sport, but so are so many other sports. In the World Cup Rugby last weekend one England player was attacked by five French players.'

Asked what safety measures he would like to see introduced, Bruno said: 'Apart from having well-qualified doctors around the ring and ambulances waiting close to the venue, I feel that perhaps championship fights should be minimised to ten rounds rather than twelve. In those two extra rounds boxers are running out of stamina and less able to defend themselves.'

Having talked to Bruno, heard him speak so confidently about himself and watched a dazzling workout, I would have thought ten rounds quite enough – for his opponent!

Helen really made me exercise my mind, and the point I made to her about a maximum of ten rounds is something that the boxing authorities might like to consider. I talk from painful experience about those extra two rounds. Many good judges had me ahead on points of Tim Witherspoon after ten rounds of our world title fight which was scheduled for fifteen rounds. The eleventh round was my bridge too far. I ran out of stamina and was in no position to defend myself as Tim started to unload his bombs. I wonder what the outcome would have been if the match had been made for ten rounds?

I took a much heavier grilling when the *Sun* had the imaginative idea of getting me to go twenty rounds of questions with their readers. I agreed not to duck anything, and these were some of my answers:

Q: How come you have never held the British title yet you have twice been given cracks at the world championship after fighting mostly bums? − asks A. Smith, of Hastings House, Leicester.

A: That's a nice opening shot. I suppose it's something to do with the fact that by beating bums as you call them I manage to put bums on seats. I would never be so disrespectful to call any of my opponents bums. They've all had two hands, two legs and a heart the same as me, and they've had the courage to climb into the ring.

The main reason that I've never fought for the British title is that Terry Lawless, my manager for the first ten years of my career, considered it more important to go for the European championship.

Let's be honest, boxing is big business and there

was not a British title fight that could have generated sufficient money and television interest. And that's the truth of the matter. I would love to win the British championship and own a Lonsdale Belt, but any fight has to be worthwhile for the promoters to want to put it on.

Please don't call any boxer a bum unless you've had the bottle to get into the ring and prove what you can do. There's no tougher sport in the world, and I admire anybody who climbs through the ropes. You won't catch me calling any boxer a bum.

Q: Why are you no longer with Terry Lawless after all that you've been through together? – asks Gillian Tucker, of Norwich.

A: I don't know what you do for a living, Gillian, but do you still have the same boss as ten years ago? People move on in life, and Terry and I were together for longer than most partnerships last. I appreciate everything that Terry has done for me, but the time came when a change seemed right. I want to see if I can stand on my own two feet.

Mickey Duff is promoting my first three fights, and I have surrounded myself with the best possible advisers. I could not have a better trainer than George Francis, and my wife, Laura, is doing a great job looking after the administration side of things.

Q: If your wife, Laura, had demonstrated more forcefully against your return to the ring would you have had second thoughts? – asks Mrs Josephine Stainton, of Kimberley, Notts.

A: Laura and I talk everything through, and she knows just what boxing means to me. We have weighed up all the risks, and I am making my comeback with Laura's full support and understanding.

I celebrated my thirtieth birthday on Saturday. That's too young for me to settle for slippers and a pipe. I've still got a lot of energy to burn, and Laura fully appreciates that I need to answer the call of the ring again. Otherwise I would become really hard to live with.

Q: Don't you think, Frank, that for the sake of your wife and children you should concentrate on being an entertainer rather than a boxer? – asks A. Thorpe, of Sale, Manchester.

A: I can give my family a better future by boxing. I am an entertainer by accident and a boxer by design. While I enjoy going on stage, I promise you that I find it harder work than climbing into the ring. I want to get into the position where I go on stage because I want to not because I have to. D'you understand?

Q: Why don't you face up to the fact that you have no style, no finesse and box like a machine . . . and that you're just not good enough to become world champion? – asks S. Richards, of Upperthorpe, Sheffield.

A: Why don't you say what you really mean! You're entitled to your opinion, but I reckon I'm not the robot boxer you make me out to be. Watch out for improvements when I make my comeback against John Emmen. George Francis and I have been working hard on new punch combinations and leg movement.

I admit to having been too stiff in the early stages of my career, but I feel I have become more relaxed and natural in the ring since I got the Bonecrusher defeat out of my system.

It will take me some time to shake off the ring rust, but I'm confident I can silence my critics with my attitude and my ability. Give me a chance, and I promise to try not to disappoint any of my fans.

Q: They say hungry fighters make the best fighters. Don't you think you're too rich to develop the necessary mean streak to win the world title? – asks Terry Jones, of Woolton, Liverpool.

A: How rich is rich? I have a lot of commitments and overheads that eat into my money, and the taxman and VAT man are two opponents that nobody beats. Money is not coming into my thoughts as I prepare for my comeback. I am hungry for success and am desperate to prove both to myself and to the British public that I have still got the best to come in the ring.

We all like money, but it's not my God.

Q: As an out-of-work actor I take great exception to the likes of you and Ian Botham taking the bread and butter out of my mouth by stealing starring roles in pantomime.

Why don't you stick to boxing and leave the acting to us professionals? – asks Geoff Harman, of Southampton.

A: Sorry you're resting, Geoff, and I hope you get some work soon. I have to say in my defence that people like Ian Botham and I generate interest at the box office. Again, it's all about putting bums on seats. By pulling in the audiences we are getting work for actors like yourself. I hope this doesn't sound conceited. It's just a fact of life. People like to come to see us so-called celebrities on stage.

Q: Never mind Mike Tyson, how about Lennox Lewis? Do you honestly think you could beat him? – asks Michael Gifford, of Gateshead.

A: Lennox Lewis does not figure in my immediate plans simply because I am taking one fight at a time. At the moment I do not want to look beyond John Emmen.

I have a lot of respect for Lewis, but I do not fear him. I have to have faith in myself, and I am confident that I could beat him. But that is something for the future. I don't wish to think about it at this moment.

Q: How many more fights do you plan to have before finally retiring? – asks J. Pearce, of Brighton.

A: Sorry, but that is an unanswerable question. I shall be taking each fight as it comes, and I have no definite figure in my mind. All I can tell you is that I won't be around as a boxer in my late thirties. Just for the record, Henry Cooper was still boxing at thirty-seven, Joe Bugner at thirty-eight and George Foreman and Larry Holmes are still rolling along like Old Man River. Right through history heavyweights have boxed on as long as they possibly could. I think I will get the boxing bug out of my system within the next two or three years, but who can say for sure?

Q: Don't you think you would have been wiser to have gone over to the United States to start your comeback with the expert help of a top American trainer? − asks L. Russell, of Liverpool.

A: It's a myth about American trainers. There are good and bad trainers in the States just as there are good and bad trainers over here. A bad trainer can destroy a boxer. A good one can make a good boxer great. In George Francis I have as good a trainer as there is in the world. He was behind the world title triumphs of John Conteh and Cornelius Boza-Edwards, and I have total confidence in him to get me in the best possible shape for my comeback.

If anything, George is an even bigger fitness fanatic than me, and even though he is in what I respectfully call the veteran stage he still pounds the roads and does explosive exercises. There is nothing that he does not know about the fitness aspect of both a boxer's body and mind.

Q: Imagine it's the year 2000, Frank. What do you think they will be writing about you? − asks G. Broad, of Neath.

A: That's a good question. I hope they will be writing something like, 'Frank Bruno, who retired as undefeated world heavyweight champion four years ago, is in the best of health and is enjoying his retirement with his loving family.' But who knows. Perhaps by then they'll be saying, 'Frank who?'

Q: *If and when Mike Tyson and Evander Holyfield fight, who do you think will win? – asks Peter Holland, of Hanley.*

A: If Tyson can get himself into the right condition both physically and mentally then I have no doubt at all that he will be too powerful for Holyfield. In my opinion Mike is still the best heavyweight around, but who knows what his present out-of-the-ring troubles are doing to him psychologically. He's got serious problems.

Holyfield is a pumped-up cruiserweight, but has enormous talent and good punching power. It will be a great fight if and when they do meet, and my money will be on Tyson if he is in anything like the right shape. (This, of course, was all said before the rape trial.)

After that interrogation by the *Sun* readers, I was glad to get back to my preparations for the Emmen fight. My only break from the daily grind was to visit the local church. I would telephone Laura four or five times every day. I was aching to see her and the girls, but it was important that I focused my mind on the fight and I could not afford any distractions. The hardest job was getting sparring partners to stay around long enough to give me a useful workout. Four of them quit after just a few rounds. In a way it was satisfying because it proved I had not lost any of my power, but it was frustrating having them walking out before they had given me a full workout. One interesting visitor was young Joseph Bugner, the son of Old Joe. He was just starting out on a professional career under the watchful eye of Andy Smith, who was the man who launched Joseph's dad. Young Joe has an excellent physique and moves well in the ring. It will be fascinating to watch his progress.

I kept a count of my sparring rounds from the moment I decided on a comeback. They totalled one hundred and eighty, but no amount of sparring can match the real thing. I felt in as good a shape as at anytime in my career, but until that first bell I would not know how I would perform.

While I was piling into my training routine, the press were pulling apart my opponent John Emmen. He was being dismissed as a no-hoper by sportswriters punching their keyboards. But it was me he would be punching not them. I had to take him seriously, and refused to get sucked into the dangerous trap of thinking he would be a pushover. When I came face to face with Emmen at a press conference he looked very impressive and anything but a no-hoper. At six feet four inches he was slightly taller than me, and he certainly talked a good fight. John, a bar-owner in Amsterdam, is a television commentator and speaks six languages. He is a charming character, and if it wasn't for the fact that I knew I was soon going to have to try to punch him on the nose I could have really taken to him.

You need tunnel vision when you are preparing for a fight, and boxers – all top sportsmen, I suppose – tend to become very self-centred before the big event. It was brought home to me how I forget the pressures that Laura feels when I read the following interview she gave to a magazine on the eve of my fight with Emmen . . .

This will sound strange, perhaps heartless, but I worry more about my husband Frank climbing into his car and driving on the M25 than I do about him climbing back into the ring.

Only people who understand boxing and boxers will understand why I say that.

Boxers, I promise you, are a breed apart. A very special breed. I have got to know dozens of professional fighters since first meeting up with Frank when he was eighteen and working on a building site. But I don't think any of them have quite matched Frank's unbelievable dedication.

To try to stop Frank boxing would be like taking the engine out of a car. He would be lost without it.

Yes, it is a violent sport.

Yes, I do worry myself sick every time he climbs into the ring.

Yes, I will be happy and relieved when he at last hangs up his gloves for good.

But I would be the last person in the world who

would try to tell him to retire from the ring because I know better than anybody else just how much it means to him.

If I thought Frank had lost the rhythm and timing that is so important to boxers, then obviously I would be honest and tell him. But Frank will know without me having to say a word. He is his own fiercest critic.

The near-tragedy with Michael Watson really brought home the dangers of the sport. I cried for Michael and his family.

My grief would have been just as great had he been injured in a car smash.

And I am of the view that there are more chances of a boxer being badly hurt outside the ring than in it.

So why does Frank want to fight on? And why am I supporting his comeback plans?

It's not just the money. Frank is chasing a dream. Ever since I have known him he has talked of one day becoming the first British-born boxer this century to win the world heavyweight title. I will encourage him all the way, yes, even with all the risks involved.

I get angry for Frank when I see him being mis-represented as a thick-headed boxer with his brains in his fists. Yes, he does mangle the grammar book at times, but he has a razor-sharp mind and is much brighter than people imagine.

A lot of people have found out that he is nobody's fool.

Frank laughs at the way he is represented by his

Spitting Image dummy, but I get annoyed by some of the drivel that comes out of the dummy's mouth.

My husband is much funnier than the scriptwriters who produce the childish material. They should get him to write the scripts. I'm sure he could do a better job.

For a boy who did not give much attention to anything but sport at school he has not done badly for himself.

How many people could stand up and make a speech in front of the Queen? Frank has, as well as making scores of speeches around the country.

How many people could memorise an entire pantomime script, and then go out in front of a packed audience and perform on stage? Frank has for the last three years, and each panto he has appeared in has set box-office records.

How many people could present a peak-viewing programme on television? Frank has, and while he was wooden in his early appearances on *People* he quickly got the hang of it and was complimented by the producers on the way he had conquered a really difficult job.

As you will no doubt by now have gathered this is a devoted wife talking. And Frank does his lovely Mum and brothers and sisters proud with the way he presents himself.

I bet wives reading this will be thinking how cold I am, but until you have been married to a boxer you cannot begin to understand their attitude to life and to their sport. I myself wonder how the wives of men in real high-risk jobs like policemen, security guards and oil-rig workers cope with the pressure of knowing the danger their husbands face every single day.

Of course I shall be nervous and jumpy when he climbs back into the ring at the Royal Albert Hall on November 20. But I shall be at the ringside cheering him on, and I shall be in the ring with him in mind and spirit.

Frank knows all the risks, and is prepared to take them. I shall support him every inch of the way.

During all the debates about the dangers of boxing the one that moved me most of all was when I watched Dick Owen on television talking about his son, Johnny.

Johnny died from brain damage after a world title fight in the United States in 1980.

Mr Owen said clearly and concisely that if he had another son who wanted to box he would encourage him, provided he was disciplined and dedicated.

If Frank and I were to have a son, we would not want him to become a professional boxer. It would not be fair for him to always have to be compared with his Dad. But we would not stand in his way if it was what he wanted and he was willing to make the necessary sacrifices.

I just want Frank to know that as he makes his comeback he has every ounce of my support. Every ounce of my love.

I was surprised at how nervous I felt when I arrived at the Royal Albert Hall on the evening of my comeback fight against Emmen. My feelings were not unlike those I had when making my professional debut at the same venue back in 1982. It was my first contest at the Albert Hall since I had knocked out Larry Frazier in two rounds in December 1985, but the crowd immediately made me feel at home with a fantastic welcome. They cheered me into the ring as if I were a world champion, and all my nerves disappeared once I had ducked under the ropes. This was the buzz I had been missing.

Sadly, the fight developed into something of a farce. It took me a couple of minutes to find my range as Emmen backed away at a fast pace. I landed with a good left hook to the body of the Dutchman and his wince was a give-away that he did not like it. A long right to the side of his head sent him tumbling over. He got up straight away and held on to me with a leech-like grip.

One newspaper reporter had predicted that I would try to 'carry' Emmen for several rounds so that I could get some much-needed action. Don't you believe it! Once the first bell goes you want to get rid of your opponent as quickly as possible. I was determined to sweep Emmen out of my path. In fact I was too keen to get the demolition job finished. I landed a sequence of clubbing rights to his head and as he sank towards the canvas I caught him with a sweeping left to the face. It must have been the influence of Mike Tyson.

Emmen seemed to twist his left knee as he went down and was whimpering like a dog as referee Mickey Vann helped him up and massaged his leg. To be honest, at this stage I don't think the Dutchman fancied the job and he was making the most of his injured knee and was also complaining that I had hit him while he was down.

In my determination to get the fight over and done with I had let go a loose punch as he was on his way to the canvas. Technically it was a foul, but there was no way that it was deliberate and the referee let me off with a lecture.

As Mr Vann waved us to continue boxing Emmen was still looking reluctant to fight and I caught him with a full-weight left hook – my 'Hook of Holland' punch – that spreadeagled him along the bottom rope near his own corner. He was trying to scramble up as the referee waved the fight all over just as the bell rang to end the round. Mr Vann revealed that he had counted out the Dutchman.

The Albert Hall fans gave me a tremendous ovation, and I was relieved to have got my comeback contest out of the way without any problems. But from the press I got over the next couple of days you would have thought I had robbed a bank. I could not understand the savage criticism because I felt that I had done all that I could against Emmen. It convinced me I was ready for a step up in class, but who was to know how I would perform after only five rounds of boxing in the previous four years?

Laura and I nipped off quietly to Jamaica for a break immediately after the Emmen fight. We had been under enormous pressure ever since I had first announced my intention to fight again. Laura had carried a heavy load because she had to run the home, look after the children and also organise my daily schedule. It was a relief to get away to think through our future plans out of sight of prying eyes, and by the time our week in the sun was over I was convinced I wanted at least another year in professional boxing.

The gloss was taken off our Jamaican holiday by a nightmare flight home. We had to make two emergency landings, first at Kingston and then after diverting to New York. Laura put her foot down and insisted that we were not going to get back on to the same plane for a third time, and we were switched to a Concorde flight to Heathrow.

The frightening experience of those two emergency landings convinced me that I would much rather take the risk of climbing into a ring than into an aircraft.

Soon after the holiday in Jamaica, I went along to the Sky television studios and watched Evander Holyfield struggle in a world championship defence against Bert Cooper. Holyfield showed great character to come through a rough patch to win the fight, but it was a contest that exposed his limitations. I have always considered him a pumped-up cruiserweight without the real explosive power needed against today's super-heavyweights. His sluggish performance convinced me that he was not the power on the throne that Mike Tyson had been.

I could suddenly see another place for myself in the world title queue, and I was itching to get back into action as quickly as possible. But I had committed myself to an appearance in pantomime as Robin Hood at Bristol.

Gary Mason, my former stablemate, led the voices

of people saying that I should drop out of the panto and concentrate full-time on my boxing career. But the box office had done such good business that I could not possibly disappoint all the youngsters who were looking forward to their Christmas treat.

It would have been unprofessional and selfish of me to have let down the management and the other members of the panto cast.

So I temporarily dropped the curtain on my boxing comeback ready for the curtain to rise on the panto-mime stage. It was time to tread the boards again.

Chapter Twelve

'Look Behind You!'

Here I am firm as a rock
I'm Sweenie the Genie
What's up Doc?

These are the sort of bone-shaking lines I have been delivering since first arriving on stage in a puff of smoke as the genial genie in the 1989 Christmas pantomime *Aladdin* at the Dominion Theatre in London's Tottenham Court Road. I'll tell you something – until you've played in pantomime you haven't lived. It's a riot of fun as much for the cast as the audience, and I really enjoy what is becoming the annual ritual of being told 'look behind you!'

It is, of course, a million miles away from the world of boxing, and perhaps that is one of its strong attractions for me. Though basically I am a shy person (you must have seen me blush!), there is an exhibitionist inside me fighting to get out and so I love parading on stage or in front of a camera. I first got the taste for treading the boards when Lenny Henry persuaded me to dress up as Juliet to his Romeo at the Shaftesbury Theatre in a Comic Relief charity show in 1985.

It all started with one of the strangest telephone conversations I've ever had.

'Frank,' said Lenny Henry, 'we'd like you to appear on next month's Comic Relief show.'

'Great,' I said.

'You'll appear on stage with me.'

'Fine, Lenny. I look forward to it.'

'We're going to do the balcony scene from *Romeo and Juliet*.'

'Err . . . great. You did say *Romeo and Juliet*, Lenny?'

'That's right, Frank. And I'm going to play the part of Romeo.'

'I see, Lenny. And dare I ask what you want me to do?'

'Well we don't want you to play the part of the balcony, Frank. So that only leaves the part of Juliet . . . Hello, Frank. Are you still there, Frank?'

'You're not joking are you, Lenny.'

'No, Frank. I'm perfectly serious. It'll bring the house down. And maybe the balcony as well.'

What Lenny − a good friend of Laura's and mine, along with his lovely wife Dawn French − did not tell me was that he was going to impersonate me while playing Romeo. We had just one rehearsal and I was petrified about making a mess of it on the night, but − as Lenny predicted − the sketch brought the house down. That was mainly due to his brilliant takeoff of me. It was so good that even I wasn't sure which of

us was which! We did three successive nights, and
every time I fluffed a line Lenny got me out of trouble
with a brilliant ad-lib.

I thought that Lenny was the king of the ad-libbers
until I played a supporting role to Michael Barrymore
in my pantomime debut in *Aladdin*. It was an education to watch him during every show making
hilarious spontaneous remarks to the audience,
bouncing off people with whippet-quick cracks off the
top of his head. Michael is a dangerous guy to cross
tongues with, and I learned very early on not to try
to get laughs at his expense. When I tried an ad-lib
while on stage with him, he said, 'Nice one, Frankie.
Now lie down and have a rub down with the *Sporting
Life*.' He can be vicious with his tongue, but you
cannot take offence because while he is insulting you
he is making you laugh. Sometimes his humour gets
close to ridicule, but nobody on the receiving end
seems to mind. He is a master at knowing just how
far he can go with a joke. Michael is such a bundle
of atomic energy that he keeps as slim as a stick
insect, and he produces a work rate on and off stage
that would burn out most people in a week. I have
an enormous respect for his professionalism, and I
really appreciate having been able to watch him at
work from close quarters. After eighty-five shows
together we had got to know each other well, and I
hope I earned his respect – not that I would ever
know because he has such a biting sense of humour
you are never quite sure if and when he is being
serious with an opinion.

There was a lot of criticism of the likes of me, Ian

Botham and Barry McGuigan getting treasured actors' union Equity cards which allowed us to play in pantomime. I can understand the anger and frustration of young actors and actresses desperate to get their hands on a card, but show business is just like boxing. At the end of the day the main thing that matters is how many bums you can get on seats. I am not being big-headed when I say that I know a lot of the people are drawn to the panto to see me. Some of them may even come just to see me fall flat on my face, but the important thing is that they buy their tickets for the theatre. So therefore everybody in the panto with me benefits, because while there are bums on seats they are earning – just like me.

My experiences in pantomime have been among the most enjoyable of my life. When you join a panto cast it is like becoming a member of a close-knit family for a couple of months. Everything boils down to teamwork, with everybody pulling for everybody else, and the atmosphere in the three pantos in which I have appeared has been marvellous. I have always been made to feel welcome, even though there are people in the cast with three times my talent and ability. They accept that I am a novice doing my best, and from the response I get from audiences I think my efforts are appreciated by the people who really matter – the punters. There were some occasions when I would forget my lines, and I would call down into the pit to ask the band members to see if they knew what came next. It was pointless trying to hide the fact that I had dried, and so I made it look as if it was part of the show, and it was always good for a laugh from the audience.

I got tremendous help and encouragement from most members of the cast, and even some of the children in the chorus showed me dance steps that helped me move with more rhythm during the numbers choreographed by a lovely mover called Rosita Yarboy. My best mate at the Dominion was a Liverpool comedian called Hal Nolan, whose Scouse wit continually cracked me up. He was kind enough to take time out to advise me how to improve the timing and delivery of my lines, and I used to stand in the wings watching his solo spot when he would always have the kids in the audience in the palm of his hands. Hal is a master of comedy who deserves much bigger billing than he gets. He has developed a style that suggests he is totally oppressed and trampled on, whereas off stage he is a happy, outgoing family man who gets a lot of fun out of life.

The lovely Roly Polys were appearing as the Chinese policemen, and I used to watch in wonder as they danced with the grace of ballerinas despite their tonnage. They made me seem as heavy-footed as an elephant (no, not Jumbo Cummings!).

It was Les Dawson who came up with the idea of forming a heavy-weight dancing group for his television series, and the Roly Polys have – no joking – got bigger and bigger in their popularity every year. Mo Moreland, their gifted lead singer and dancer, was good enough to take time out to show me how I could become better balanced when performing my dance routines. I honestly feel that learning to dance properly has helped give me better balance in the ring. But back to the panto . . .

Alyson McInnes, as a beautiful Aladdin, was never quite sure what to expect of me when I appeared with my lamp, particularly when I used to zoom around the stage on a motorbike! In pantomime, anything goes. The magic ingredient was provided by Geoffrey Durham, Victoria Wood's charmer of a husband who doubled as the Emperor and the Great Soprendo. His mind-reading act is quite mind-boggling, and I wondered if perhaps he would be worth employing as an extra second in my corner so that I would know what my opponent was thinking.

It was an unbelievably fast-moving show that included such diverse acts as Lia Malcolm in a flying ballet and Dooby Duck with his disco friends, but director Stewart Morris – skilfully piecing it all together like a giant jigsaw – managed to retain the traditions of the pantomime and we saw to it that the kids in the audience, aged from seven to seventy, gave us plenty of 'look behind you' warnings.

A writer from one of the posh papers tried to wind me up during my debut appearance at the Dominion Theatre. While we were standing in the wings waiting for my cue he suggested that by treading the stage in pantomime I was lowering my dignity. I really flew at him. Let me quote you how he quoted me:

'What you saying? You saying I got no dignity? Listen, my dignity is in my private life with my wife. My dignity is in my two little girls. My dignity is in the way I fight my fights. And in how I handle myself outside the ring. Are you saying that playing in panto for kids is the wrong thing for a sports star? Are you saying that I should be yelling "I am the baddest dude" and all that crap, just to show you that I'm hard? Is your article going to be one of those hatchet jobs? Hey, you could always be my next opponent.'

I don't like anybody questioning my dignity. From day one of my boxing career I have tried to be dignified and honourable both inside and outside the ring. Terry and Laura have always encouraged me to give the right lead to the youngsters who look up to me, and the writer from the posh paper really touched a nerve when he suggested that I was losing dignity by appearing in panto.

There was just one nasty moment during my run at the Dominion. Some of us had been out for a late-night meal at a West End restaurant after one of the shows, and I was standing at the counter paying the bill when I was suddenly grabbed from behind by a drunken slob. I pushed him off and managed to control my temper while waiters bundled him out of the restaurant. He caught me where you wouldn't show your mum, and I was shocked as much as hurt. It was the old problem of some idiot wanting to make a name for himself, and I was grateful to all the people who saw the incident that they did not tip off the media. We had a laugh about it later when I told my panto pals off for not having shouted, 'Look behind you!' When the press asked me what had happened I played it down because I did not want the panto to get the wrong sort of publicity, and I did not want to give one twit the satisfaction of getting his name in the headlines at my expense.

A year later I had an even more enjoyable panto experience when I again played the genie with the magic lamp, this time with star billing at the Theatre Royal, Nottingham. My co-stars were Scottish entertainer Allan Stewart and his beautiful wife, Jane Danielle; with the part of Aladdin being played to perfection by Anne, one of the Nolan Sisters. Allan, a Glaswegian with a wicked sense of fun, was a joy to work with. He has no arrogance or the sort of super ego you find with many stars, and he often had me doubled up with laughter on and off stage with his crazy humour.

Allan has been treading the boards since he was twelve, and is an expert at working the audience. He is a brilliant all-round entertainer who can sing, dance, tell jokes with perfect timing and, of course, impersonate just about anybody who is anybody. We used to have running gags that were not written into the show, things like water fights that would start in the dressing-room and continue on stage and using different props to try to catch each other out. Producer Barrie Stead and Bryan Blackburn, the writer and director of the panto, encouraged us to have fun because they knew this spread to the audience. Allan started trying to throw me by changing his lines. It gave me the confidence to try some ad-libs of my own, and our friendly rivalry gave the show an added sparkle.

I cannot claim that the lines we were spouting would have won us a place in the comedy hall of fame. Example:

Allan (playing Wishee-Washee): 'In Africa they have lions, rhinos and the great white bison.'

Me (playing the genie and shuddering with horror): 'You frightened me there for a minute. I thought you said the great white Tyson.'

Anyway, the audience – particularly the kids – seemed to love it, and their laughter was just as big a reward as the cheers that greet me when I'm climbing into (and sometimes out of) the ring.

We had a wonderful 'family' at Nottingham, with no personality problems whatsoever. Wyn Calvin (Widow Twankey), George Reibbitt (Abanazar) and famous circus ringmaster Norman Barrett (as the Emperor) all gave marvellous support, and Lewis and Payne (a double act appearing as the Chinese policemen) joined forces with me in trying to get the better of Allan Stewart in our nonstop leg-pulling pranks. My dancing started to become almost passable thanks to the expert tuition of choreographer Trudi Moffatt, and musical director Maurice Merry along with his orchestra were surprised to find there were even times when I was in tune and time with them!

I went on training runs every day, and almost the entire cast caught the fitness fever and we used to go for runs and workouts together. But our training programme was disrupted in the last week when the entire Midlands became buried under a blanket of snow, and one day I got stuck in my hotel at the Hilton until I was dug out just in time for me to get to the theatre for the curtain-up.

My only other problem at Nottingham was the trap door through which I had to make each entry with a crash of cymbals and a puff of smoke. Two stage-hands pulled ropes that worked the door and I kept kidding them that they should pull faster so that I could make my entrance more spectacular. So it was my fault when they pulled too quickly and the door got stuck halfway open. I had to almost do a limbo dance to get on to the stage, and as I crawled out I managed the ad-lib: 'Sorry to keep you waiting, oh master. My magic lamp needs oiling.'

It wasn't the greatest ad-lib of all time, but it got me a laugh and the audience accepted it as all part of the act.

The final scene was the spectacular wedding celebration as Aladdin married the beautiful princess. I wondered what Allan Stewart felt during each performance as he watched his wife, Jane, walking off hand in hand with her new 'husband' Aladdin in the lovely shape of Anne Nolan. That's pantomime for you. A real world of make-believe.

My pantomime commitments in 1990 meant that I had to turn down the chance to appear in the Hollywood film *Rocky V*. It was reported in the press that the offer was $400,000. If that had been the case I would have been there like a shot, but the truth is that we did not get around to talking money. I lost interest when I learned that my part would feature me in a losing contest against the great white hope Tommy Morrison, who was building a reputation for himself as a real-life heavyweight prospect. If the offer had been to give Rocky − or Sylvester Stallone

– a punch on the nose I would have tried to fit the film into my schedule.

I have managed to crowd a lot of experience in front of the television camera away from boxing, but it is difficult to relax and be yourself and I am still learning the techniques of the business. The list of people I have been lucky enough to appear with on the small screen reads like a Who's Who of British comedy. They include Freddie Starr, Little and Large, Cannon and Ball, Les Dawson, Michael Barrymore, Saint and Greavsie, Jim Davidson, Norman Wisdom, Frank Carson and, of course, Lenny Henry.

I impressed the BBC enough with my appearances to land a contract to succeed Derek Jameson as the presenter of the *People* series. This took me the length and the breadth of the country meeting Britain's most eccentric, heroic and extraordinary characters. The critics gave me a lot of stick for some of my wooden performances in front of the camera, but I gradually improved and by the end of the series felt I was becoming reasonably accomplished and more relaxed. I would have paid the BBC for the experience. The one thing I could not conquer was the Autocue – which is the system the newscasters use when reading the news on television. My eyes would open wide like Louis Armstrong clowning when I was concentrating on reading and it all became so stilted that we found it easier for the producer to tell me what to say and then for me to repeat it parrot-fashion. It was not very professional, but I had simply not had sufficient time to conquer the Autocue.

I got a lot more in-front-of-camera experience in the

world of advertising, and was lucky enough to be selected to help promote HP Sauce, Kleenex Tissues and Applause chocolate bars in television commercials. It brought the power of advertising home to me because I could not go anywhere without people shouting 'Pass the sauce, Harry' following my appearances in the HP commercial. In 1990 I was flattered to come out top in a marketing evaluation survey. Ten planning directors from Britain's top advertising agencies drew up what was called a Q-list – basing their choices on what was described as the 'quotient of popularity and likeability'. It was all a bit over my head, but what it finally amounted to was that they picked me as being the British personality who is 'the best known and most appealing' to a cross-section of the public. Michael Aspel and Cilla Black were second and third on the list, so I was in very good company.

The man who has taught me most about how to talk to the camera as though it is a friend rather than an enemy is my old mate Harry Carpenter. We have developed a sort of double act since he started interviewing me in the ring after fights, and we have made some corn together on the after-dinner speaking circuit. It's a pleasure doing business with Harry because he is such an old charmer, a true English gentleman with perfect manners and a subtle sense of humour. There are few people in television who can match his long experience at the microphone, and I listen respectfully to everything he tells me. He's semi-retired these days, and spends much of his time with his lovely wife Phyllis in their home in France close to their son, Clive, and French daughter-in-law.

Clive, a dead ringer for Harry, is a high-powered executive with a brandy company (which reminds me: Harry has not bought me a drink in the dozen or so years that we have known each other). The thing that most impresses me about Harry is his all-round sports knowledge. He is not only a walking record book on boxing, but also knows all there is to know about the worlds of golf, lawn tennis, rowing and greyhound racing – in fact he started out as a journalist writing about greyhounds, and the family joke is that he has been going to the dogs ever since.

In the spring of 1991 I was delighted to be asked by Michael Aspel to help him trap Harry for a *This Is Your Life* tribute. BBC executive Brian Barwick was in on the secret, and he told Harry that he should go to the Royal Oak gymnasium in Canning Town to interview me about the possibility of a comeback.

Michael hid in Terry's office at the back of the gym, and when Harry came in I was working out on the punch bag. To distract his attention from what was going on behind him I started playfully sparring with Harry, who must have wondered if I had gone off my rocker. The look on Harry's face when Michael stepped in and presented him with the famous red book was a picture. He is not the swearing kind, but he came close to using a few choice words when he realised that I had helped hook him. 'You've done me good and proper,' he said. 'I did not have the slightest suspicion that I was being set up.'

The highlight of our association has got to be the Royal Command performance when we were invited to take our double act on to the stage at the Palladium in front of the Queen. Harry won't mind me saying this, but I think he was more starry-eyed than I was. 'All the years I've been in the broadcasting business and it takes you to get me on to the stage of the London Palladium,' he said.

'Yeah, 'Arry,' I said. 'I know what you mean!'

It was organised chaos behind the scenes at the Palladium where you could not move an inch without tripping over a superstar, but while we were treading on each other's toes it somehow worked like clockwork once the curtain went up. The only mistake Harry and I made was standing in the wrong line when the Queen came backstage to meet everybody who had taken part in the show. We had been told to stand in the front, but I misheard and Harry followed me into the second line where you look on rather than get introduced. As the Queen went past us, I whispered: 'Well done Harry. You've been given the elbow by Her Majesty!'

Harry got his consolation when he was invited to Buckingham Palace to receive his well-deserved OBE. He is into semi-retirement now, but will, thank goodness, continue to cover boxing for the Beeb. It just wouldn't be the same without having him to chat to after fights – know what I mean, Harry?

I was back treading the boards in pantomime at the Bristol Hippodrome for Christmas 1991–2. It was some eight months earlier in the spring that I committed myself to the panto by signing a contract with Apollo Leisure. This was before I knew that I would be getting involved in a comeback contest at around about the same time that the show was scheduled to open.

There were some sniping criticisms by people in boxing who thought I was taking my comeback less than seriously. They thought I should have pulled out of the pantomime to give all my concentration to training and fighting. There were two things my critics did not understand: one, that I owed it to the cast and management – and those people who had bought tickets – not to back out of the show at the last minute; two, that I get a kick out of playing in panto and find it a release from the pressures of boxing.

When Barry Clayman and Paul Gregg of Apollo Leisure and executive producer Barrie Stead first contacted me about the panto in Bristol I thought they were winding me up. 'We want you to play the part of Robin Hood,' said Mr Gregg.

I had a good laugh and then sat waiting to see which character they *really* had in mind. After two consecutive years as the genie in *Aladdin* I fancied a change. They let me have my laugh and then insisted they were serious. Bryan Blackburn, who was to write and direct the show, said: 'We are going to do a gentle mix of the traditional Babes in the Wood, dropping them into Sherwood Forest where you will appear as Robin Hood.'

'Yeah, all right, Bryan,' I said, still thinking it was a leg-pull. 'There's just one little thing that might have escaped your notice. I've got rather dark skin.'

Bryan, a comedy genius who has written for every top British comedian and also the likes of Bob Hope, Jack Benny and Jerry Lewis on the other side of the

Atlantic, looked at me and gave a mischievous smile. 'Don't worry about it, Frank,' he said. 'Leave it to me.'

He got his vivid imagination to work, and came up with a fairy who could not quite get her magic spells to work properly. She waves her magic wand to conjure up Robin Hood to look after the Babes in the Wood and manages to produce a dark version of the legendary outlaw of Sherwood. It seemed odd reading it on paper, but it worked to perfection on stage thanks mainly to the marvellous performance of Sarah Thomas as the heavy-footed and dotty 'Airy Fairy'. You would quickly recognise Sarah for her amusing portrayal of Glenda, Thora Hird's daughter in *Last of the Summer Wine*.

I was given the honour of sharing the top-of-the-bill spot with Little and Large, with whom I had worked before as a guest on a couple of their television specials. They were cast as two robbers who are too nice to be able to carry out their orders to kill the babes in the wood.

When you read this strange mixture of storylines here in black and white you would never think it would make sense on stage, but thanks to the words of Bryan Blackburn and the expert delivery of Little and Large we had all our audiences roaring with laughter every night and twice on Wednesdays and Saturdays.

Because I got my attention diverted by my comeback contest, Bryan thoughtfully chopped a couple of pages of dialogue from my script yet I still had more lines to handle than in my previous panto performances. Once the Emmen fight – some people called it a pantomime – was out of the way, I had to give all my concentration to learning my lines. It was several shows before I was word-perfect, but whenever I 'dried' there was always a willing member of the cast to either prompt me or ad-lib to make sure there was continuity.

No two shows were the same because Little and Large could not resist tossing in hilarious ad-libs that were as topical as the latest news headlines. For instance, we had a scene in which I had to try to hit the bullseye with an arrow during an archery tournament. Eddie Large, a master impressionist, would slip into his Jim Bowen role and introduce the tournament as if it were *Bullseye* and he kept changing the list of prizes available at every show. One night, at the peak of the Maxwell scandal, he said: 'And Bully's star prize tonight is a Robert Maxwell pension.'

I have never come across a sharper comedy brain than Eddie's. With the general election looming he kept introducing Syd as John Major – there is a real likeness – and he would continually get on at him about whatever political issue was the talk of the media on that day.

'I'll only vote for you, Mr Major, if you give the Ninja Turtles a place in your Cabinet . . . or even in your drawers,' he'd say. I know it looks corny sitting on this page, but the kids (and many of the adults) in the audience loved it.

Syd Little deliberately plays the poker-faced straight man to 'Machine Gun' Eddie, but anybody who saw the show will know he is extremely talented in his own right. He is a fine singer and plays a real mean guitar. His hobby offstage is making model sailboats, and he has patiently created scaled-down versions of Drake's *Golden Hind* and Nelson's *Victory*. Not a lot of people know that! He just ignores Eddie when he makes cracks about how he is never first to push the boat out. Syd takes as much stick offstage from Eddie as on, but they get on famously – unlike some warring double acts that you hear about.

Eddie – whose Bristol-born wife Patsy Ann Scott was a knockout in our panto as Maid Marion – is sports daft. He would have made the grade as a professional footballer but for getting knocked down by a bus after passing a trial to play for his favourite club, Manchester City. Now he spends every spare second on the golf course, and is a low-handicapper who doesn't mind whose money he wins. As a rabbit who can't hit a ball straight, I was too smart to take up any of his challenges to play him.

Anyway, I was too busy training every day to spare the time to go onto the golf course. Throughout the run of the panto I worked each morning at the superbly equipped Spaniorium Farm gymnasium owned by Bristol's two most popular boxing characters, Tex and Kirk Woodward. I ran six or seven miles before going through a series of explosive exercises and then sharpening up on the punchbags and punchball. I found a 1-in-7 hill at Ashton Park that really tested my legs, and so by the time I had finished my evening show I was always ready to flop straight into bed. I may not have been the best entertainer in any of the pantos over Christmas, but I was definitely the fittest!

We had great characters in two of the other leading roles in the Bristol panto. Forbes Collins played a marvellous villain as the Sheriff, and at every show inspired hurricanes of hisses and boos. A Bristol connection was nothing new to this talented Shakespearian actor. He stars as Attila the Hun in the Bristol Cream Sherry advertisement in which he delivers the deep-throated line, 'How very civilised.'

Our dame – playing the big-bosomed children's nurse with lots of Bristol City gags! – was Frankie Desmond, who had the audience eating out of the palm of his hand throughout the run of the panto. No wonder, because Frankie is literally one of the country's great communicators. Entertaining on a cruise to the Southern Seas several years back he became aware of the plight of deaf children on the island of Tonga. He helped set up two schools for deaf children on that tropical paradise in the South Pacific, and his work has been the subject of a special *See Hear* documentary on BBC television. A scriptwriter and composer when he's not on stage, Freddie was the first songwriter to compose a hymn exclusively for deaf children that they could 'sing' using sign language. There ain't nothing like this dame!

There were just a couple of silly incidents that were small scars on my enjoyable stay in Bristol. One night after a show I still had a lot of energy left and decided to go for a run. It was asking for trouble because the pubs were just starting to close. A crowd of drunken yobs began to follow me, and were showing off to their mates by shouting what they would do to me 'if you've got the guts to stand still and fight'.

I had the guts . . . but I also had the sense to get away from there as fast as my legs would carry me.

Suddenly I was like Linford Christie as I sprinted from the trouble spot and back to the Swallow Royal Hotel where I was staying. By going for that run I had broken a rule I always try to observe, and that is not to go near any places where trouble is waiting. Once you go into any pub, nightclub or disco environment where there is music, alcohol and mixed company, then you are a sitting target for troublemakers. Generally I find people pleasant and genuinely happy to meet me, but − as the likes of Gazza and Ian Botham have discovered to their cost − there is always somebody stupidly looking to make a name for themselves at your expense. So I have no-go areas. I have been lucky during my pantomime appearances to have Apollo Leisure company manager Don Auty acting as a sort of unofficial minder for me. He is able to spot any potential problems that are brewing when I am relaxing backstage, and he is quick to use his cutting Yorkshire tongue on anybody who is threatening to make a pest of themselves.

I could have done with Don looking after my interests at the hotel one evening when a muck-raking newspaper sent a glamorous reporter to interview me. She arrived at the reception desk at midnight! The duty manager was alert enough to tell her that there was no way in the world that I would agree to talk to her at that time of night. The reporter waited until the Manager had gone off duty, and she then sweet-talked a member of the night staff into ringing my room at two o'clock in the morning. I came out of a deep sleep as if I was answering the first bell, and when I had collected my senses I told the staffman to tell her where to go and suggested he might follow her! I just couldn't believe that he would trouble me at that time of night.

It turned out that the reporter was trying to break a story about me having gone to a lady in Bristol for a massage. Big deal! Yes, it was true. The newspaper really thought they were onto something, knowing the nudge-nudge-wink-wink reactions that the story of Bruno going to a masseuse would bring.

I had to politely let them know that if they wrote the story giving the wrong emphasis they would hear from my solicitors. The fact was that I had been to see the masseuse to get the stiffness out of my wrists following too long a session on the punchbag. Oh yeah, I hear you say. It just so happened that while I was having the healing massage there were two other people in the room with us – my trainer, George Francis, and the husband of the lady expertly using her hands to ease my problem.

This little incident illustrates the lengths to which some newspapers will go to dig up dirt. Most media people I meet are likeable and genuine, but they are given a bad name by a minority of reporters who crawl out from the woodwork.

The show at the Bristol Hippodrome was such a box-office success that before the run was halfway through Apollo Leisure were offering me a leading role for a 1992–3 panto. But I delayed giving them a decision because I needed to know where my boxing career was leading me. To be honest, if I had the choice I would much rather be topping the bill at Wembley against Evander Holyfield than, say, topping the bill at the Palladium in *Puss and Boots*.

'Oh no you wouldn't!'

'Oh yes I would!'

Chapter Thirteen

By Royal Command

The most satisfying thing about the fame that has come my way is that I am able to put something back for all the good fortune that I've enjoyed. I hope nobody interprets this as me indulging myself and claiming what a good boy I am, but I want to take this opportunity to bang the drum for some deserving causes with which I am happy to be associated. Laura keeps my diary and she has counted that in the year leading up to my boxing comeback ninety-three of my days were taken up with charity work. I am not complaining because I am flattered that people want me to help them, but it started to get so time-consuming that we had to select just a handful of charities on which to concentrate my effort. This has meant having to disappoint a lot of people, but there is only so much that I can do and I have had to learn the tough task of saying 'no'.

The charity with which I have become most closely associated is the Prince's Trust, which Prince Charles set up to help underprivileged and deserving youngsters. I link up with the Prince's associate Jock Barr, who is a smashing bloke with the energy of four people. I go anywhere he asks to help promote the Trust, and I have travelled up and down the country meeting and encouraging young people who have been, indirectly, given a helping hand by the Prince of Wales. During my travels I am often in the Prince's company, and occasionally Princess Diana is with him. I was really sad for them when news broke of their marriage problems, and I just wish everybody would leave them alone to sort out their lives in which ever way they want to. There was just no way they could stand up to the daily pressure of being under the media microscope. There are cameras and nosy reporters everywhere they go, and I reckon I would go crazy under such intense scrutiny. I would like to go into battle for the Prince and Princess of Wales and to tell the media to back off and give them some precious space, but that would be sticking my nose in where it does not belong. But I am sure a lot of you out there share my feelings.

The time when I was most thrilled to meet Prince Charles was when I was summoned to Buckingham Palace to receive the MBE just a few weeks after my marriage to Laura. It was the Prince who presented it to me, and I look on it as one of the most memorable and proudest moments of my life. I hired my morning dress from Moss Bros and like to think I looked the bee's knees in my topper and tails. I had been to the Palace several times and had been privileged to have met most of the Royal Family, but this was really special and I felt a million dollars as I was driven through the Buck House gates with Laura, Rachel and Nicola alongside me all dressed in identical blue dresses. In fact I felt like a king. Wandsworth – a fifteen-minute drive across the Thames – seemed a million miles away.

It's just mind-boggling in the Palace, and you go pop-eyed looking at all the magnificent paintings, massive chandeliers and ornate furnishings and beautiful tapestries. It's everything you can imagine and more. I got quite nervous in the gallery alongside the investiture room, waiting for my name to be called and trying to remember what I had been told about bowing before and after receiving the award and reversing to avoid turning my back on His Royal Highness.

There were about fifty people who received awards before me and I thought the Prince would be just about sick to death by the time my name was called, but he gave me a friendly smile as I walked towards him. 'Congratulations, Frank,' he said as he shook my hand and presented me with my medal. 'This is well deserved.'

He then asked me how the wedding had gone and enquired about my future plans. 'Don't you think you're a bit old to want to keep on boxing?' he asked, with a twinkle in his eye.

'I'm still a young man, sir,' I said, laughing.

'Well good luck in whatever you decide to do,' he said. 'And I hope you and your wife have a long and happy marriage.'

It was all over in a few moments, but the Prince had managed to make me feel as if I was really special. And he had achieved the same effect for everybody else receiving their awards. It's incredible how he finds something personal to say to all those who are invested.

Thanks to Jarvis Astaire and the National Sporting Club, my day was made even more memorable by a buffet lunch with a gathering of my family and closest friends. A few years earlier Jarvis had arranged for the Variety Club to honour me with a lunch after the Witherspoon fight, and I want to go on record with my appreciation of all the efforts Jarvis has always made to get me public recognition. He is now the main driving force behind the International Variety Club that raises millions of pounds for children worldwide, and if anybody deserves a pat on the back it's him. Jarvis – an out-and-out boxing fan, vice-chairman of Wembley and a high-powered business-man – likes to stay in the background, but there are thousands of underprivileged kids who have ben-efited from his tireless money-raising charity work. Nice one, Jarvis.

Anyway, getting back to my Royal name-dropping. Nearly all my associations with the Royal Family are through charity work. I met the Duke and Duchess of York when appearing in a Northern Royal Variety Show in Newcastle, which is one of my favourite towns and where I am always made welcome for the Great North Run. I attended the Queen Mother's ninetieth birthday party in the gardens of Buck-ingham Palace, and saw close-up just why she is the most adored lady in the land. And I have discovered that Prince Charles has inherited his sense of humour from his father, who always manages to make me laugh. I help out whenever I am asked with Duke of Edinburgh Award projects, and I recall during one function Prince Philip asking me: 'Can't you find an easier job than boxing?'

I came back with my usual line about not being bright enough to be a barrister, an accountant or a doctor, and that boxing is all that I could do.

Prince Philip did a Lenny Henry on me and replied using one of my little catchphrases. 'Wicked,' he said.

I couldn't believe my ears. 'Pardon, sir?' I said.

And he repeated: 'Wicked.'

That really broke me up and I made the room boom with the sound of my laughter.

Another time I was helping out with a Duke of Edinburgh Award Scheme project and I managed to go to the wrong place. I drove myself to Windsor Great Park where the function was being staged, and I followed the queue of cars and found myself at the polo grounds where Prince Charles was playing. The Duke of Edinburgh's presentations were being made a mile away over the other side of the park. It was a mistake anybody could have made, and I did not take kindly to one newspaper dubbing me Wally of the Week. I wonder how many of that newspaper's reporters could find their way around Windsor Great Park on their own when there are two major Royal affairs in progress? In fact that Wally of the Week headline was probably written by a sub-editor who has never been on any assignment outside his office. Bloody clever dick.

Laura and I were honoured to be invited to attend Prince Philip's seventieth birthday bash on board the QE2 when it was docked at Southampton. I found myself sitting next to Prince Edward, and I almost died when it was suggested that I should propose the Loyal Toast to Her Majesty the Queen. I had done this at previous dinners, but how many people have been asked to propose the toast while members of the Royal Family are sitting at the table?

I gulped a few times, and said to Prince Edward: 'Suppose I go blank when I stand up?'

The Prince took a piece of paper from his pocket and wrote my script on it: 'Your Royal Highnesses . . . my lords, ladies and gentlemen . . . the toast is Her Majesty The Queen.'

I hope Prince Edward's dad was happy with my delivery.

You will have gathered by now that I am a fiercely patriotic Royalist, and consider myself British to the bone. I've had taunts of 'Go home nigger' shouted at me in the street by misguided idiots. It makes me laugh because to go home would cost me about 50p fare on the bus across Battersea Bridge to Wandsworth.

I was a dedicated fan of Maggie Thatcher's when she was at No. 10 Downing Street. I have never met anybody as strong-minded and as confident as she was. Just by her very presence she could make you feel a foot taller at the thought of being British. When I shook her hand I almost expected her to break into a verse from 'Land of Hope and Glory'. I have also had the honour of meeting John Major, and have been tremendously impressed. He has not quite the same aura about him as Maggie, but he has a quiet confidence that gave me good vibes. His knowledge of sport is extraordinary, and he is really comfortable in the company of sportsmen and sportswomen. It does not make sense to me when I hear people describing him as a grey man. I have found him very colourful and with a good sense of humour. I became an even bigger fan of his when he stood up in the House and said that he was not in favour of boxing being banned.

While I am on about impressive people let me name the one who has impressed me most of all: Take a bow, Sir Jimmy Savile. A lot of celebrities have crossed my path, but none have matched Sir James. We have run side by side in marathons and he has been kind enough to invite me to several of his charity functions. I have never seen anybody work harder for the benefit of others. Before I knew him I used to think a lot of his charity involvement was just a big self-publicity act. How wrong can you be. This amazing man has raised millions – yes, millions – of pounds for charity, and he keeps a high profile simply to make his money-raising efforts easier. He is larger than life, and puts action where his mouth is. Sir Jimmy does not just visit Broadmoor. He *works* there. He is not too proud to pick up a bucket and mop to clean out a ward, and for many years he would broadcast on radio during the day and work as a porter at a Leeds hospital through the night. He did not do that for publicity, but because of a genuine desire to help others. You have only got to visit the Stoke Mandeville Hospital for paraplegics to get an idea of the mountains that Jimmy has climbed in the name of charity. He has almost single-handedly raised enough money to build a complete new wing, and talk to anybody there and they will tell you that Sir Jimmy is a saint. Yes, Jim'll fix it.

He has a dream of one day getting the money together to build a special children's hospital that will be like a magic castle from a fairy story. If there's anything I can do to help your dream come true, Sir James, just call me. I just wish it was as easy as rubbing my magic lamp but, believe me, raising money on the scale that Jimmy does is pure hard work. There is nothing I would not do for that man. He is a world champion.

I am a pygmy alongside Sir James when it comes to charity work, but I do my best and other charities with which I am proud to be linked on a regular basis include the British Sports Association for the Disabled, the Variety Club of Great Britain, the Stars Organisation for Spastics and The President's Sporting Club, which is a children-supporting charity run by caring Essex policeman Mike Jackson.

Another charity that has a special place in my heart is the Paul O'Gorman Foundation that has its sights set on raising £2 million to maintain and improve the centre for children with leukaemia at Great Ormond Street. A great character called Eddie O'Gorman has thrown himself into the job of reaching the target after losing first his son, Paul, and then his daughter,

Jean, to the killer disease. Eddie will not stop when he has satisfied himself that he has done all he can for the Great Ormond Street centre. The Foundation will then set out to maintain other centres at hospitals around the country. Professor Judith Chessells and her hardworking research team at Great Ormond Street deserve all the support they can get. I know a book like this is not the sort of place where charity requests should be made, but if you do happen to have some spare cash looking for a good home then it would be greatly appreciated at the Paul O'Gorman Foundation care of Great Ormond Street Hospital in London.

I hope I have not made you feel uncomfortable with this information, but I have seen the way Eddie O'Gorman worries himself sick trying to raise money for this great cause. He is a man with a very special mission, and I have promised him my total support.

When there are caring people like Sir Jimmy Savile, Mike Jackson, Eddie O'Gorman and Jock Barr around it fills me with hope and optimism for the future, and I cannot think of a better way to end this book of mine than on that note of hope. They have shown me that there is a lot for me to do in life once my boxing career is finally over.

Thank you for going the distance with me, and just remember – it's all in *the eye of the tiger!*

The Fight File

A lady called Laura has faithfully kept newspaper cuttings of all my fights, and I would like to place on record my thanks to all those boxing writers who have reported my fortunes in the ring – the ups and the downs. My thanks to the editors of each named newspaper and magazine for allowing me to reproduce the following words by their boxing reporters. Here from my scrapbooks are reports on all of my professional contests, plus my own brief, honest verdict on each performance . . .

Fight No. 1 v. LUPE GUERRA
Date: 17 March 1982
Venue: Royal Albert Hall
Reporter: Sydney Hulls, *Daily Express*

FRANK BRUNO, Britain's new heavyweight hope, pounded his way to victory in just 151 seconds at London's Royal Albert Hall last night. In that sliver of fighting time, his unfortunate opponent Lupe Guerra, from Nebraska via Mexico, subsided twice for counts of seven and eight. Then a crisp left and right to the jaw sent the Mexican down on his back, to be counted out. So after two expensive years spent on an eye operation, persuading the Boxing Board to grant him a licence, and the final hurdle of a High Court legal wrangle, Frank Bruno finally arrived. But this encounter was far too brief to judge whether he is going to become one of the giant-killers of his division. Still, no fighter in my memory has had such a spectacular send-off for his professional debut. At 15st 7.5lbs Bruno looked a super-heavyweight compared to the stone-and-a-half lighter Mexican-American. He came out for the start of his career, moving forward confidently. After a scramble, Guerra collapsed for a count of seven, rose to take a right uppercut to the jaw and go down for eight. And then came a touch of class from the Wandsworth twenty-year-old – a nifty two-punch combination that ended the fight.

Bruno's Verdict: *Considering I was a bundle of nerves, I was satisfied with my debut. I had been under enormous pressure before the fight, what with my eye problem and the dispute over my management with Burt McCarthy. It was hardly the ideal preparation for my professional career. I was just pleased to be back in the ring two years after winning the ABA heavyweight championship.*

Fight No. 2 v. HARVEY STEICHEN
Date: 30 March 1982
Venue: Wembley Arena
Reporter: Colin Hart, *Sun*

FRANK BRUNO destroyed his second professional opponent, Harvey Steichen, at Wembley last night in under two rounds. The twenty-year-old London heavyweight blasted Steichen to defeat in just 5 minutes 30 seconds – and showed what a fine boxer he is. Bruno, at 6ft 2ins and 15st 4.5lbs, was outweighed by twelve pounds. But he jolted Steichen's head back with a biting left jab throughout the first round. And midway through the second, he sent the Nevada man down for a count of five with a crushing right, before a flurry of punches finished off the American. Steichen, with a cut over his left eye, crashed to the floor and referee Harry Gibbs called a halt to the fight.

Bruno's Verdict: *I got my first taste of the 'psyching' that goes on in professional boxing when, at the weigh-in, Steichen told me: 'You're gonna be in big trouble tonight, Bruno. I'm gonna bust your ass.' But he looked so fat I don't think he could have busted his way out of a paper bag. He was puffing like a steam train at the end of the first round, and I could hardly miss him with my big punches in the second. I was happy to win, but I knew I had not beaten the greatest fighter in the world.*

Fight No. 3 v. TOM STEVENSON
Date: 20 April 1982
Venue: Royal Albert Hall
Reporter: Peter Moss, *Daily Mail*

FRANK BRUNO moved from the fight to the farce business last night and was howled out of the Royal

Albert Hall ring after only 2 minutes 25 seconds. It will be some consolation to the irate spectators that his beaten opponent, Tom Stevenson, will return to Indianapolis without his promised $1,000 purse. That has been withheld pending an inquiry by the British Boxing Board of Control, whose members were as furious as the paying public. Why, they will ask, did Stevenson fail to get back into the ring from the apron while the referee was counting to ten? It did not seem much of a body punch which had him sagging on the ropes and even less of one which bundled him through them. Once he found himself on the apron Stevenson sat there as if he had landed in Superglue.

He looked around and, moving like a turned turtle, made a feeble gesture to crawl back which was never going to succeed.

'I was homesick,' he said in the security of the dressing room. 'Bruno hit hard but I was all confused. I wasn't concentrating like I should.'

This was Bruno's third appearance in his five-week professional career, all matches with Americans who have lasted a total of 10 minutes 26 seconds.

There was doubt from the start about the wisdom of feeding these little-known Americans to Britain's twenty-year-old prospect and something needs to be done before Bruno is badly hurt by the derision.

Bruno's Verdict: *It was not my fault that Stevenson had little or no heart for the fight. This was my first taste of a crowd booing one of my contests, and it was a really disturbing experience – even though most of the boos were directed at my opponent. The warning signals were there* *that the public would not stand for me being fed soft touches.*

Fight No. 4 v. RON GIBBS
Date: 4 May 1982
Venue: Wembley Arena
Reporter: Harry Mullan, *Boxing News*

HEAVYWEIGHT hope Frank Bruno, Wandsworth (15st 4lbs) produced a magnificent left hook to beat game trier Ron Gibbs from Carson City, USA, in the fourth of a scheduled eight-rounder. The punch dropped Gibbs (14st 12lb) against the ropes and although he beat the count referee Roland Dakin was right to stop it after two minutes of the round as Bruno opened up on a dazed opponent. The perfection of the knock-down punch erased the memories of the three plodding rounds that preceded it. Bruno, still too stiff and tense, poked out a long left jab to keep the shorter American away, but was caught once or twice by long rights. Gibbs, the last in a long line of suggested rivals for Bruno, did his best and performed acceptably. He even caught Bruno with a decent right uppercut early in the fourth – but then over came the left hook, and that was win number four for Bruno. The dramatic finish will probably give Bruno a confidence boost, and we can expect a more relaxed and professional look about him next time out.

Bruno's Verdict: *I was doing my best to loosen up, but when I look back at the video recordings of my early fights I can see that I was as stiff as starch. I was also pawing* *with my jab, but at least I was pleased with what was a belter of a left hook.*

Fight No. 5 v. TONY MOORE
Date: 1 June 1982
Venue: Royal Albert Hall
Reporter: Ken Mays, *Daily Telegraph*

DAVID PEARCE, from Newport, earned the right to challenge for the British heavyweight title at the Royal Albert Hall last night, but it was Frank Bruno who looked the heir apparent. Bruno, having his fifth contest, stopped his first British opponent, Tony Moore, in the second after a rather one-sided 5 minutes 12 seconds of boxing. The Wandsworth heavyweight was in relentless form against an opponent who wilted under his hammer-like punches, and the sixteen-pound weight difference was obvious as the experienced Moore succumbed. Bruno caught Moore with a superb left to the head and then sent him down with a right. Although his opponent got to his feet after a count of nine, he took only a little more punishment before referee Sid Nathan rightly stepped in.

Bruno's Verdict: *Tony's best was behind him after a gruelling twelve-year career during which he adopted a have-gloves-will-travel policy, fighting all over the world. He was a nice chap, but could not forget that I had once been his sparring partner when I was a young amateur and he resented all the publicity that I was attracting. Tony was noted as something of an 'iron man' of the ring with a* *strong chin, but he made himself a sitting target for my punches by continually resting on the ropes. It was easily the most satisfying of my wins to date.*

Fight No. 6 v. GEORGE SCOTT
Date: 14 September 1982
Venue: Wembley Arena
Reporter: Martin Creasy, *Boxing News*

AFTER half a dozen pro fights, none of which has gone past the fourth round, Wandsworth heavyweight Frank Bruno must now be regarded as a serious contender for the British title. He crushed a markedly reluctant George Scott, Newcastle (15st 10lb), in just 2 minutes 42 seconds of the first round of their scheduled eight-rounder, and this result, taken with his second-round stoppage of Tony Moore in his previous outing, makes him a match for anyone in the country. Scott looked thoroughly intimidated by the powerful, menacing figure of Bruno (15st 8lbs), and was on the floor in Bruno's corner after about a minute, from a right uppercut. He took a count of eight, was pummelled along the ropes and back again towards Bruno's corner, and sagged for the second count, this time after a flurry capped with a left hook. Boos sounded all around the arena as referee Sid Nathan counted, with Scott up at eight, and increased in volume when Mr Nathan stopped it moments later as Scott cupped his head in his gloves.

Bruno's Verdict: *Scott, known as the 'King of Geordieland', talked a great fight before we climbed into the ring,* *but the moment the first bell rang he froze. It was almost embarrassing hitting an opponent who suddenly wanted to be a million miles away. I got little satisfaction out of the victory because Scott virtually gave up from the moment I landed my first big punch. I got on with my job, and all the boos were aimed at the Geordie, who must have known in his heart that he had let himself down against me.*

Fight No. 7 v. ALI LUKUSA
Date: 23 October 1982
Venue: West Berlin
Reporter: Alan Thompson, *Daily Express*

FRANK BRUNO is no nearer a crack at the British heavyweight title after scoring his seventh knockout in double-quick time. Bruno, twenty, put the lights out for Ali Lukusa (Zaire) in just under four minutes of controlled aggression in West Berlin. But manager Terry Lawless has no intention of bowing to public pressure and aiming too high too soon for his novice with the knockout drop. Lawless says: 'I want to move one step at a time, going up in class steadily. Frank needs as much experience under every type of condition that he can possibly get.' Bruno spent just over one minute sizing up an opponent who has twice fought European champions, then he let loose putting Lukusa down twice in the round. The end came early and humanely with the first decent punch of the second round, a right hook chopping down on his crouching opponent from which there was no hope of recovery.

Bruno's Verdict: *Terry was concerned about the pressure being put on me by the press because so much was expected of me even though I had fought less than twelve rounds as a professional. He slipped in this fight in Berlin to get me away from the media microscope. It was expected that Lukusa would give me a decent fight, but he folded as soon as I let my biggest punches go. It just wasn't his night. On the way home from the stadium he got mugged!*

Fight No. 8 v. RUDI GAUWE
Date: 9 November 1982
Venue: Royal Albert Hall
Reporter: James Dobson, *Daily Star*

FRANK BRUNO crashed his mighty right hand on to Belgian Rudi Gauwe's jaw at the Royal Albert Hall last night and put him in hospital – with a broken right ankle. Gauwe crashed to the floor after twenty seconds of the second round, twisting his ankle as he fell, to become the Wandsworth Walloper's eighth victim, all stopped so quickly that the twenty-year-old has still fought less than fifteen rounds as a pro. Bruno, four pounds heavier at 15st 6lbs, punished Gauwe from the start. He hurt him with his first left jab and then clobbered him with his first big hit of the second round – a perfect right cross landing flush on the chin. Joe Bugner watched from the ringside, but the thirty-two-year-old former British and European champion will not be meeting Bruno for quite a while. 'I would not consider a Bugner match at the moment,' said manager Terry Lawless. 'I might think Bruno would win, but if he did where could I go to get him experience? I'm delighted with him, but he has a long way to go yet.' Bugner, accompanied by promoter Frank Warren, said: 'Bruno's fighting a load of nobodies. It is not doing him or boxing any good. I am ready to take him now.'

Bruno's Verdict: *Gauwe was my most experienced opponent to date, and had gone nine rounds in a European title challenge against John L. Gardner in 1980. For the first time since turning professional I managed to produce my gymnasium form in the ring, and was less stiff and tense. The crowd booed the Belgian when he failed to beat the count, but I think they would have been more sympathetic had they realised he had broken his ankle as he fell to the canvas. As Harry Carpenter interviewed me in the ring after the fight, Joe Bugner kept holding up an open hand to signal that he would beat me in five rounds. I mimed that I would stop him in two. But Terry was having none of it. 'There are two reasons why we are not interested in Bugner at the moment,' he told me. 'One, the longer we keep him waiting the bigger the interest and the purse will be. Two, you need a lot more experience. Joe knows all the tricks and could mess you about. I think you could beat him now. I know you will beat him in six months' time. Let him wait. He needs you more than you need him. You have all the time in the world.' That six months actually stretched to five years.*

Fight No. 9 v. GEORGE BUTZBACH
Date: 23 November 1982
Venue: Wembley Arena
Reporter: Colin Hart, *Sun*

FRANK BRUNO took only two minutes to dispose of West German George Butzbach at Wembley last night. The giant 15st 5lbs British heavyweight hope needed only one punch to end the visitor's interest in proceedings. George looked as if he had been training on sauerkraut and dumplings. And Bruno's left hook seemed to disappear right up to his elbow into George's stomach as if he was plunging his fist into a barrel of dough. Butzbach sank to his knees, his face screwed up in both pain and alarm. As he knelt, the air hissed out of his open mouth like a Zeppelin that had been punctured. The German rose at seven, but as soon as he realised he was being ordered to continue by referee Roland Dakin, he held up his right hand in surrender and fell to the canvas. He stayed there for several minutes until he got his wind back, and was justifiably booed by the sparse crowd of 2,000. Bruno was surprised that Butzbach had folded so quickly. He said: 'I only meant that punch to soften him up. I'd love to meet Joe Bugner, to show I really have world potential, but Terry tells me that I am not yet ready for a showdown with Joe. And Terry is the boss.' Butzbach, a former German champion, has had only one fight in the last twelve months. I'm afraid such poor opponents don't do Bruno or the paying public any favours.

Bruno's Verdict: *Butzbach had such a big belly on him that he looked better prepared for a beer-drinking competition than a boxing match. I made his body my target and he squealed like a wounded pig as I sunk in a vicious left hook. It knocked all his interest in the fight right out of*

*him. There were boos again, and all I could do was shrug
my shoulders. I did not select my opponents, and all I could
do was get on with my job. Terry and matchmaker Mickey
Duff were put under tremendous pressure the next day
when British Boxing Board of Control secretary Ray Clarke
announced: 'The honeymoon is over. Bruno must now meet
men with more experience and of more substance.' Terry
made the reasonable point that it was not my fault that my
opponents seemed intimidated the moment they got into the
ring with me. Terry warned through the press: 'If the Board
try to make me put Frank in with men that I consider over
his head we will pack our bags and go to the States. There
he can get the experience he needs without the inquests.'*

Fight No. 10 v. GILBERTO ACUNA
Date: 7 December 1982
Venue: Royal Albert Hall
Reporter: James Dobson, *Daily Star*

ANOTHER serious boxing injury was prevented last
night by Britain's most famous referee Harry Gibbs.
He stepped in after just 40 seconds at London's Royal
Albert Hall to rescue Costa Rican Gilberto Acuna,
who had been bowled over by an enormous right
hand from Frank Bruno. Acuna folded at the knees
and tried to get up at the count of six. But Gibbs
ended the fight and then said: 'My job is not to look
after the promoter or the fans. My job is to look after
the boxers. I will not be as daft as to say that had I
allowed him to continue he might have been killed.
But he was certainly in no position to defend himself
and he was certainly in a position to be hurt much

worse.' Bruno, the twenty-one-year-old heavyweight from Wandsworth, had in fact stopped Acuna with the only punch of the scheduled eight-round contest. There was, of course, disappointment in the crowd with stamping and booing and jeering. But Harry Gibbs was quite right. Had Acuna taken another punch to the head, boxing could have taken another blow it can do without. Another fatality. It is the eternal dilemma with which this sport has to contend. Where Bruno can go from here is unclear. It is hard for anyone to suggest that he should now fight opposition who can do him the same damage he did to Acuna. But there can, as I have said, be no further point in pitting this giant against pygmies. It is a problem that his manager Terry Lawless has to solve before the fans start showing their resentment by staying at home.

Bruno's Verdict: *The booing from the fans signalled their disappointment that referee Harry Gibbs had stepped in so quickly, but believe me Acuna was in no position to defend himself. A few weeks earlier I had the power of my right-hand punch tested by scientists who measured it as travelling at twenty miles an hour and landing with a force of half a ton. It was travelling at full power when I made contact with Acuna's face. If it had connected just an inch or two lower I am sure he would have gone down for the full count. As it was the punch scattered his senses and when he got up his legs betrayed him with a sort of delayed impact effect. That was my boxing programme for 1982 finished. Ten fights, ten inside-the-distance wins and they* *had lasted less than seventeen rounds in total. All in all it had been a year to remember.*

Fight No. 11 v. STEWART LITHGO
Date: 18 January 1983
Venue: Royal Albert Hall
Reporter: Frank Keating, *Guardian*

WELL, Frank Bruno has at least seen the end of a fourth round after eleven professional fights. But at the Royal Albert Hall last night Britain's extremely promising new heavyweight was given a whirligig twelve minutes before Stewart Lithgo of Hartlepool retired on his stool with blood cascading down his cheek. Another easy victory for Bruno perhaps, but this time the records will not show how game, not to say unorthodox, was the challenge. Not that we learned any more about Bruno's real potential. Lithgo threw a thousand swats last night, but in truth you couldn't call one of them a real haymaker on the very button.

Lithgo charged in with reckless fearlessness, a freckle terrier baiting the big black bear – and if Bruno wasn't thinking that his head was actually in a mincing machine he must have felt at times like a test pilot in a wind tunnel. Certainly Bruno, with his puzzled mien and furrowed brow, had never before seen anything like the crazed, flailing fists that kept coming at him. Nor had the packed crowd, and as once or twice Bruno was forced to weather the storm on the ropes against a man 24lbs lighter, the old pile at Kensington Gore rattled to the rafters as the cheers for an unlikely hero reverberated. At odd times Bruno stood up and hit back, and the North-Easterner unquestionably felt the punches. Certainly Bruno looks very menacing.

The Londoner was played in to a snatch of the *Planets* suite, and dressed in the West Indian cricket colours of deep cherry red, he looked as intensely murderous as Colin Croft walking back to bowl.

The overture music did not quite suit Lithgo as well. He is an unlikely gladiator – lanky, all legs, knees and elbows, with National Service haircut and squaddie moustache to match. Shades of Jack Gardner.

For each of the four rounds Lithgo came out with marvellous, even jokey guts standing upright in the stance of an olde-tyme pugilist coming up to scratch, whirring and shaking his fists.

'Bend those legs, boy . . . off those bloody ropes . . . Move around and think what you're effin doin'!' shouted Lithgo's corner. Whether he took any notice or not, he certainly kept coming. Bruno had not come across anything like this before.

In the second round a small nick appeared on Lithgo's left cheek and it got worse through the fight even as he kept harrying the bemused Bruno, once or twice into the corners.

By the middle of the fourth the crowd were as demented as the gallant Lithgo as the crazy man still charged in, as hopelessly and bravely as a British infantryman extra auditioning for *Zulu*. The unlikely white man had an awful lot of bottle.

Bruno's Verdict: *Lithgo was the gamest opponent I had ever met. I found him an awkward cuss, and felt so frustrated at my failure to nail him that the next morning I was up at five o'clock pounding the road as I attempted to run the excess energy out of my system. When I told Terry what I had done he went spare. I had become not so much a workaholic as a trainaholic, and he warned me that I should lift my foot off the accelerator or risk burning myself out. I took the advice and started to relax more in my training, putting in the same effort but in shorter bursts. It was still hard work, but a lot better than slaving on the building site.*

Fight No. 12 v. PETER MULENDWA
Date: 8 February 1983
Venue: Royal Albert Hall
Reporter: Srikumar Sen, *The Times*

BEFORE Peter Mulendwa, of Uganda, came here we knew nothing about him; now that he is on his way back to his coal-heaving job in Rome we still know nothing about him except that he is built like Joe Frazier, with muscles to match, and knows little about boxing. He would not have been here if Alfredo Evangelista, the experienced Spanish heavyweight, had not cried off with a damaged wrist at the last moment and left Frank Bruno to take on Mulendwa at the Albert Hall. Bruno disposed of him in 1 minute 37 seconds of the third round. A right to the ribs that sent a stab of pain through the Ugandan's frame, followed up by a couple of taps, had him rolling on the floor. He stayed down there while Harry Gibbs counted him out. Though Bruno did what was expected of him, Terry Lawless his manager said: 'He did everything right; it could have all gone wrong if he had tried to get the job done quickly.' It was a far from satisfactory bout for the big Wandsworth heavyweight, who was making his first top-of-the-bill appearance.

'I was completely relaxed,' Bruno said. No wonder. He was not only 34lbs heavier than the Ugandan but six inches taller. Bruno could box with all his concentration on the crouched figure in front of him trying to get in but getting nowhere. Mulendwa did not know enough to be able to get to grips with the British boxer, who had no difficulty in keeping him out with the right which had a kind of tolerant air a father might show to a son learning to box. But every so often Bruno clouted him with the right just in case the Ugandan was thinking of taking liberties. Mulendwa threatened to go to work on the vast expanse of middle in front of him at eye level but when I looked at the washboard facade before the Ugandan I had grave doubts whether his blows would have the slightest effect.

Bruno's Verdict: *I had got myself psyched up for the biggest examination of my career against former European champion Alfredo Evangelista for my first top-of-the-bill contest. It was an almighty anticlimax to find myself facing short-notice substitute Peter Mulendwa. In all honesty he should not have been in the same ring with me. I towered over him, and hated every minute of the contest because I was on a hiding to nothing. If I beat him, the press were*

*going to say 'so what?' If I lost it would be a disaster. It
was one of the most frustrating fights of my life.*

Fight No. 13 v. WINSTON ALLEN
Date: 1 March 1983
Venue: Royal Albert Hall
Reporter: Peter Batt, *Daily Star*

BIG Frank Bruno proved last night that he is, indeed,
the genuine heavyweight thoroughbred British boxing
has been waiting for. He took only 4 minutes 25
seconds to scatter wild Welshman Winston Allen's
challenge to the winds. But in that short, sensational
passage of time, frisky Frank answered almost all the
questions that have been haunting him. Could he
take a wallop, the cynics demanded to know. The
answer came in a double-barrelled affirmative as
Allen clobbered him with two mighty rights inside
the first minute. Delighted Royal Albert Hall fans
roared their approval as this big brown superboy
calmly blinked out the vital answers. But it was the
corrective left jabs with which he chose to chastise
Allen that really left the onlookers gasping. The first
of them almost lifted the 14st 10lb Allen off his feet
and brought shuddering echoes of the fearsome
Sonny Liston. Yet, as any boxing buff knows, the left
jab was designed simply as a tool to feel your way
with. With a merciless searchlight like this flushing
him out, fugitive Winston must have known then that
he was destined for darkness and despair. It did not
take long to descend. After being cautioned for holding at the end of the first round, Allen cast aside the

last remnants of discretion and charged headlong in. A brutal two-handed clubbing assault left him hanging helplessly over the ropes. And Welsh referee Jim Brimmell was left with the sad St David's Day task of leading his headstrong countryman back to obscurity.

Let the purists insist that Bruno is still a gangling novice, but let them add in future the word 'fabulous' as a prefix. It was a real man-sized job he did here in his thirteenth lightning-fast win. And it overshadowed Joe Bugner's similar performance against the same opponent.

Predictably, Bruno's manager Terry Lawless refused to compare his twenty-one-year-old star's showing with that of Bugner. He said: 'Frank did the job he has been taught and he controlled himself perfectly.'

Woeful Winston lamented: 'I'm not making excuses, but I over-trained. I was tired as early as the first round. I just couldn't bring anything else out of the bag.'

But Bruno joked: 'After all I'd read about Winston biting and butting an opponent, I had my eyes on his head and teeth. But I guess he had other things on his mind.'

Bruno's Verdict: *I had the satisfaction of stopping Allen quicker than Joe Bugner, who was getting me worked up boasting about what he would do to me if he ever got me in the same ring. For the first time I had my chin tested when Allen caught me with a looping right hand flush on the jaw in the first minute. It felt as if I'd had an electric* *shock, but I did not let Winston know that he had hurt me. I had proved that I could take it as well as give it.*

Fight No. 14 v. EDDIE NEILSON
Date: 5 April 1983
Venue: Royal Albert Hall
Reporter: Tim Mo, *Boxing News*

FRANK BRUNO barely had to extend himself in a one-sided rout of the amazingly brave but outclassed Eddie Neilson of Swindon whom he halted in the third of their scheduled ten-rounder, officially on cuts. The cut above Eddie's right eye was the worst injury I have seen in eight years at ringside. In fact cut is hardly adequate to describe the awful wound which seemed to burst open, the flesh falling away in a terrible gash. Referee Sid Nathan started to take up the timekeeper's count but at about six was able to see the eye and then and there correctly decided enough was enough. Eddie got to his feet, raised his gloves and was turning to Bruno to go on before being restrained by Mr Nathan.

If the wound and the four knockdowns Neilson suffered were sickening, the man's bravery and uncrushable spirit were almost sublime. Although the cut was the official reason for the stoppage, Bruno would inevitably have knocked out or stopped Neilson otherwise.

In the opening seconds southpaw Neilson was over from a left-right of Bruno's to the top of the head, which was not thrown with Bruno's maximum power. Eddie was up, game but flustered, and was driven round the ring as Bruno flurried. He looked in big trouble. More punches put him over as he tried to stay close and cover up.

Neilson was up at eight and ran into more punches. Bruno was always icily composed. There was nothing wild about the punches and he was in no haste to end matters. Eddie tried to stay low and bob and weave. He got out of the way of some. Then more blows put him over. This time he was up at two and he might sensibly have gone over to regroup himself. When he rose Bruno drove him round the ring. Eddie covered but was being belted.

Somehow Eddie found the punches to fight back; they were disorganised, feeble blows but at least he was providing resistance. Now he got low and tried to weave in. Eddie's eye started to bleed slightly in this opening round.

The second round was fought at a quieter pace. Bruno contented himself with left jabs. Eddie was still crouching and weaving his way in. He had some success with hardish body blows, though they weren't full-blooded Neilson shots and certainly didn't distress Bruno.

Bruno, lighter than Neilson at 15st 7.5lbs to Eddie's 15st 9lbs, looked the bigger man, height disparity exaggerated by Neilson's crouch.

Neilson came out for the third, again bobbing and weaving and looking to work the body over. He put Bruno with his back to the ropes near Eddie's own corner. Now as Neilson came forward in a crouch, Bruno set himself to throw the first full power right of the night.

He threw it in a downwards arc and it landed smack on Neilson's cut right eye – the same eye which brought about his loss to Joe Bugner in five rounds.

It was a blow which landed flush and it floored Neilson. Eddie screwed his face up in pain, which had the effect of disguising the injury for a few moments. Then the flesh fell away and it began to pour blood. Mr Nathan's intervention at 25 seconds of the round was the only possible action.

Bruno's Verdict: Mrs Neilson had talked a better fight than Eddie fought. His wife, who would have been a good match for Marlene Bugner, grabbed all the headlines in the pre-fight build-up with statements about what her husband was going to do to me. He was my first southpaw opponent, and I had no trouble working out his wrong-way-round style. Again, I had the satisfaction of doing it quicker than Bugner. It was not a fight for the squeamish. There was a horrible popping noise as my final right-hand punch landed on Neilson's eye. Poor old Eddie was not ready.

Fight No. 15 v. SCOTT LE DOUX
Date: 3 May 1983
Venue: Wembley Arena
Reporter: Donald Saunders, *Daily Telegraph*

FRANK BRUNO, unbeaten young heavyweight from Wandsworth, earned his fifteenth and most impressive victory at Wembley Arena last night, stopping Scott Le Doux, a veteran American, after 1 minute 35 seconds of the third round. Although Larry

O'Connell, the referee, intervened because Le Doux had suffered a bad cut over his left eye, there was no doubt that Bruno was destined, in any case, for decisive victory. His long, bludgeoning straight left had given him command of the contest from the opening seconds, and by the time the referee had called a halt Le Doux was bleeding from the cut over the eye and from another wound on the left cheekbone. He clearly had no answer to the accuracy and power of Bruno's punches and despite his commendable courage and long experience surely would have been dispatched before the ten rounds had ended.

Some of the crowd thought Mr O'Connell had acted prematurely and booed their disapproval, but I did not share their opinion. The cut was so serious that it required six stitches and, in any case, there was absolutely no point in the American continuing.

This was by far the most important of Bruno's fifteen quick victories. Indeed, last night, he moved out of the novice ranks and took a firm step forward. True, Le Doux, looking flabby at 16st 2lbs, nearly half a stone heavier than his opponent, is thirty-four and well past his best. But he has mixed in good company, including five world champions, and learned his trade on the tough American circuit. Bruno built his success on those long, straight lefts but hurt the American with hooks and crosses. Le Doux was on the floor from a left hook when the bell ended the first round. He must have known then that his immediate future held only the prospect of pain and punishment.

'Bruno is one of the heaviest punchers I have ever

met,' he said. 'I would put him in the top five, alongside men like George Foreman and Ken Norton,
though it was the cut that beat me.'

Bruno's Verdict: *Le Doux tried to wind me up before the
fight by slapping into my hand a photograph of a battered
boxer. 'Here, boy, this is for you,' he said. 'That's a picture
of my last opponent after I'd gotten through beating him
up. And that's how you're gonna look when I'm finished
with you, boy.' He made me feel as if I was a slave in the
cotton fields, and I boiled with anger. But Terry cooled me
down and said: 'He's just trying an old pro's trick on you.
Save your anger for the ring, and show him who's the real
boss.' Le Doux, a schoolteacher when he was not scrapping,
had drawn with two former world champions – Ken Norton
and Leon Spinks – and had given a good account of himself
against Mike Weaver and Larry Holmes, so I was delighted
to beat him in style. He dropped his slave-boss act after the
fight, and proved to be a pleasant and friendly man. 'You're
gonna go all the way to the top,' he told me, which did
wonders for my confidence. Floyd Patterson, former world
heavyweight king who had spent a couple of days showing
me some tricks of the trade in the gymnasium, was at the
ringside, and he said that my left jab rated with the best
he had seen in the current heavyweight division. I felt that
I was now a fully-fledged professional.*

Fight No. 16 v. BARRY FUNCHES
Date: 31 May 1983
Venue: Royal Albert Hall
Reporter: Peter Moss, *Daily Mail*

FRANK BRUNO stopped Barry Funches in the fifth round at London's Royal Albert Hall last night and the truth is that Big Bruno was in no hurry. Boxing to orders, the twenty-one-year-old black Londoner used the occasion to sharpen his jab to near-perfection. The thirty-four-year-old New Yorker, allowed to stay longer with Bruno than any of his fifteen previous opponents, is known for his left lead. He relies on it. He has little other weaponry. He is Funches not Punches, yet Bruno outclassed him at his own game. The crowd who packed the hall, drawn to the exciting young prospect, had become a little impatient. Bruno had made little attempt to land bigger punches, but after four rounds, he had jabbed his man silly. In the fifth, they took away the reins, told him to finish it, and he needed just 52 seconds more. He swung the left hook and missed. He tried a right uppercut to the jaw and it swept to the target with devastating effect. Funches, thirty-four today, was still on his knees at nine. Referee Harry Gibbs decided to let him continue, but after one flurry from Bruno and a stagger from Funches, he realised his mistake and stepped in. Funches said: 'Bruno would beat 90 per cent of American heavyweights right now. He has real power and was a lot quicker than expected.'

Bruno's Verdict: *This was just a learning fight. There was nothing to gain but experience. Terry wanted me to get some rounds under my belt and I deliberately carried Funches until I was allowed to cut loose in the fifth* *round. My education then continued in the United States.*

Fight No. 17 v. MIKE JAMESON
Date: 9 July 1983
Venue: De Vinci Manor, Chicago
Reporter: John Hiscock, *News Of The World*

FRANK BRUNO, Britain's exciting heavyweight hope, last night produced two explosive punches to show the Americans he means business. An electrifying second round burst in the London lad's first fight Stateside dumped over delivery man Mike Jameson on his back like a lorry-load of stale ale. Bruno caught the brawling, mauling Jameson with a left hook that lifted him off his feet. He followed up with a right uppercut that finished off Jameson, who had never been knocked out in sixteen fights. Jameson was floored for a minute after being counted out and he was helped out of the ring with blood pouring from his right temple. He admitted: 'Bruno is a devastating puncher. He mixes his punches and he hits very hard indeed.'

Big Frank, twenty-one, flies back tomorrow for a short holiday, while manager Terry Lawless goes to Las Vegas to check out the Tim Witherspoon–Jumbo Cummings fight, with a view to matching the big Briton against Cummings. A cautious Lawless said: 'I am checking out possible opponents for him in America, but at the moment I think his next fight will be in Britain, probably in October.'

Bruno began cautiously, jabbing at Jameson's face

and fending off the big Californian's attempts to wrestle him on to the ropes. Frank won the first round and in the second, he moved in for the kill. Lawless said: 'That was Frank's best performance so far. Jameson had never been knocked out until now, and Frank did it without too much difficulty. My problem now is getting Frank to take a short holiday. He is a fanatic about training and that is why he is always in such good shape.'

Bruno's Verdict: *The two punches I unleashed to knock out the giant Jameson added up to the best combination I had ever thrown. It was the sort of one-two I had practised many times in the gymnasium, but this was the first time that they came together so perfectly in the ring. Angelo Dundee, trainer of Muhammad Ali and Sugar Ray Leonard, was at the ringside and said: 'Bruno is the best prospect to come out of Britain in a long, long time. He hits like a mule, but there are still some faults to iron out before he is the finished article. He walks in instead of gliding in on the balls of his feet, and he could get knocked cold with a left hook as he comes in.' I respected Angelo's constructive criticism, and accepted that I still had plenty to learn.*

Fight No. 18 v. BILL SHARKEY
Date: 27 September 1983
Venue: Wembley Arena
Reporter: Ian Gibb, *Sun*

FRANK BRUNO, Britain's heavyweight boxing sensation, blasted his way to his eighteenth straight win at Wembley last night. Inadequate American Bill Sharkey lasted just 2 minutes 8 seconds in what was hardly a decent warm-up for Bruno. Sharkey, stopped only once before, praised the power of our twenty-one-year-old Londoner, saying: 'I've been in the ring with George Foreman and Bruno's punching was comparable – he destroyed my pride.' Sharkey, hopelessly dwarfed and almost two stone lighter, might have had pride – but he didn't have heart for a battle. Bruno toyed with the New Yorker's puny efforts until the abrupt finish. The Wandsworth Walloper pushed out several light jabs before delivering the finisher with a right uppercut. Sharkey almost threw himself on the floor where he lay face down quite prudently until the count had reached nine. By then, he had no chance of beating referee Roland Dakin's count – and he was thankfully on the way back to the haven of his dressing-room.

Bruno's Verdict: *Sharkey was deliberately picked as my first opponent of the new season to try to give me some distance experience. He was noted for his stamina and staying power and had gone the distance with former WBA world champion Mike Weaver, and had held Scott Le Doux to a draw. In my seventeen professional fights I had travelled a total of only thirty-nine rounds, and I needed to be tested by somebody who could take my best punches and still keep on his feet. But Sharkey just was not big enough for the job. He looked like a pumped-up light-heavyweight and he went down and out to the first full-powered punch that I threw.*

Fight No. 19 v. FLOYD CUMMINGS
Date: 11 October 1983
Venue: Royal Albert Hall
Reporter: Jack Steggles, *Daily Mirror*

FRANK BRUNO survived an almighty shock last night before stretching his impressive record to nineteen wins − all inside the distance − with a performance that warmed the heart. He was hit as he has never been hit before by giant American jailbird Floyd 'Jumbo' Cummings, who promised to come and fight but kept his word only in flashes at London's Royal Albert Hall.

Britain's big heavyweight hope proved he could take it, as well as dish it out, by coming back in magnificent style to stop Cummings in the seventh round. That at least gave the battered Cummings the consolation of taking Bruno further than any man has ever done before.

Cummings made his mark in the first round when he thumped Big Frank with a crashing right hand that caught him flush on the jaw. Every nerve and muscle in Bruno's massive body shuddered as the punch landed. He had no idea where he was and was out on his feet as the bell came to his rescue.

His cornermen worked feverishly on him during the break and they revived him enough to survive the predictable onslaught Jumbo launched early in the second round. Things slowly turned Bruno's way. He stalked his man relentlessly and referee Mike Jacobs was forced to work overtime as the Yank resorted to holding tactics that angered the crowd and frustrated Frank.

As Jumbo began to wilt under the pressure, Bruno stepped up his efforts to make the opening for a big final punch. He could not afford to hang about because a cut had opened over his left eye. The big chance came in the seventh when a right cross rocked Cummings and sent him back to the ropes.

Although he got away there was to be no reprieve. Bruno chased him across the ring and another flurry of punches, finishing with two clubbing right-handers, dropped Cummings.

He got up at six, but his legs would not hold him and as he staggered again Jacobs stepped in after 2 minutes 43 seconds of the round.

Bruno's Verdict: *It was after this fight that the press first started writing about me having a suspect chin. But the punch that knocked me out on my feet at the end of the first round would have flattened any heavyweight in the world. I thought that I did well to survive it. If there had been just a couple of seconds left before the bell I reckon I would have been going down to my first defeat. My revival, watched by millions on television, won me a lot of new fans, and I got a standing ovation as I left the ring. But I was not happy with my performance, and I returned to the gymnasium to work on tightening my defence.*

Fight No. 20 v. WALTER SANTEMORE
Date: 6 December 1983
Venue: Royal Albert Hall
Reporter: John Rodda, *Guardian*

FRANK BRUNO knocked out American Walter Santemore after 50 seconds of the fourth round at the Royal
Albert Hall last night. It was a clean, clinical finish
by Britain's heavyweight prospect – a short left followed by a ramrod right cross which sent Santemore
crashing in a neutral corner with absolutely no chance
of beating referee Roland Dakin's count. Santemore,
from New Orleans, became the twentieth fighter to
feel the power of Bruno's right hand. All 16st 3lbs of
the American toppled over and finished up rolling
beneath the bottom rope dangerously towards the
front seats. The crowd roared approval when Roland
Dakin reached the count of ten as the American tried
to regain his feet.

While Santemore was larger and heavier, Bruno
was given something of a start for there was recent
scar tissue above the American's left eyebrow and on
the cheekbone. After only a sampling of the Bruno
jab, blood appeared and troubled the American from
the second round.

Santemore tried a poor imitation of the Ali shuffle
to distract the Briton, but Bruno's concentration was
unaffected and he worked assiduously throughout
the rounds.

It was noticeable that Bruno spent much time with
his back to the ropes. That is an extremely vulnerable
position which will concern his manager Terry Lawless.

Santemore's seconds worked hard to quell the blood flow. But that was not the American's downfall. After the opening exchanges of the fourth round Bruno's left jab went home and the right came devastatingly behind it.

Bruno's Verdict: *Santemore told me at the weigh-in: 'Back home I'm known as "Mad Dog". Tonight you're gonna find out just why.' But I reckon he was more of an old fox, and I refused to fall for his clowning tricks because I knew he was trying to lure me into a trap. All the time that he was clowning he was looking for the chance to throw the sort of overhand right that had brought Jumbo Cummings close to a victory, but I had learned my lesson and had my chin tucked into my shoulder. He started the fourth round with a sort of clumsy tap dance, but I quickly had him doing a break dance on the canvas. I measured him with a left lead and then put all my bodyweight behind a follow-through right that landed high on the side of Santemore's left cheek. He crashed on his back and I knew that was my night's work finished. The best punches are those you hardly feel as you land. It's like when you hit a sweet shot at golf. It's all in the timing and you instinctively follow through. It's not necessarily the hardest punches that knock boxers out. It's those that are best timed. The punch that put Santemore on his back was perfect to the split second.*

Fight No. 21 v. JUAN FIGUEROA
Date: 13 March 1984
Venue: Wembley Arena
Reporter: John Pyke, *Daily Star*

FRANK BRUNO took just 67 seconds to knock out Argentine champion Juan Figueroa at Wembley last night. The quickness of Bruno's twenty-first victory inside the distance has set him up for a money-spinning return to Wembley in the spring. Bruno is now due to meet James 'Bonecrusher' Smith there on Sunday, May 13. With the fight beamed live to America, it would be an opportunity for Bruno to live up to his claim after beating Figueroa: 'Having seen Greg Page and Tim Witherspoon fight for the world title last week, I could beat either of them. I'm only twenty-two and I am fitter than either of them. You haven't seen the best of Frank Bruno yet.'

The £40-a-seat ringsiders were stunned by the speed of the win, but they must be certain now that Bruno has earned the right to be ranked in the world's top ten.

Figueroa got a mixed reception when he climbed into the ring, with the cheers mixing with the boos for the first Argentinian to fight in this country since the Falklands war. However, it was nothing to the reception that Bruno gave him. Having softened the Argentinian up with a solid left hook, Bruno missed with a right but his second right landed flush on Figueroa's jaw. Down he went on one knee in his corner and he could not climb back on his wobbly legs before referee Harry Gibbs counted him out.

Sid Martin, Figueroa's American manager, said: 'The booing did not upset Juan who is a professional. He stood in the corner too long, froze and got caught with a good right. He just couldn't beat the count. It's as simple as that.'

Bruno's Verdict: *I caught Figueroa cold with a combination left hook, right cross, but little praise came my way for the victory. A lot of the critics felt I was being fed too many low-category opponents, and my pride was demanding that I should be given a real test by somebody who was well established on the world heavyweight scene. Terry agreed that my apprenticeship was over, and live television was arranged for my next fight to give me vital projection in the United States. Coming out of the opposite corner would be a fighter glorying in the name James 'Bonecrusher' Smith . . .*

Fight No. 22 v. JAMES SMITH
Date: 13 May 1984
Venue: Wembley Arena
Reporter: Sydney Hulls, *Daily Express*

FRANK BRUNO, London's world heavyweight title hope, and British middleweight champion Mark Kaylor were both flattened at Wembley Arena last night in our greatest double fighting disaster for years. Millions of pounds were wiped off the 'sock' exchange as Bruno, blood trickling from his mouth, suffered a terrible last-ditch barrage from American James 'Bonecrusher' Smith and was counted out after 1 minute 46 seconds of the tenth and final round. And more box office bonanza dreams were blasted into nightmares when Bruno's pal Kaylor, of West Ham, was knocked out by another American, Buster Drayton, after 2 minutes 33 seconds of the seventh round.

Sadly, both Bruno and Kaylor had been miles ahead

on points when they were floored. On my scorecard, twenty-two-year-old Bruno, previously undefeated in twenty-one professional fights, had only to last out another seventy-four seconds to score win No. 22.

Smith's trainer, ex-world champion Emile Griffith, told his man before the start of the tenth round: 'You've got to knock this guy out or we go home losers.' Then it happened.

The unhappy-looking Smith, his bruised face showing all the effects of Bruno's left jab from the nine previous rounds, suddenly landed a left hook to the jaw and big Frank was hurt. It was the opportunity the powerful, but novice-like Smith had awaited through all the earlier pain and discouragement and he immediately produced the hitting power that has won him his last thirteen fights and earned him the reputation of America's most improved heavyweight in 1983. He pinned his man back against the ropes just above me and unleashed punch after punch until Bruno went down flat on his back.

Bruno courageously tried to rise, but his legs betrayed him and he was still on the floor as referee Harry Gibbs completed the full count. His anxious cornermen had to cross the ring and help the stricken 15st 12.5lb Bruno back to his corner.

Bruno, who had hoped for victory to celebrate the seventieth anniversary of the birth of his hero Joe Louis, said later: 'Every great fighter – including Joe Frazier, Muhammad Ali and Joe Louis – came back after being beaten. I think I let the earlier defeat of my great chum Mark Kaylor get to me, but I'm not crying. I will be back.'

Terry Lawless, his manager who has brought Bruno along with kid gloves, was almost too shocked to talk. 'What a Sunday the 13th,' he said. 'I am going to go home and sleep on this. When I wake up I hope to find it has all been a bad dream. Frank had the fight won, but his pride made him try to clinch victory in spectacular style. He only had to stand up to win on points, but Smith deserves credit for the way he finished the fight when he got his opening.'

British boxing has tears in its eyes this morning because Bruno was beaten – if the brutal truth be told – by a near-novice. After this fight the ultra-cautious Lawless had intended to take his giant off the leash and put him in for a big pay day with ex-world heavyweight champion Mike Weaver. Now he has to go back to the drawing board and start all over again.

Bruno's Verdict: *As silly as it sounds, the last-round hiding that I got from Bonecrusher did me good. I had dished out plenty of punishment against my previous opponents, and now I knew what it was like to be on the receiving end. At least I was free of the pressure of carrying round the 'unbeaten' tag that gets heavier after every fight. The defeat had made a man of me. There were a lot of people out there saying that I had got what I deserved because I had been fed a diet of easy opponents. Little did they know it, but their sniping remarks were giving me the motivation I needed to climb back up and show that I had what it takes to go all the way to a world championship fight.*

Fight No. 23 v. KEN LAKUSTA
Date: 25 September 1984
Venue: Wembley Arena
Reporter: Neil Allen, *Evening Standard*

FRANK BRUNO, welcomed back with a roar of public approval worthy of Henry Cooper as he scored the twenty-second stoppage of his twenty-three-fight career, may well have his next contest abroad in France, Italy or the United States. That's the hope, anyway, of manager Terry Lawless. Having nervously chewed his way through a wad of gum at Wembley ringside, Lawless now wants to take his 6ft 4in, 16-stone black heavyweight hope away from the magnifying glass of pressure which he claims the twenty-two-year-old from Wandsworth invariably has to endure here.

'Ideally, I'd like Frank to continue learning his trade by sparring with men like Larry Holmes or Pinklon Thomas, the new World Boxing Council champion,' said Lawless after Bruno had knocked out Canadian Ken Lakusta in 1 minute 30 seconds of the second round. 'But the answer we get from people like Holmes is that they are just very happy for Frank to work with their sparring partners rather than with themselves. That's understandable because there's no reason why they should want to go in with a big youngster who wants to work hard all the time – and we'd be getting much more out of the experience than they would.'

Following the round and a half which it took Bruno to dispose of Lakusta, who gave a good imitation of a yo-yo, no one could surely say for certain that Our Frank had proved himself totally recovered from the knockout defeat by James 'Bonecrusher' Smith in the same ring last May. After all, Lakusta was so busy rushing in and claiming his taller opponent whenever he could, that Bruno never had to stand up and take a real wallop on the whiskers.

On the other hand Bruno's short-range biffs to the head were impressive, the Canadian's head being almost swivelled off his shoulders. Long after the applause – and just a few cynical boos – had died away, twenty-nine-year-old Lakusta was almost painfully honest about what had happened to him as he tried to stay in there with a young man who had so much to prove.

'Bruno caught me with two punches on the back of the neck,' he said, 'and those were the shots that put me down. Even now, my legs are still trembling. At the time that he first connected I thought to myself "I'm not going to come out of this one." Of course, I was disappointed with my performance. But I really rank Frank up with the best so I'm not ashamed. He was much too strong for me and I was never really in the fight at all. His combination punching was just too much. Trevor Berbick, who is world-ranked, was the last fighter before Frank to KO me, and it took him ten rounds. That must say something for Frank's punching power.'

Bruno's Verdict: *I instinctively dropped to my knees in a gesture of thanks to God as the referee stopped the fight. It was an enormous relief to get this victory under my belt. I* *felt like a racing driver who had climbed out of a wrecked car and had then gone out and won the next race. This was the first time in my career that I had weighed in at over sixteen stone, and I really felt comfortable with the extra weight, and Lakusta could vouch for the fact that I was punching with more authority and power. I had managed to make the Bonecrusher defeat work for me, and had used it as a motivation to prove to everybody that I could go all the way to the top. Lakusta was just the start as far as I was concerned. I felt more relaxed, more mature and more in control of myself. Bonecrusher was just a bad memory.*

Fight No. 24 v. JEFF JORDAN
Date: 6 November 1984
Venue: Royal Albert Hall
Reporter: Tom Lyons, *Daily Mirror*

FRANK BRUNO predictably beat American Jeff Jordan at the Royal Albert Hall last night, stopping him in the third round of a completely one-sided fight – if fight is the right word. The American, who had nine stitches put in a cut over his left eye afterwards, should never have been allowed in the same ring as Bruno. Indeed, he did not land a single telling punch in the first round. No wonder, because apart from being vastly inferior in boxing skill, he was at an enormous physical disadvantage as well. For Jordan, standing just six feet tall, was nearly three inches shorter and twenty-three pounds lighter than Bruno. The Wandsworth battler was just too big and too strong for his opponent, who simply couldn't get near enough to do any damage.

Ringsiders who paid up to £30 a seat must have felt cheated by this mismatch. Bruno rocked his man with left and right-hand punches in the opening round and did the same in the next. At the end of the second round referee Sid Nathan went over to Jordan's corner and asked for more action. It came, sure enough, in the next round. But it was all from Bruno, who thumped Jordan round the ring and along the ropes before the referee mercifully stepped between them and called a halt after 1 minute 50 seconds. The ashen-faced Jordan was buckling at the knees and blood was pouring from the cut over his left eye as well as from his nose.

'Bruno is just a big sucker,' Jordan said later in the safety of the dressing-room. 'He hit me with his best shots but couldn't put me down. I reckon he will get eaten alive if he takes on the top heavyweights in the States.'

Bruno's Verdict: *Jordan was nothing like as capable as we had been led to believe, and I had an easy but hardly satisfying night against him. He talked a great fight, and kept telling me in the ring that I was not hurting him. He could have fooled me. 'You ain't got nuthin', sucker,' he kept saying as he made a meal of my jabs, hooks and crosses. He was such an easy target that it became embarrassing, and I was more relieved than he was when referee Sid Nathan stopped it. I had never heard instructions quite like those being shouted from his corner. 'Come on, Jeff baby, let's get acquainted,' was one classic as he hid behind a* *high guard. I was told that the final instruction to him as he came out for round two was, 'If he tags you, run like hell.'*

Fight No. 25 v. PHIL BROWN
Date: 27 November 1984
Venue: Wembley Arena
Reporter: Bob Driscoll, *Daily Star*

THE SAGA of heavyweight Frank Bruno's dopey opponents reached rock bottom at Wembley last night. He recorded a points win over ten rounds. But it was a formality, because his American match Phil Brown virtually refused to fight. After four rounds Brown had failed to land a punch, and he was warned that he would be thrown out of the ring unless he bucked up. The warning had little effect, as the Yank continued to shadowbox. Bruno saw the fight as a prelude to a match against European champion Steffen Tangstad of Norway. But his ponderous performance, and failure to drop the hopeless Yank despite landing a couple of solid rights, was way below championship class. No wonder the packed Wembley crowd, expecting so much, booed both men out of the ring.

Bruno said later: 'I know it must have been a stinker to watch, but it wasn't my fault. It takes two to tango, but Brown just did not want to know.'

Manager Terry Lawless shrugged as he said: 'What can you do when only one man wants to fight? But in a way I am pleased he has had the experience of going the distance. He now knows just how to pace himself against this type of spoiling opponent.'

Bruno's Verdict: *Brown came merely to survive, and produced a performance that was so negative I sometimes felt as if he was more of a sparring partner than an opponent. Referee Larry O'Connell scored every round for me and I got a maximum 100 points, but I have rarely been so frustrated in a fight. I did not blame the fans for feeling they had been given poor value for money, but at least I knew I had tried my best. I wonder if Brown considered he had earned his money?*

Fight No. 26 v. LUCIEN RODRIGUEZ
Date: 26 March 1985
Venue: Wembley Arena
Reporter: Tim Mo, *Boxing News*

FORMER European heavyweight champion Lucien Rodriguez was a sorry disappointment as he crashed out to Frank Bruno in just 2 minutes 39 seconds of the first round of their scheduled ten. Rodriguez (14st 13.5lbs) had been dropped for a count of nine and when he rose shook his head at Harry Gibbs indicating that he did not wish to continue. Mr Gibbs obliged by stopping the fight.

Bruno (15st 12lbs) had jabbed heavily with the left as Rodriguez retreated in an uneventful round. Then he got Rodriguez by the ropes, threw punches, landed a right, and in a delayed action effect, Rodriguez sagged. He was half down to the floor when Bruno hit him some more to the head. Down went the Frenchman and he barely beat the count before indicating his wishes to the referee.

All in all, it was a remarkably poor fight. We gave the bout an 'A' grading and were very wrong. Its entertainment value was 'D'.

Bruno was his usual lumbering, jabbing self, and when he threw the right the blows were fair. It was an undemanding warm-up for his European title challenge to Anders Eklund, who was at ringside.

Eklund stopped Steffen Tangstad who outpointed Rodriguez to win the EBU title. Previously, Rodriguez outpointed British heavyweight champion David Pearce, although he had to come from the brink of being stopped to do so.

It looks like the end of the line for Rodriguez and it is a sorry exit for a world title challenger who took the great Larry Holmes the distance for the WBC championship two years ago almost to the day.

Bruno's Verdict: *I was very tense before the bell because so much was riding on this fight. I had already signed to challenge Anders Eklund for the European title, and a defeat by Rodriguez would have thrown a spanner – or a hammer – in the works. Rodriguez was past his best, but he was still a dangerous opponent who had been one of the world's leading heavyweights at his peak. I knew I had to get to him early, because he was the cagey sort of boxer who could have messed me around if I had given him time to find his rhythm. As soon as I landed with a right uppercut followed by a right hook I knew that he would not be around for long. His eyes glazed over, and he sank slowly to the canvas as I threw a left-right combination to the head. The press* *were less than kind with some of their comments on the fight, but I thought I deserved credit for decisively beating a man who exactly two years earlier had gone the distance in a world title fight against Larry Holmes. Anders Eklund came into my dressing-room after the fight, and as we shook hands for the photographers he told me: 'You beat an old man tonight. I am young, and I have a strong chin and a strong punch, you'll see.' I replied in an exaggerated English accent: 'Just make sure you turn up, old chap. We can make a fortune together.' Little did I then realise that it would be more than six months before we finally climbed into the ring for our championship contest.*

Fight No. 27 v. ANDERS EKLUND
Date: 1 October 1985
Venue: Wembley Arena
Reporter: Peter Moss, *Daily Mail*

FRANK BRUNO could be no more than a year and a couple of fights away from becoming the first British fighter to win the world heavyweight title. That is my belief after watching the twenty-three-year-old Londoner's awesome destruction of European champion Anders Eklund in the ten seconds that last night's fourth round lasted before the Swedish giant hit the floor of the Wembley Arena ring. At 17st 6.5lbs he was the biggest European champion since the Ambling Alp Primo Carnera in the 1930s. He was twenty pounds heavier than the home man but Bruno took him apart.

In the time it took Carl Lewis to win the Olympic sprint title, Bruno threw many punches from many angles and all of them packed with power. Eklund's left eye was cut, his senses scrambled and when the ring boards shook with his fall, there was always considerable doubt that he would get up. As early as three he was looking up at Swiss referee Franz Marti but the stare was vacant.

What has to be taken into consideration of Bruno's world chances are the limitations of the trio who currently claim the ultimate crown. Bruno also has his faults but the way he performed last night, the way he turned that huge power of his into a machine of destruction gives him a chance against any man.

Last night Bruno might even have won it in the first round. Certainly he tried – maybe too hard – for a decisive punch. His left jab, a thundering punch in its own right, gave him immediate control. The timing of his bigger punches was just a little awry but that was understandable.

In the previous eleven months he had had less than a round of action which was all the time it took him to demolish former European champion Lucien Rodriguez.

Eklund kept him waiting for six months and there were two postponements, but he was just building up more trouble for himself because Bruno has never stopped working and improving in the gym. Just how much he has learned became obvious. Through the second round and for much of the third he showed commendable patience and skill setting up his man with that left and containing the few rushes by the Swede. In the final minute of the third Bruno tried a big left. Eklund ducked but ran into a right. The next

left hook was bang on target and the right that followed staggered the Swede. He grabbed at Bruno.
The referee parted them and as Eklund stepped back
he staggered again. Then the bell and a minute's rest
for Eklund but he walked straight into that ten
seconds of cold fury which will remain long in the
mind.

Bruno's Verdict: *The four punches I threw to finish the
fight were among the most explosive I had ever thrown –
and they were all right-handers. First of all there was a
right over the top of his left lead, then I quickly followed
with a right uppercut and then two more right crosses.
Eklund's leg came up as if it was being worked by a puppet-
eer, and it was like watching a giant tree falling as he sank
to the canvas. A big worry had been removed for me on
the eve of the fight. I had been scheduled to appear in the
High Court the morning after challenging Eklund. This
was for the hearing to settle the long-running dispute over
the piece of paper I had signed with Burt McCarthy four
years earlier. Terry knew it was weighing on my mind,
and he decided to settle out of court. It meant I climbed
into the ring against Eklund in a perfect frame of mind.*

Fight No. 28 v. LARRY FRAZIER
Date: 4 December 1985
Venue: Royal Albert Hall
Reporter: Donald Saunders, *Daily Telegraph*

FRANK BRUNO, the European heavyweight champion
from Wandsworth, completed a highly successful
year, at the Royal Albert Hall last night, with a

spectacular second-round victory over Larry Frazier, of the United States. Two ferocious left hooks to the body sent the huge American sinking to the canvas for the full count, after 2 minutes 14 seconds of the second round.

Only once before – very early in his career – had Frazier failed to last the distance in twenty-seven bouts spread over the last thirteen years. Yet, as Roland Dakin, the referee, tolled the ten seconds above him last night, there was never the slightest suggestion that this giant of a man would get up unassisted.

Frazier was obviously in pain, gasping for air, as he lay on his side, while a doctor and seconds from both corners worked to revive him. Let me make it clear that Frazier took this contest at only four days' notice, after Larry Alexander, another American, had been ruled out on medical grounds. Moreover, it must be emphasised that, at thirty-six, he was twelve years older than Bruno.

Nevertheless, Frazier mixed in some good company in the ring and in the gym – either side of a two-year stretch in San Quentin. Though well past his moderate best, he had learned during long years of sparring with such champions as George Foreman, Larry Holmes and Ken Norton how to take good care of himself.

It looked as if he was going to do just that – and cause Bruno some problems in the process – in the first round last night. The American, a couple of inches taller than his young opponent, and at 16st 3.5lbs, nine pounds heavier, moved backwards round the ring pushing out a left jab, covering up and holding frequently inside.

Bruno remained admirably patient, ramming his long lefts into Frazier's face whenever the opening was presented and occasionally hammering the American about the body with his right. The second round followed much the same pattern with Frazier seemingly quite happy just to stay there, push out that left, steal the odd point – and keep out of trouble. Then, suddenly, Bruno showed the American his right and sank those two rib-bending lefts to the body. Poor Frazier grunted with pain, dropped heavily to the canvas, and we all knew it was over.

If this victory showed nothing else, it clearly demonstrated that Bruno really does possess a destructive punch, whether it lands on the chin or sinks into the body. Moreover, he hits as hard with his left as he does with his right. Consequently, this autumn, he has won the European title with a fourth-round knockout of Anders Eklund and has reconfirmed his number six position in the world rankings by destroying a man who has only once before failed to travel the full distance.

Manager Terry Lawless said after the fight: 'Frank proved tonight that he is one of the best body punchers in the business. The body shots that put Frazier away would have knocked the breath out of anybody. I know that Frazier was a late substitute, but he has a good record and has only been stopped inside the distance once before tonight. It has been a marvellous year for Frank, and I think we can look forward to him challenging for the world title next year.'

Bruno said: 'Those punches to the body were so hard that Frazier grunted as they went in. I have been working on my combinations to the body in the gymnasium, and tonight all the practice paid off.'

When he had recovered, Frazier said: 'All that I have heard about Bruno is true. He is a tremendous prospect. He's got concrete in his gloves. I've worked with George Foreman, Joe Frazier, Ken Norton and Earnie Shavers – all the big punchers. And none of them hurt me downstairs the way he did tonight.'

Bruno's Verdict: *What I didn't tell the press is that I did not want to go through with the fight. I had been keyed up for a challenging battle against highly regarded American Larry Alexander when, just three days before the fight, he failed the British Boxing Board of Control's strict medical check after a brain scan had revealed an irregularity. When the veteran Frazier was brought in as a last-minute substitute I was reluctant to take the fight. I told Terry that I was on a hiding to nothing, and that there was too much at stake to risk losing it against a late substitute. It is really difficult to pump yourself up for a contest against – and I'm not trying to be flash – a lesser opponent. But Terry told me to be professional about it, and that I should treat Frazier as seriously as if he were the top contender for the title. I pushed all negative thoughts out of my mind, and set out to beat 'old man' Frazier as convincingly as possible. A secret I carried into the ring with me was that I had been lined up for a world championship eliminator against former title-holder Gerrie Coetzee, of South Africa.*

Fight No. 29 v. GERRIE COETZEE
Date: 4 March 1986
Venue: Wembley Arena
Reporter: Mike Donovan, *Today*

THE DREAM is a step nearer reality. Frank Bruno, carrying the burden of a nation's expectation, knocked out South African Gerrie Coetzee at Wembley last night in just 1 minute 50 seconds. The referee declared he had stopped the fight, but Coetzee was out cold, prostrate across the bottom ropes. He was floored by an explosive straight right following a series of blows to the head.

There must be a question mark over whether Coetzee deserved his reported £150,000 split of the £250,000 purse after this. But that should not detract from the performance of Bruno. He said before the fight that he would destroy the South African and that is precisely what he did.

There were the critics who said he had not had enough top class experience; that the defeat by Bonecrusher Smith had shown flaws in the twenty-four-year-old Londoner's ability to take a punch. But it seems as if Bruno doesn't need to manufacture more punches and improve on his ring craft if he can deal with his opponents the way he finished off the sad Afrikaaner.

We still don't know how fluid a boxer Lawless has produced. But last night he dipped his feet in the water and was not found wanting. It was never going to be a fight for the boxing purist. Coetzee's strong chin suddenly weakened and we discovered just who was the hungrier for a crack at Tim Witherspoon's title. Now the £5m match for the world title between Bruno and Witherspoon should come off in front of 75,000 at Wembley Stadium on June 14, provided Terrible Tim isn't stripped because of the drugs problem he ran into while taking Tony Tubbs' title.

Forget Henry Cooper, Joe Bugner, Richard Dunn and all the other British heavyweights who were so near yet so far. Bruno is now a genuine prospect and the lads from the Royal Oak gym in Canning Town where he trains will be forgiven for being a bit hung over this morning.

Bruno's Verdict: *There were never any hangovers at the Royal Oak. Terry would have kicked out any boxer he suspected of drinking or taking drugs. I can vouch for the fact that Terry is the Mr Clean of boxing. I was high on my performance against Coetzee. My critics said that I had beaten a washed-up fighter. But if he was so washed-up how did he get his rating as No. 1 contender for Tim Witherspoon's title? I know that I would have beaten Coetzee on that night regardless of what fight plan he had. I had never been so stoked up for a contest, and I was ready to walk through a brick wall to get myself the shot at the world title. I saw Coetzee as a safe door barring my way to the crown jewels, and I was determined to blast him out of the way. We had noticed when studying film of him that when he threw his left jab his head would come up. I waited for his first jab and then fired my right over the top of it just as I had practised in training. I have never seen such a look of shock come over an opponent's face as much as it* *did with Coetzee when he felt the weight of that first right hand that dropped him briefly right at the start of the round. I knocked him cold with an even more devastating right, but it was that first punch that knocked the heart out of him.*

Fight No. 30 v. TIM WITHERSPOON
Date: 19 July 1986
Venue: Wembley Stadium
Reporter: Nick Pitt, *Sunday Times*

FRANK BRUNO's bid to become the first Briton this century to win a world heavyweight title ended in dramatic but very brave failure at the Wembley Stadium in the early hours of this morning. The fight was stopped during the eleventh round after Bruno had been hammered to the canvas by a succession of punches by the champion Tim Witherspoon which left him totally helpless and unable to continue. But Bruno's challenge was a courageous and worthwhile attempt to realise a dream which is among the hardest in sport to achieve.

For much of the fight Bruno matched everything the American could do. He boxed better than we knew he could, he took many of Witherspoon's best punches, and he launched several attacks of his own that troubled the American, damaged his face considerably, and which made it seem that for much of the fight he had a real chance of winning.

But finally his stamina and his chin gave out. Just when Witherspoon appeared to be tiring and sucking for breath, he found the right-hand punch that broke down Bruno's admirable resistance and left him suddenly and totally vulnerable.

Bruno had crossed himself immediately before the first bell. He was wise to take that precaution for Witherspoon immediately went on to the attack, throwing the first punch of the fight, a long right-hand punch that grazed the side of Bruno's face. The home hero worked busily, and opened up with a flurry of punches midway through the first round, but these brought nothing but a smile from Witherspoon.

The smile soon disappeared, however, when Bruno caught the American off guard with a right hand to the side of the face. For a second Witherspoon staggered but immediately recovered. The first round ended with a hard exchange which must have told our man that his opponent was fresh and dangerous, and as the bell went Bruno gave a hard long glance at Witherspoon, and Witherspoon raised his arms to the crowd. But when he took a mouthful of water and spat it into the bucket it was noticeable that his spit was coloured bright red.

Both fighters attacked hard at the start of the second round. Indeed both opened the round with punches which landed simultaneously, Witherspoon's left hook seeming the more damaging. Bruno's plan seemed clear. He was attacking Witherspoon's fleshy body with a succession of hooks, hoping to persuade the champion to lower his hands and provide an opportunity upstairs. But Witherspoon took the punches well, as his record always suggested he would, and he was catching Bruno often enough with counter-punches to cause disquiet. It was clear already, however, that Bruno was not being outboxed to the extent that many had feared.

It was also clear that Witherspoon had come to fight. In the third round he kept Bruno occupied on the end of his left jab, and then suddenly, with a flurry of punches, caught Bruno exposed, hitting him three times to the chin. He looked at Bruno's legs, and they were still as firm as when he entered the ring.

Bruno himself was soon handing out the heavy stuff, and he caught Witherspoon against the ropes in a neutral corner and hit him with a succession of punches to the head. Witherspoon tried all he knew to avoid the barrage, but before he managed to escape from the corner he had been hit cleanly several times.

As we entered round five it had become clear that this was an even contest. Witherspoon settled down to a period of clever boxing, trying not to work too hard to conserve energy, but catching Bruno on occasions with sharp left hooks. Bruno took these punches well, and still looked the part in a world title fight, but he appeared to have slowed down a little. In the interval after round five he was given a sharp talking to by his corner and urged to step up the pace.

Witherspoon's jab seemed to be becoming the most significant punch in either man's arsenal. He threw it out repeatedly, catching Bruno more often than he should have been allowed to. Bruno was caught time after time, and blood began to trickle around his nose.

He seemed to have little defence to this punch, and could only blink, move forward, and be hit again.

Suddenly, in the seventh round, Bruno was in trouble. He caught Witherspoon with a good right-hand punch in a neutral corner, but Witherspoon replied with two hooks to Bruno's chin. Witherspoon followed up quickly, catching Bruno repeatedly and punching him across the ring. Bruno rode the storm, and briefly fought back, but as the bell sounded he was caught again with a right-hand punch flush to the chin. It was a worried corner that he returned to.

It was Bruno, whose defences were now clearly inferior, who was having to take the worst punches. Even when Witherspoon was hit himself, he was always fast to reply with hurtful punches of unerring accuracy. Bruno was beginning to discover just how hard the hardest game can be. In round nine his mouth was open as he took some fearful punishment.

But he suddenly found some encouragement, turning Witherspoon cleverly on the ropes and hitting him hard himself. It was a brave rally, and Bruno still looked amazingly strong, but it was Witherspoon who delivered another telling punch as the bell sounded.

Witherspoon may have looked awful in training, and he may have weighed far more than his best fighting weight, but he was lasting the course well, fighting in bursts of activity but bursts which were undeniably threatening.

In the tenth round Bruno at last achieved what he had been trying to do for so long. He threw a right hand, one of his best punches, and hit Witherspoon exactly where he wanted, on the chin. For a moment, Witherspoon's legs began to buckle, but he held on to the challenger and the danger passed.

Both fighters were beginning to show the wear and tear of battle and both corners were busy between rounds in attending to cuts and lumps around the faces. Stamina was becoming critical, and both men needed the luxury of large gulps of air to sustain their activity. But it appeared that Witherspoon needed a breather more than Bruno, for he slowed noticeably during the eleventh round.

But how deceptive Witherspoon's appearance proved to be. Suddenly he started the attack that was to bring him victory. Bruno was on the attack late in the eleventh round when he was suddenly caught by a massive right-hand punch which went over his guard and slammed into his defenceless chin. Bruno wobbled, and his legs shook. Champions know how to finish, and Witherspoon was no exception. He tore into Bruno catching him again with a right hook, then a left, and then another right. The first punch put Bruno in trouble, the ones that succeeded it left him quite defenceless and helpless.

Bruno staggered and was hammered to the canvas. His eyes were uncomprehending and he stared balefully towards his corner, which threw a white towel into the centre of the ring. The towel was superfluous, for the referee had already decided that Bruno's brave and worthwhile challenge had come to an end.

Bruno's Verdict: *It was tiredness as much as Tim that beat me. All the pre-fight tension must have got to me* *because from about the ninth round I was feeling as if my arms weighed a ton and my legs had gone heavy. Going into that eleventh round a lot of ringside experts had me even, and some had me a point ahead. If only I'd had the sense to claim Witherspoon when he hit me with that first big right. But what's the point of 'if onlys'? It's all blood under the bridge, and I have to give Tim credit for the professional way he finished me off. He knew he had been in a fight. And, boy, so did I!*

Fight No. 31 v. JAMES TILLIS
Date: 24 March 1987
Venue: Wembley Arena
Reporter: Ken Jones, *Independent*

FRANK BRUNO took a considerable step towards another fight for the world heavyweight championship and the riches that go with it when he stopped James 'Quick' Tillis after 1 minute 50 seconds of the fifth round at Wembley Arena last night. After feeling his man out with left jabs, trying to get the range, Bruno launched an attack that drove Tillis back into a neutral corner and the American was forced to wrestle his way out of trouble.

At 16st 2.5lbs Bruno heavily outweighed Tillis who scaled at 15st 4lbs and that advantage plus a longer reach gave Bruno an edge. The former European title-holder waded into Tillis again to set up the customary chant 'Bruno, Bruno'. This seemed to have some effect on the American, who had been vigorously slapped about the face by his manager during the interval and he surprised Bruno suddenly with a sharp combination, a left hook and a right thrust that reached the target.

Tillis was boxing with more confidence but Bruno showed no concern for the effect of counter-attacks and at the bell he had taken up the initiative again. They have been trying to make Bruno more aggressive in training and he showed plenty of fire and more mobility. When Tillis chose to lead with a right hand instead of the more orthodox left the punch found its way through Bruno's guard, but it did not seem to bother him and he sent the American back into the ropes with a long left. Tillis began to make a real fight of it and a short right sent spray flying from Bruno's head.

Tillis showed some smart moves, catching Bruno once more with a sharp combination, but there did not appear to be any real power in the punches and Bruno appeared to be setting himself up for one big punch.

Before Bruno could settle at the start of the fourth Tillis was across the ring to catch him with a long left high on the temple and Bruno had to back away to regain his composure. He then switched to the body with a powerful left, but Tillis was making him work although his habit of backing up on the ropes, allowing Bruno to come forward, was an invitation to big trouble.

Tillis was still on his toes but his punches became wilder and after he had missed with a left hook Bruno landed his best combination so far, a left, a right and another left that caused a tremor in the American's legs as he found himself backed up and hanging on just to the left of Bruno's corner.

He retaliated with a fast straight attack reminiscent of Muhammad Ali, but it was still Bruno's round and Tillis no longer appeared to be as confident. Bruno's corner were imploring their man to come forward and when a cut appeared over Tillis's left eye midway through the fifth round the referee stopped the contest.

Bruno's Verdict: *I was happy with my performance considering that it was my first outing after the disappointment of losing to Witherspoon. Tillis was a good-class opponent, and Mike Tyson was at the ringside to see me give him quite a tanking. Tillis had taken Tyson the distance.*

Fight No. 32 v. CHUCK GARDNER
Date: 27 June 1987
Venue: Cannes
Reporter: Patrick Collins, *Mail on Sunday*

ON A night of low and predictable farce, Frank Bruno knocked out a sad American named Chuck Gardner in precisely one minute here in Cannes. The first real punch of the fight was the blow which ended it, a sweeping long left hook detonating on the side of Gardner's jaw and spreading him across the bottom rope like a pained and lifeless walrus.

Bruno had the grace to seem embarrassed, even a trifle concerned that such a mundane blow should have brought such dramatic results.

Gardner, who had been knocked out on six previous occasions, simply wore an expression of dazed *déjà vu*. Even by the eccentric standards of modern matchmaking, this was a preposterously ill-fated event.

It was difficult to discern what benefit Bruno expected to reap from such a fight, other than a spot of useful pocket money. For a man whose ambitions involve Mike Tyson's world heavyweight title, it was an utterly irrelevant exercise, like preparing to attack China by invading the Isle of Wight.

Gardner had arrived from Minneapolis just two days before the bout after an intricate, protracted and cut-price flight. He had indulged in a little light work which made no significant dent in the folds of flesh which clung to the 17.5 stones.

He had spent much of yesterday afternoon wandering around his hotel pool, watching with approval some infinitely superior physical specimens. The flesh around waist and chest wobbled alarmingly as he tried to dance about the ring in the opening seconds but he winked outrageously when Bruno landed the first inquisitive jab.

Gardner had claimed, unconvincingly, to be thirty-three years old but he looked a decade older as Bruno moved into the conclusive attack.

Most pundits had given Gardner only the slimmest chance of surviving the opening round; in the event he failed to negotiate that opening minute.

Bruno's Verdict: *I've said all I want to say about this nightmare. It was a disgrace. My Oscar for the best line I read about the fight goes to Pat Collins – '. . . – like*

*preparing to attack China by invading the Isle of Wight'.
Nice one, Pat.*

Fight No. 33 v. REGGIE GROSS
Date: 30 August 1987
Venue: Marbella
Reporter: Ken Gorman, *Daily Star*

FRANK BRUNO moved a stage closer to his planned
showdown with Mike Tyson next summer with an
overwhelming victory over American Reggie Gross
here last night. It was a workmanlike rather than
spectacular performance from Britain's world heavyweight hopeful – hardly the deft and deadly touch of
the matador's sword we had hoped for in the local
bullring. But in fairness to Frank, he faced an
opponent who was rarely prepared to play the part
of an enraged bull or even a half-angry rhino.

Gross had felt the power of Bruno's punching from
the first round and seemed intent only on survival
until the one-way demolition was eventually halted
in the eighth. I felt the slaughter could have ended
much earlier and the watching John Morris, secretary
of the British Boxing Board of Control, echoed my
feelings.

'It was a disgrace to allow it to go on that long.
Gross could have been badly hurt,' he said.

There was an air of aggression, an edge of real
meanness about Bruno, and twice he was warned for
hitting and holding. But the power and strength of
his punches began to tell by the second round.

Reggie did raise the siege with one brief counter

attack, but spent virtually all of round four with his arms covering his head and body – almost a human punchbag.

Bruno's manager Terry Lawless fumed: 'The refereeing was a total disgrace. Gross had been barely able to defend himself for several rounds.'

Bruno's Verdict: *It takes two to tango, and Gross just did not want to know. The referee should have put him out of his misery at least three rounds earlier.*

Fight No. 34 v. JOE BUGNER
Date: 24 October 1987
Venue: White Hart Lane
Reporter: James Mossop, *Sunday Express*

As OLD Joe Bugner pitched forward, dead eyed and legless, the last word really was goodbye – and some may say good riddance. In the chill night air of White Hart Lane he was battered to an eighth-round defeat by our own heavyweight Frank Bruno and goes back to Australia with £250,000 and what must feel like as many bruises.

For all the pre-fight hype, the end was chilling and dramatic – and not without a hint of controversy. Bugner, lurching away from the younger man most of the time, frequently spitting blood and breathing heavily, was stunned by a banging right-hander. He dropped to the bottom rope where he seemed to sit as Bruno's iron fists pumped into his head. Then he slumped grotesquely forward in a drunken lurch and was halfway through the ropes. He was up at nine, his eyes glazed, his mind numbed and his arms dangling.

As the towel came flying in from his corner the referee – who perhaps should not have allowed the punching to go on when Bugner was in the sitting position – was waving the fight to an end and bringing the old fellow out of his trance.

For the invading Australian, the mouth behind most of the pre-fight hype, it was an undignified end.

He announced his retirement and croaked: 'I was not happy with the verdict, but Frank did a good job on me.'

Bugner had caused a gasp of surprise when he weighed in at a lumbering 18st 4lbs, almost two stones heavier than his supremely fit opponent.

Bruno fought cleanly and efficiently. His jab was always too quick for a slowing opponent who showed only bravery and an instinct for survival. In that sense he earned the respect of the 35,000 fans who had greeted his entry with a storm of boos.

Bugner began with a burst of aggression that few people had ever seen from him before. But Bruno soon pulled him up with a couple of banging left hooks. They tussled furiously after the bell at the end of the first round, but from then on Bruno, with some handy combinations, began to pile up the points.

Bugner had stood proudly in his fancy dressing gown beforehand, clutching the Australian flag in his right glove, as they played 'Advance Australia Fair'. But Bruno did most of the advancing.

Whether he is ready to go forward to meet undisputed world heavyweight champion Mike Tyson is another matter. While a huge crowd created a Cup Final atmosphere at the home of Tottenham Hotspur it must be remembered that a has-been who, at best, is a survivor, is no yardstick.

Bugner said later: 'I have to take my hat off to Bruno. I underestimated him. His punches hurt and he has got more class than I gave him credit for. He puts some good combinations together, and he will give Mike Tyson plenty to think about. I'm not saying that he would beat Tyson, but it is not going to be easy for the champion.'

Bruno's Verdict: *Old Joe had angered me for years, yet when it was all over I could not help but have a soft spot for him. He had talked a good fight, and it was thanks to all his blarney that so many people bought tickets. Most people thought there were more than 30,000 fans packed into White Hart Lane, and as I was 'on the gate' that was good news for me. You can imagine how shocked and choked I was to be told later that there were only 25,000 paying customers.*

Fight No. 35 v. MIKE TYSON
Date: 25 February 1989
Venue: Las Vegas
Reporter: Srikumar Sen, *The Times*

FRANK BRUNO may not have won the world heavyweight championship boxing title, few thought he would, but he won the admiration of none other than Mike Tyson, the champion, and that was enough to show that Bruno did everyone proud here on Saturday. 'It was a very difficult fight,' Tyson said.

Although Bruno was knocked into a helpless state in the fifth round, he had the satisfaction of hearing Tyson say at the interview after the bout: 'It's the hardest I've been hit by anyone. He was pumped up. He came to fight.'

When Tyson says 'he came to fight' it is praise indeed.

The most significant outcome of the bout is that Bruno can at last believe in himself and in his chin and fear nobody anymore. Every heavyweight in the world will now respect him. After all the years of soft opponents and manoeuvrings round difficult obstacles and lobbying the boxing councils of the world that brought Bruno money but not respect, he has at last emerged as a true contender.

Bruno's performance was a triumph for his trainers, Terry Lawless, George Francis and Frank Black. They did a magnificent job with him. While not boxing any better he at last learned to hold and fight and there was even one moment late in the bout when he ducked out of trouble. Even Sugar Ray Leonard, the HBO commentator, said: 'He has definitely improved his left hand since his last fight. He did things we never thought he could do.'

Bruno proved also that he does not have too bad a chin − it took some tremendous punches in every round. The gentle giant even matched Tyson stare for stare, rough stuff for rough stuff. And there was some really dirty work from Tyson going on inside: elbows, shoulders, and Tyson's use of the head would have brought Bobby Robson to his feet in excitement.

Of course Bruno brought much of this on himself. By using the survivor's tactic of holding on to Tyson's neck with his left hand, as if Tyson was his little brother, he angered the champion. Even though the referee, Richard Steele, deducted a point in the first round for holding and told him in the interval after the second 'the next time you're out', Steele did not do anything about it. He allowed Bruno to continue holding. When the protests from Tyson's corner were ignored Tyson 'went to work' inside. 'He was pulling my head so hard that I thought it would come off,' Tyson said. 'He hit me with some hard punches, the hardest I've been hit. But this is the hurt business. From the third round I knew I would break him. How dare they challenge me with their somewhat primitive skills? They're as good as dead.'

The contest opened with Tyson going straight for Bruno. Surprisingly though, Bruno met him head on and came off the worse when a right hand struck him high on the head and sent him staggering towards the floor. It was eighteen seconds into the bout and a record for the quickest knockout in the world heavyweight championship looked likely.

But luckily for Bruno, it was only a glancing blow and Tyson's follow-up went over Bruno's shoulder and knocked him to the floor. A count of eight gave him a rest. A further delay for the warning for holding allowed him another respite.

Instead of running, Bruno came for Tyson. A fight exploded. For the first time in his career Bruno was hitting out in self-defence. Tyson leapt up but missed with a left hook and Bruno caught him with his left. Tyson was knocked out for a good few seconds. He was still in the air. You could tell because his right leg wriggled like a lizard's tail that has dropped off.

Tyson then crash-landed against Bruno, who had no idea at all that he could have caused the greatest upset in the history of the world heavyweight championship at that moment. Instead of stepping back (something he cannot do) and dropping a right on Tyson's chin, Bruno imagined that the horror on him was about to start another assault and he gathered Tyson in his arms and involuntarily helped him to recover.

Bruno had lost his biggest chance and he paid for it. Tyson, even though rusty after six months' lay-off because of marital and managerial problems, went for Bruno in the second and caught him with three good punches. Bruno stayed on his feet, although only just.

From that point Bruno could do little but brace himself for Tyson – three inches shorter at 5ft 11in and ten pounds lighter at 218lbs – to come barging in. All Bruno could do was hook his left arm round Tyson's neck and pummel pathetically against the champion's body.

As the blows fell on Bruno's face one had to marvel at his new-found resilience. A right hand and a left exploded in Bruno's face in the fourth, but to cheers from his 2,000 or so supporters, not only did Bruno not go down but rushed at Tyson and held on again. It was only because Tyson had not been able to 'unload' his bombs because of Bruno's spoiling tactics, that the championship bout went as far as the fifth.

Now Tyson caught Bruno with a right in the middle of the ring. Bruno tried to clear his head. But another left hook and Bruno was on the ropes. The ropes gave and Bruno seemed to be leaning against the railings on the boat deck on a bad day in the Bay of Biscay.

Tyson launched his final onslaught from which there is usually no return. There was not. A left, a right, followed by a right uppercut, then a big uppercut that almost took Bruno's head off, and a short right.

Bruno was gone, held up only by the middle rope. Tyson was loading up for another barrage. Terry Lawless was running along the ring apron with his towel in his hand. Someone ringside held the towel. Lawless jerked the towel away and threw it into the ring. But Steele had already stepped in between the boxers. Tyson threw one more punch at Bruno. One more or less did not matter for the challenger was rapidly collapsing into Steele's arms.

Bruno did not take long to recover. Harry Carpenter, glasses awry, leapt into the ring for an interview and Bruno was glad to be talking to 'Arry. Bruno had come out of a horrific experience in one piece.

One cannot tell whether the blows of the final assault by Tyson will adversely affect Bruno, but until such time as it does his backers will be able to risk him against better opposition than he has faced since his victory against Joe Bugner in 1987.

Bruno can confidently work himself into a No. 1 position for a return. Since Tyson is beginning to do the rounds of old opponents such as Jose Ribalta, a Cuban living in New York, a return with Bruno, in London perhaps, looks more than likely. The cries of 'Brun-o, Brun-o' could be with us for some time.

Bruno's Verdict: *For months after the defeat I dreamt of getting a return with Tyson. I spoke to him twice and each time he agreed that he would be prepared to come to London to fight me. But behind my back he made jokes about me being 'a coconut . . . we Americans like beating up on good old Frank.' It was a strange thing to say as I have beaten all but three of the Americans I have fought, and particularly as Mike knows that I had him out on his feet in that first round of our title fight. I am convinced that it was my first round performance that gave Buster Douglas the heart to beat him when he took the title off Tyson in Tokyo. Mike is a great fighter, no doubt about it, but I will always remember the day I shook him to the soles of his boots. What a pity I didn't follow up . . . and what a tragedy for him that his personal life became such a tangled mess. I will be proud to tell my grandchildren that I fought – and hurt – one of the greatest heavyweights of all time.*

Fight No. 36 v. JOHN EMMEN
Date: 20 November 1991
Venue: Royal Albert Hall
Reporter: Ken Mays, *Daily Telegraph*

FRANK BRUNO made an impressive, if slightly farcical, return to the ring after a thirty-three-month absence when he knocked out hapless Dutchman John Emmen after only three minutes at the Royal Albert Hall last night. Bruno, making his comeback after being stopped in five rounds by Mike Tyson when challenging for the world title, wasted no time in beating a boxer who, on his record, should not have been in the same ring.

The Dutchman, who had failed as a cruiserweight before becoming the Benelux champion, looked game enough at the start but really never had a look-in.

Bruno, who scaled eighteen pounds more at 16st 4lbs, just a few ounces heavier than when he fought Tyson, really punished a boxer who combines the sport with part-time modelling and TV commentating.

In this contest Emmen appeared brave for a few seconds, but when Bruno produced the powerful right hand which had seen him win thirty-one of his previous fights inside the distance, Emmen looked hopeless.

The British boxer appeared slightly ring-rusty with his timing, but the power behind the punch was there and when Emmen stood in front of him he was punished for his boldness.

Bruno thrashed home a left and then a late right to put him down for the first time. Emmen bravely climbed to his feet only to be battered once more.

Bruno appeared to throw a late punch as the Dutchman was falling. For this he received a severe warning from referee Mickey Vann, of Leeds, as Emmen appeared to react to a leg injury. But once Mr Vann allowed Bruno to continue, the former European champion went straight at him and a long left had the Dutchman reeling once more and down in almost the same spot.

Although Emmen wobbled to his feet, the referee counted him out just as the bell sounded, and it was a merciful release for both him and the audience.

The victory continued Bruno's successes at this Victorian venue, for it was his fourteenth victory here since 1981, and it was his eleventh victory in the opening round. It was hard to gauge what Bruno's chances would be as he progresses, for this farce could be classed as the possible walkover of the decade.

Bruno, who has a three-fight contract with promoter Mickey Duff before he seriously thinks of challenging for a third attempt at the world title, would have to be given tougher opposition than the promoter offered last night.

Bruno's Verdict: *I know I am biased, but I do not think enough consideration was given to the pressure I was under when I climbed into the ring against Emmen. There had been months of hassle because of my eye problem, and then the unfortunate incident with Michael Watson put me even further under the media microscope. Add all that to the fact that I had boxed only five rounds in four years and you might understand the weight I felt on my shoulders. It was not my fault that Emmen seemed to lose heart for the job from the moment I landed my first big punch. I was just relieved to get the job over and done with. Now I could start dreaming again about one day making a winning challenge for the heavyweight championship of the world.*

Fight No. 37 v. JOSE RIBALTA
Date: 22 April 1992
Venue: Wembley Arena
Reporter: Harry Mullan, *Boxing News*

FRANK BRUNO produced one of the finest punches of his career to dispose of Jose Ribalta, the man whom we had confidently expected to give him a decent comeback test. The booming right which set up the Cuban for the knockout, in one minute 44 seconds of the second round, would have flattened most of the world's heavyweights and lent instant credibility to the hitherto unjustified talk of Bruno as a viable world title contender.

But at the inevitable risk of sounding churlish and begrudging, I have to say immediately that Ribalta (16st 8lbs) was a serious disappointment; in fact even the pathetic John Emmen, whom Bruno dismissed in a round on his first comeback appearance in November, threw more punches and fought more aggressively.

Ribalta's record showed him to be capable and hard hitting, and close points losses to Bonecrusher Smith, Tim Witherspoon and Pierre Coetzer suggested a toughness which was conspiciously absent from this performance. Of course, Bruno (16st 10lbs) seized control of the fight from the opening second, using a stiff left jab to keep the Cuban backed up and under sustained pressure, so it could be argued that Ribalta was never given a chance to show what he could do.

But even under pressure, a fighter with the Cuban's world-class level of experience can fairly be expected to throw the occasional counter. I noted one sloppy right in the first moments of the fight and five pawing left jabs, as Ribalta's total contribution to the evening. By any standard that is not an acceptable level of effort.

If he were a racehorse there would be a Steward's Enquiry, or a one-way canter to the nearest glue factory.

There was nothing wrong with Bruno's work: it has been a long time since we have seen him so positive, controlled and accurate, and the finishing punch was an absolute stunner. However, he has always looked good against opponents who don't hit back, so praise for the positive qualities of Bruno's display must be tempered by serious reservations about Ribalta's attitude to the fight.

It seems absurd that a man who warred with the young Mike Tyson for ten rounds, and who went the distance in hard fights with Tim Witherspoon and Bonecrusher Smith, would be intimidated by the prospect of facing a man who had been stopped by two of that trio and knocked out by the third, yet that was exactly how it seemed.

Ribalta looked unhappy and demoralised from the moment he was booed into the ring by a sparse crowd of fewer than 4,000, and the only forward move he made all night was to walk towards Bruno at the first bell and miss with a long, loose right hand. Bruno immediately put him on the retreat, snapping out left jabs and curving a left hook around Ribalta's guard which may have had the effect of convincing the

Cuban inside the first 30 seconds that there was no point in wasting effort in a lost cause.

Even when he tried to tie up Bruno against the ropes, it was done with the desperate floundering actions of a novice rather than the crafty spoiling of an old pro.

There was a moment of low farce when Ribalta got off his stool before the bell to start the second round, and then changed his mind and sat back down again, only to find that the stool had been removed. The sheepish embarrassment of the moment seemed to pile on the misery for a man who was demonstrably unhappy to be there in the first place.

The second round was a rerun of the opener, with Bruno forcing him back around the ring perimeter until, nearly halfway into the round, he fired a long right from far back which smashed onto Ribalta's chin with an audible impact.

Ribalta was out from the moment it landed, but fell awkwardly onto his side with the ropes holding him up. Bruno, legitimately, continued to throw punches while referee Roy Francis moved into stop it. A final left, which landed as Ribalta's back was to Bruno and his body draped at right angles along the rope, sent him crashing onto his back to be counted out.

Bruno's Verdict: *Ribalta got me really steamed up before the fight by telling the press how the power of his punches could blind me. It was not a cheap publicity gimmick to sell tickets. He really meant it. From the moment of the first bell I was determined to give him a good hiding, and I did not give him a chance to get into the fight. The right* *hand that knocked him out on his feet in the second round was a special blow that trainer George Francis and I had been working on in the gymnasium. I call it my 'Banana Bomb'. It is a mixture of a cross and a hook and it comes down on the side of the jaw on a curve. Ribalta did not know what had hit him. The way I finished him off made many people inside the fight game sit up and take notice. They suddenly knew that I really meant business. I had been under enormous pressure, what with my long run in the pantomime with Little and Large at Bristol and then going straight into a strict training schedule. Laura and I nipped off to Jamaica for a quiet holiday while I recharged my batteries. There was an amazing co-incidence during my first week winding down in Jamaica. I hired a motorbike and went off on my own exploring the winding roads in the heart of that paradise island. Coming off a bend I noticed another motorbike coming towards me, and we both slowed down. And would you believe that sitting on the other bike was none other than Lennox Lewis. At home, everybody in boxing was talking about if and when we would meet, and here we were face to face in the middle of Jamaica sitting on hired motorbikes! Lennox had also dropped off in Jamaica on holiday, and I wondered what the odds were of us meeting like this. We had a friendly chat and agreed that all the nasty things we were being quoted as saying about each other was pure hype. I have a great deal of time for Lennox. I like him as a man outside the ring, and respect him as an exceptional boxer. We enjoyed our chat, had a good laugh and then whizzed off on our bikes, both of us wondering in what circumstances we would next meet. Laura and I returned home and I went back into training for a fight against a South African called Pierre Coetzer, who had been*

*rated number one contender for the world heavyweight title
until beaten in an eliminator by Riddick Bowe.*

Fight No. 38 v. PIERRE COETZER
Date: 17 October 1992
Venue: Wembley Arena
Reporter: Frank Field, *Sunday Times*

FRANK BRUNO was forced to find grim determination
as well as the big punches to cut down South Africa's
Pierre Coetzer in a brutally hard IBF heavyweight title
eliminator at Wembley last night.

Bruno finally knocked the fighting spirit out of
Coetzer in the eighth round after the towel floated in
and referee Roy Francis halted the pulsating proceedings, often outstanding in terms of sheer willpower.

Monster strength brought Bruno a triumph which
puts him another step closer to a third attempt at the
world title.

But Coetzer came to fight until his last breath.
Often in the early stages he pushed Bruno's bulk back
into the ropes, and, though outweighed by a stone
and a half, was never intimidated by the British
favourite's sheer physical presence.

Bruno's chin also stood up to examination. Coetzer
found it with his left hook too often for comfort, and
it was fortunate that the South African did not carry
more venom in his punches.

Bruno, however, said a lot about himself in this
title eliminator. When things were going against him,
he dug deep and kept Coetzer at bay.

He weighed in at his heaviest ever, 17 stone 6

pounds, and his high poundage slowed down his movements and there were signs of him tiring around the halfway point as Coetzer refused to capitulate.

But by the time the fight reached the fifth round, Coetzer's injury-prone face was looking the worse for wear under the assault from Bruno's mighty fists.

The 30-year-old Coetzer posed Bruno more problems than he cared for in his third campaign for a crack at the world heavyweight title.

Coetzer, coming virtually straight off a clash with Riddick Bowe, simply refused to give ground and Bruno had to use all his armoury to fight him off.

Indeed, big Frank looked a trifle flustered in the opening round as he could not keep Coetzer off with his heavy left. Coetzer simply walked forward and fought back, oblivious to the weight difference of a stone and a half – and Bruno was twice guilty of hitting and holding in the opening session.

Bruno shaded the opening round, and gained encouragement when a cut appeared on Coetzer's left eye.

Bruno got his jab going, generally boxed better, but still had to be supremely careful. Time and again he was pushed back into the ropes and into positions he had rarely experienced in his professional career.

And he took two cracking left hooks on the ropes from Coetzer which clearly shook him, but the darling of British boxing fought back well.

There were times it seemed Coetzer might fold, but he kept coming back and stung Bruno in the sixth, and there were signs that Bruno could be tiring by the halfway stage of a brutally hard fight.

Bruno clubbed Coetzer with a big right at the start of the seventh as the British hero dug deep against the rock-hard South African, who refused to capitulate. But it was then Coetzer's turn to cause Bruno more problems with two solid left hooks that had Bruno retreating with blood appearing on his mouth.

But Bruno was back on top by the end of the round with Coetzer looking distinctly the worse for wear.

Suddenly in the eighth round the fight went emphatically Bruno's way as Coetzer took a left uppercut from close in, then two bombing rights sent him crashing through the ropes on to the apron. He pulled himself back into the ring and the mandatory count continued as he scrambled to his feet.

Bruno was now only moments from victory as he unloaded against Coetzer in his own corner. As the South African's chief second threw in the towel that wrapped around the top rope, referee Roy Francis stepped in to halt the contest after two minutes 17 seconds of the eighth round to ignite the usual celebrations associated with a Bruno triumph.

Bruno's Verdict: *I deliberately came in at my heaviest ever weight of 17 stone 6 pounds because I knew I would need all my strength to wear down Coetzer. I had studied him on video, and knew that he was a tough nut who would take some stopping. He had a jaw like Desperate Dan, and tremendous courage. After only three rounds of boxing in more than three and a half years, I had a lot of ring rust to shake off and for the early part of the fight my timing was off. But once I got into my rhythm I knew it was only a question of time before I stopped him. He was* awkward and dangerous, and I had to resort to some rough, tough stuff when he started getting careless with his head. There were accusations that I fought a dirty fight, but all I was guilty of was giving it everything I had and my determination and enthusiasm got the better of me a couple of times. I stopped being a gentle giant the day George Francis took over as my trainer. This is a hard, hard business and once that bell goes you have to give it all you've got. It was vital for me to win against Coetzer because a defeat would have meant that I had nowhere else to go. But the victory kept alive my dream of winning the world heavyweight title. **The eye of the tiger was still burning brightly.**

The Frank Facts

Born: Hammersmith General Hospital, 16 November 1961. Christened Franklyn Roy Bruno.
Weight at birth: nine pounds.
Star sign: Scorpio.

Mother: Lynette, a former district nurse and a Pentecostal lay-preacher.
Father: Robert, died in 1975. Robert and Lynette arrived in London from the West Indies in the 1950s and set up home in Wandsworth.
Brothers: Michael and Eddie.
Sisters: Faye, Angela and Joanne. Frank is the youngest.

Schools: Swaffield Primary, Wandsworth, and Oak Hall, Sussex. **Represented** Sussex schools at football and athletics. He was head boy in his final year at Oak Hall.

Started boxing at the age of nine with the Wandsworth Boys Club. Won an NABC title on a walkover. Boxed three times as a junior. All his contests were against Gary Hill. Each bout went the distance, with Bruno winning two and Hill one.

Amateur career: 21 contests, 20 victories (avenged his only defeat by Irish international Joe Christle). Boxed for the Sir Philip Game Amateur Boxing Club, 1977–80. In his final season as an amateur he represented Young England, and he won the London ABA and national ABA heavyweight titles. At eighteen, he was the youngest ever ABA heavyweight champion.

Professional from 1982 following an operation in Bogotá to correct short-sightedness in his right eye. **Managed** originally by Terry Lawless and is now self-managed, with his wife, Laura, supervising his commitments away from boxing. **Trainer:** George Francis.

Ring record: 38 contests, 35 victories. His only defeats have been by James 'Bonecrusher' Smith and in world title fights against Tim Witherspoon and Mike Tyson. Total rounds as a professional: 134. Has won 34 of his fights inside the distance, 16 by clean knockout. European champion 1985–86 (relinquished the title).

Tale of the tape: Height 6ft 3in; weight 17st 6lbs; reach 82in; boots 12in; calf 16in; thigh 24in; biceps

16in; neck 18in; chest 43in (47in expanded); fist 14in; forearm 14in; wrist 9in; waist 33in; ankle 10in.

Personal: Married to Laura Mooney. They live in Emerson Park, Essex, with their daughters Nicola and Rachel. He was awarded the MBE in Her Majesty the Queen's 1990 New Year's Honours List, and he was invited to Buckingham Palace to receive the award from His Royal Highness Prince Charles.

Hobbies: Road running, swimming, training, driving, eating, shopping for good clothes, listening to jazz-funk and soul records, watching old boxing videos (his favourite boxers Joe Louis and Muhammad Ali). **Books:** *Know What I Mean?* (1987); *Eye of the Tiger* (1992).

Outside the ring: Frank is a member of Equity, and has starred in pantomime with Michael Barrymore at the Dominion Theatre (with record box office sales). He topped the bill as Aladdin in pantomime at Nottingham during Christmas 1990 (with record box office sales). In 1991–2 he played the title role in the pantomime *Robin Hood* at Bristol, and advance ticket sales for the theatre were an all-time record. He has made guest appearances on dozens of TV shows including with Cannon and Ball, Little and Large, Freddie Starr and Terry Wogan. He was the presenter of the BBC television series *People*. Voted the Stars Organisation for Spastics Sports Personality of the Year for 1989 and 1990.

For the Record

17. 3.82	Lupe Guerra	w.ko.1	Royal Albert Hall
30. 3.82	Harvey Steichen	w.rsf.2	Wembley Arena
20. 4.82	Tom Stevenson	w.ko.1	Royal Albert Hall
4. 5.82	Ron Gibbs	w.rsf.4	Wembley Arena
1. 6.82	Tony Moore	w.rsf.2	Royal Albert Hall
14. 9.82	George Scott	w.rsf.1	Wembley Arena
23.10.82	Ali Lukusa	w.ko.2	Berlin
9.11.82	Rudi Gauwe	w.ko.2	Royal Albert Hall
23.11.82	George Butzbach	w.ret.1	Wembley Arena
7.12.82	Gilberto Acuna	w.rsf.1	Royal Albert Hall
18. 1.83	Stewart Lithgo	w.ret.4	Royal Albert Hall
8. 2.83	Peter Mulendwa	w.ko.3	Royal Albert Hall
1. 3.83	Winston Allen	w.rsf.2	Royal Albert Hall
5. 4.83	Eddie Neilson	w.rsf.3	Royal Albert Hall
3. 5.83	Scott Le Doux	w.rsf.3	Wembley Arena
31. 5.83	Barry Funches	w.rsf.5	Royal Albert Hall
9. 7.83	Mike Jameson	w.ko.2	Chicago
27. 9.83	Bill Sharkey	w.ko.1	Wembley Arena
11.10.83	Floyd Cummings	w.rsf.7	Royal Albert Hall
6.12.83	Walter Santemore	w.ko.4	Royal Albert Hall
13. 3.84	Juan Figueroa	w.ko.1	Wembley Arena
13. 5.84	James Smith	l.ko.10	Wembley Arena
25. 9.84	Ken Lakusta	w.ko.2	Wembley Arena

(Commonwealth championship eliminator)
6.11.84	Jeff Jordan	w.rsf.3	Royal Albert Hall
27.11.84	Phil Brown	w.pts 10	Wembley Arena
26. 3.85	Lucien Rodriguez	w.rsf.1	Wembley Arena
1.10.85	Anders Eklund	w.ko.4	Wembley Arena

(European heavyweight championship)
| 4.12.85 | Larry Frazier | w.ko.2 | Royal Albert Hall |
| 4. 3.86 | Gerrie Coetzee | w.rsf.1 | Wembley Arena |

(WBA world heavyweight championship eliminator)
| 19. 7.86 | Tim Witherspoon | l.rsf.11 | Wembley Stadium |

(WBA world heavyweight championship)
24. 3.87	James Tillis	w.rsf.5	Wembley Arena
27. 6.87	Chuck Gardner	w.ko.1	Cannes
30. 8.87	Reggie Gross	w.rsf.8	Marbella
24.10.87	Joe Bugner	w.rsf.8	White Hart Lane
25. 2.89	Mike Tyson	l.rsf.5	Las Vegas

(WBC world heavyweight championship)
20.11.91	John Emmen	w.ko.1	Royal Albert Hall
22.4.92	Jose Ribalta	w.ko.2	Wembley Arena
17.10.92	Pierre Coetzer	w.rsf.8	Wembley Arena

Index

<u>INSIDE TRACK</u>

Carl Lewis

Carl Lewis is officially rated the fastest man alive. He has dominated track and field events throughout the 80s, winning four Olympic gold medals in 1984 (equalling Jesse Owens' record) and two more in 1988. But he has hit the headlines off the track as well as on it, and in this revealing autobiography, written with Pulitzer Prize-winning journalist Jeffrey Marx, he gives us the most outspoken book about track and field ever written.

For the first time, Carl Lewis talks openly about himself, his family, his volatile relationship with the world's press, and the lurid rumours about his sexuality. He also exposes some shocking truths about the profession that has made him an international superstar: the outrageous college recruiting practices, the lucrative endorsements and vast appearance fees, and the steroid scandals that blighted the career of Ben Johnson and led to speculation about the outrageous Florence Griffith Joyner.

'Draws you to him with the most intimate confidence in family, professional, spiritual, even sexual life . . .'
Independent on Sunday

'Powerful, thoughtful and honest . . . strong stuff'
Standard

AUTOBIOGRAPHY
£4.99

ARNOLD

The Unauthorised Biography of Arnold Schwarzenegger

Wendy Leigh

Wendy Leigh delves deep behind the public image and, after two years' research and scores of interviews with Arnold's friends, family, lovers, colleagues and rivals, she emerges with some startling facts. She explores his troubled boyhood in an obscure Austrian village, his tortured relationship with his Nazi father, his sexual exploits, his political ambitions and his lifelong penchant for often cruel practical jokes. The portrait that emerges is of a complex, intelligent, sometimes ruthless and often manipulative man who has allowed little to stand in the way of his meteoric rise to success.

'This book you can't put down about a man you couldn't pick up may have a significance beyond titillation . . . a sensationalist biography which may have the benevolent effect of slowing its subject's declared political ambitions'
Independent on Sunday

'Wendy Leigh spares him nothing. The father fetish, the uniform fetish, the ambition fetish: as with everything, Arnie does it in a big way . . . convincing'
Independent

BIOGRAPHY
£5.99

GRIDLOCK

Ben Elton

Gridlock is when a city dies.

Killed in the name of freedom. Killed in the name of oil and steel. Choked on carbon-monoxide and strangled with a pair of fluffy dice.

How did it come to this? How did the ultimate freedom machine end up paralysing us all? How did we end up driving to our own funeral, in somebody else's gravy train?

Deborah and Geoffrey know, but they have transport problems of their own, and anyway, whoever it was that murdered the city can just as easily murder them.

'Brilliant . . . the comedy sometimes achieves Tom Sharpe levels of outrage and the thrills sometimes match Alfred Hitchcock for malign invention . . . somewhere under the stage suit there may be a Booker candidate'
Richard Heller, *Mail on Sunday*

Also by Ben Elton in Sphere Books:
STARK   GASPING

GENERAL FICTION
£4.99

TAKING THE MIKE

Fred Eyre

Fred Eyre's first book, *Kicked into Touch*, has become a football classic. It is as popular and as educational to aspiring young footballers today as it was when it was first published in 1981.

Thanks to the written word, he was given the opportunity of *Taking the Mike*, by accepting countless invitations to travel the country to discuss his two favourite subjects – football and Fred Eyre!

As usual, his anecdotes and stories, written in his own unmistakable style, from within the game and from his career as one of the top sporting after-dinner speakers, make unusual, interesting and hilarious reading.

HUMOUR/SPORT
£4.99

INSIDE TRACK	Carl Lewis	£4.99
ARNOLD	Wendy Leigh	£5.99
TAKING THE MIKE	Fred Eyre	£4.99
GRIDLOCK	Ben Elton	£4.99

Warner Books now offers an exciting range of quality titles by both established and new authors which can be ordered from the following address:

Little, Brown and Company (UK) Limited,
P.O. Box 11,
Falmouth,
Cornwall TR10 9EN.

Alternatively you may fax your order to the above address.
Fax No. 0326 376423.

Payments can be made as follows: cheque, postal order (payable to Little, Brown and Company) or by credit cards, Visa/Access. Do not send cash or currency. UK customers and B.F.P.O please allow £1.00 for postage and packing for the first book, plus 50p for the second book, plus 30p for each additional book up to a maximum charge of £3.00 (7 books plus).

Overseas customers including Ireland please allow £2.00 for the first book plus £1.00 for the second book, plus 50p for each additional book.

NAME (Block Letters) ....

....

ADDRESS ....

....

....

☐ I enclose my remittance for _____

☐ I wish to pay by Access/Visa Card

Number

Card Expiry Date